For my
loving Jim —
much love — Rose-Mary Rummel
Dec. 1984

A Century Of Class

Public Education In Dallas
1884–1984

Rose-Mary Rumbley

EAKIN PRESS

Austin, Texas

FIRST EDITION

Copyright © 1984
By Rose-Mary Rumbley

Published in the United States of America
By Eakin Publications, Inc., P.O. Box 23066, Austin, Texas 78735

All Rights Reserved

Rumbley, Rose-Mary, 1922–
    A century of class.

    1. Public schools — Texas — Dallas — History. I. Title.
LA372.D3R85   1984   379.764′2812   84-18640
ISBN 0-89015-457-0

This is my mother, Amy Hass Brau, costumed as a flower. Her brother, Carl, is Jack Sprat.

—Author's collection.

School days, school days,
Dear old golden rule days . . .

When children used to bring
    their teachers an apple,
Instead of driving them bananas.

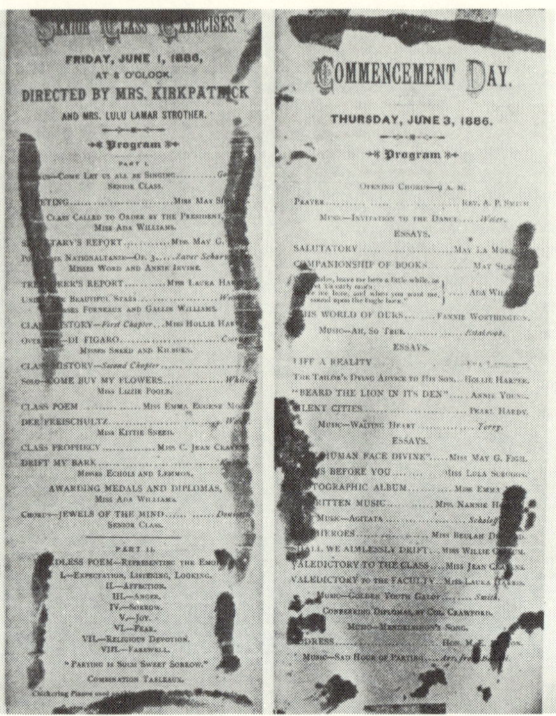

These are the programs for the first Senior Class Exercises and the Commencement ceremony, 1886. Note the dates. The printer was obviously confused.
— From the collection of the Dallas Independent School District.

Fifteen nationalities were represented in this picture of children attending Cumberland Hill School, 1915. Already the area in the northeast part of town was becoming a melting pot.
— From the collection of the Dallas Independent School District.

Contents

Two views of the Chenoweth home and a look at their general store in 1890 at 133 Nettie Street. This country home and general store were across from the old Alamo School where the Chenoweth children attended classes. Nettie Street is no more. Today it's where the Good-Latimer Expressway meets I 45.

— Courtesy Dr. John Chenoweth

Preface

This is a history of public education in Dallas, Texas, 1884–1984. However, I've done more than just write a history. I have reflected upon the subject. I have philosophized, editorialized, idealized, theorized, and cogitated. Therefore, this is my story of public education in Dallas. I was fortunate enough to attend and graduate from the Dallas schools. My children were fortunate enough to attend and graduate from the Dallas schools. My husband taught for almost twenty years in the Dallas schools. My mother enrolled as a Dallas schoolgirl in 1899. My father came home from the trenches of France after World War I and went to work for the Dallas schools. In order to complete my Ph.D. at North Texas State University I wrote a dissertation on one phase of the work in the Dallas schools. Unfortunately I never taught in the Dallas schools myself, because of the rule that husband and wife could not teach in the Dallas schools at the same time. Many of my closest friends have been and are, teachers in the Dallas schools. I have talked with these friends. I have read the school board reports. I have read annuals and school newspapers. I have looked at PTA scrapbooks. I have rummaged through all sorts of memorabilia.

Now, I wish to thank those people who shared with me so many unforgettable school stories. I thank those who shared their scrapbooks and files with me.

After reading this book, should you feel that I have left out some important people and some great stories, you will be correct. I have. Do not protest. Write your own book, because the story of education is vast and never ending. This is only a part of the whole story of public education in Dallas. There is so much more — volumes more. This is merely *my* offering to the history of public schools in Dallas — the first one hundred years. I thoroughly enjoyed putting it together.

This was one of the first classes to meet at San Jacinto School, 1891, which was on the corner of Ross and Washington where the school administration building stands today. The administration building was built on the original foundation of the San Jacinto School.

— From the collection of the Dallas Independent School District.

Joe Bob Cave, the first male to graduate from the Dallas public schools. He received his diploma in short pants, but this didn't stop him from becoming a prominent businessman in Dallas.

— Courtesy Mrs. Joe Bob Cave

Chapter One

The Beginning

The story of education in Dallas is the story of the building of a city, because positive growth of any city is brought about by intelligent, informed, and inspired citizens. On September 15, 1884, public education was offered to the children of Dallas. Houston and Fort Worth had opened public schools the year before. The citizens of Dallas, with an already strong spirit of rivalry and a healthy feeling of jealousy toward those other two growing Texas cities, couldn't be out done. There had been schools in Dallas, but they were private schools.

Texas pioneers built cities and conquered a new land, and along with their homes they built schools, churches, stores, and anything else that was needed for settling into the new territory. There were log cabin schools built in Dallas during the eighteen forties and eighteen fifties. These were supported by those parents who had money for their children's education.

As early as 1841, the state of Texas made a gesture toward public schools by authorizing an appropriation for them, but the amount was so small that it supported them for only a fraction of a term. These state incorporated academies were supposed to stimulate citizens to seek local public support for education, so in many cities the academy with partial public support was a transition step to totally supported public education. Dallas had her share of the private schools that had sprung up all over the country.

Educational transitions occurred, and these were vital and needed transitions. At the beginning of the eighteenth century a man prepared for only three professions — the ministry, the law, and medicine. However, religious liberalism, the industrial revolution, and the expanding intellectual needs of merchants and men of affairs were making themselves felt by the end of the eighteenth century, and anyone who was teaching could sense the demands that a changing society was making. New subjects and new teaching methods came about. They came about in early Dallas, for the city was filling up with merchants and men of affairs and they saw that everyone needed an education, not just the preachers, the lawyers, and the doctors. Then too, women needed to be considered!

Author Alvin Toffler in his book, *The Third Wave*, says that these nineteenth century changes caused the thrust of the second wave, the industrial revolution. This second wave created new jobs, new thinking, and new attitudes for everyone, and Dallas made ready for the push and power of this new wave.

Just recently the letters of John Milton McCoy, an early Dallas settler, have been published by the Dallas Historical Society in a book, *When Dallas Became A City*. An excerpt from a letter dated, July 7, 1872, Dallas, Texas, tells all about the changes made in the city and the excitement generated by such alterations.

> My dear parents,
>
> Well, the railroad and telegraph are here now. Yesterday the track reached the corporate limits about a mile and a half from the Court House square. The streets were crowded yesterday evening with equestrians, pedestrians, and carriages and buggies flying back and forth to the terminus of the road. Today I see a bright new omnibus upon the streets, the first that has come to town. Dallas is to be grinned at no longer as a one horse town. It has put away its petticoats and donned yesterday a new pair of 'britches' with pockets and a cigar in its mouth and is no longer a boy — a full man in feeling, strides, and gas. Talk about your Baltimores, New York, and Philadelphia, and leave Dallas out of the ring if you dare.

Baltimore is not more of a 'Hub,' New York is no more of a 'Street' and a Philadelphia lawyer isn't any sharper in his own estimation than Dallas. Dallas, the Hub Dallas, the crescent of the southwest, Dallas the bright spot of the Lone Star, Dallas the coming City of Texas, the center of the grand Eldorado of the South.

The writer of this letter, which reads like a Chamber of Commerce promotional presentation, was just one of many enthusiastic citizens who were watching the city grow and who were thinking of the expanding business opportunities.

There was a group that not only thought of business, but also thought of the educational opportunities that needed to be afforded to the lively populace. However, before there could be any educational opportunities there had to be places for the teaching — classrooms. The Tannehill Lodge provided space for education. The Masonic Temple, corner of Houston and Ross, was an early important building erected in Dallas with one of the largest halls in the city. In 1876 the first major school of Dallas was established, and it did meet on the first floor of this Masonic building. It met there on the weekdays, and the First Baptist Church Sunday School met there on Sundays. However, this school offered education only to those that could afford the tuitions — which ranged from $1.50 a month all the way up to $2.50 a month. Elocution and expression lessons were available to those children whose parents could pay $3 a month.

In Dallas's early days there were gifted and dedicated teachers like Mr. and Mrs. R.D. Coughanour. This couple with real heart for teaching came from Kentucky to Dallas in 1861, and they came to teach. Mr. Coughanour taught school here until eventually he went into practicing law. He needed to make more money. Alas, it's the age old dilemma in the teaching profession with the long debated question — how much should be paid to a teacher who is responsible for the future of the country when it is known that an effective teacher is actually priceless? The question remains unanswered.

Mrs. Coughanour continued in the educational field. She had a girls' school from 1877–1883 on Bryan Street where the old Crozier Tech High, now the Business Magnet, is today. The Bryan Street property had been the sight of various private schools for thirty-five years before 1884, when the city purchased the land and the building for $10,000 from the Methodists. That building had to be renovated for high school classes, and until it was ready, the second floor of a building on Elm at Akard was used for the high school.

Then in 1907, the present building on Bryan was built. This building and property are now up for sale. For over one hundred and thirty-five years that land has only been used for education, and many Dallas natives will be saddened to see the oldest high school in Dallas fall into dust and to see the land which has always been used for schoolhouses go for office buildings.

Mr. Coughanour, even though a successful lawyer, really never lost his heart for schools, because it was in his law office on the sixteenth of June, 1884, that the first board of education of Dallas met. The hand written minutes state that Mr. R.D. Coughanour, Colonel L.M. Martin, and E.M. Tillman were going to request authority from the council of the City of Dallas to employ a superintendent of schools and with this superintendent at the helm, to establish public education in Dallas.

John Henry Brown, termed the first historian of Dallas, was mayor at the time, and the request for schools was granted by Mr. Brown and the city council. Therefore, on September 15, 1884, young people in Dallas went to public school for the first time. Mr. W.A. Boles, superintendent, personally welcomed them to four white elementary schools and one white high school, and two black elementary schools and one black high school. The schools were numbered and not named. There were sixteen white teachers and six black teachers for the five hundred and twenty-two white students and the one hundred and eighty-one black students who enrolled that first day. The principals for the white schools were J.P. Vaughan, J.T. Weaver, Miss Blanche Aldehoff, Miss Leila P. Cowart, and Frank M. Johnson. The black principals were F.C. Long, J.W. Ray, and John Smothers.

That first school board report stated that all children of Dallas from the ages of eight years to sixteen years regardless of race and color were invited to come to school. The first Board of Education declared itself in full control of the schools with the superintendent inspecting to see that "nothing was amiss." Each year the superintendent was to make a report of all activities, and the principal of each school was to be in charge of the attendance record of each child. These job descriptions have obviously changed thorough the years. The report went on to say that school would always start on the third Monday of each September and continue until the funds for that current year were exhausted. The 1884–1885 school year ran until the middle of March when there just wasn't any more money to give to public education. Thus, the school doors shut for that year, a seven month term, but actually a good start for public education.

The opening of the schools certainly happened without incident, ceremony, or celebration, for in the Dallas Times Herald, September 15, 1884, the only notice given to school was a Sanger Brother's ad for school shoes, $2 a pair. It wasn't until a week later that a word about the public schools made the paper. *The Times Herald*, Tuesday, September 23, 1884, published this letter from a satisfied parent.

> It is a source of great encouragement and pleasure to know that our city schools have been launched for the scholastic year with entire success. They opened without a single jar — and to the satisfaction of all concerned.

On that first day, the teachers came into the classrooms and greeted the students,

"Good morning, students. Open your books to page one, and we'll begin our lessons."

The children opened the McGuffey readers. William Holmes McGuffey was a college teacher — later a college president — who compiled a text book in 1836 for the first and second grades. He collaborated with his brother, Alexander Hamilton McGuffey, to complete the whole series on through the upper grades by 1857. The McGuffeys were the most popular texts in American schools, and there were still editions of McGuffeys published as late as 1920. The texts have sold over one hundred and twenty-two million copies and for most school children including the school children of Dallas, they were the first textbooks.

McGuffey and his brother were extremely conservative in their political beliefs and support, and this was reflected in the texts. The brothers stood politically with the namesake of the younger McGuffey, Alexander Hamilton, rather than with Thomas Jefferson. The conservative readers remained in the hands of the Dallas children until the 1920s when they were traded for the less conservative Dick And Jane who had a hyper dog named Spot who ran, jumped, and looked a lot.

That September of 1884, the little first graders were taught reading, writing, and numbers. The course of study for Dallas teachers warned them to "watch for bad writing habits." At the end of that first year those beginners were to write short sentences legibly — with hands always in proper writing positions.

The first grade teachers were also urged to make the little ones conscious of the marvelous world around them — to make them alert and alive. The children looked at a picture and described in detail what they saw. This exercise definitely extended the vocabulary and made them conscious of all about them. Today, this remains a good exercise for anyone regardless of age, for unfortunately, the drudgeries of life tend to make one numb and unaware. This numbness can and often does set in after the first grade.

All was not rosy during that first year, for there was some bad news in the school report. The superintendent was distressed over the daily tardiness. His calculations on the subject showed that he really got to the nitty-gritty of the matter. There were 12,350 cases of tardiness. The superintendent, figured that one minute was lost per teacher for each class, and that thirty-four days were lost because of these ten o'clock scholars. This was one and seven-tenths of a month lost which cost the district one hundred and nineteen dollars. What a waste! Tardiness, he felt, had to be stopped.

Also, the superintendent was very distressed over the short seven month term. The nine month course could not be done in seven months. "The building of a house may be hastened by more workmen, but not so in the building of the brain."

Time was necessary for the mind to digest the mental food that was being fed to the first pupils. Superintendent Boles was determined to get more money!

Teachers were instructed to test the children carefully, and no child was to be promoted unless prepared for the next grade. The last of the nineteenth century brought about a surge of standardized testing programs all over the country, for psychologists realized that with mass education, there must be mass testing. The colleges began to see that some students would be eligible for higher learning institutions, and some would not be. Who was going to determine eligibility? In the schools, the educators knew that some kids understood everything, some understood nothing. But who was to say? Who was able to measure the mind? The Dallas report didn't state any particular mass testing program, so the creation of the tests was probably left up to the teachers.

With money for only seven months of school, there wasn't money for standardized testing, and the new testing programs really weren't popular everywhere. Most educators felt that the classroom teacher knew everything anyway. When I was teaching I always thought that I did. There was no way that I could meet everyday in a room with a group of students and not discover what they were thinking and feeling and learning. A truly dedicated and loving teacher knows all.

The superintendent pointed out that it was quite easy to discover in the elementary grades which students were live wires — the alert and aware. The teacher had only to ask the children to draw a picture of themselves. The bright child would draw a complete and detailed body of himself. The bright little girls would put bows in their hair, bracelets on their arms, rings on their fingers. The bright little boys would put buckles on their overalls, stripes on their shirts, and shoes plus socks on their feet. The child who drew a circle for a head with two arms coming out of that circle would definitely need extra help. He would need to learn that there was more to life than just a head and two arms. So far, this was all that he had noticed. This test is as effective today as it was then.

The first course of study advised that there be more numbers, more reading, and more writing in the second grade. The instruction was upgraded each year. In the third grade course of study, the instruction in numbers was called arithmetic and the writing course was termed penmanship. The fourth grade offered more of the same, but there was a change in the fifth and sixth grades. Written in capital letters was this demand. THE CHILDREN WILL LEARN ENGLISH GRAMMAR. The fifth and sixth grade students had to understand the structure of a sentence and to identify the parts of speech in that sentence. This was most important, and it still is. When a student does not learn English grammar in the fifth grade and certainly by the sixth, he is handicapped throughout his whole educational career.

When I was teaching communication at Dallas Baptist College, my lesson drifted over to the use of the gerund. I was explaining the usage of this noun/verb part of speech, when a voice piped up from the back of the room. "If I understood what you're talking about in English, I'd be passing Spanish right now."

My fifth and sixth grade language arts teacher, Mrs. Myrtle Smith, at Robert E. Lee School was responsible for my knowing English grammar. She was excellent. She had all of us diagram every sentence that we read. We wrote stories and received rewards for excellence. She awarded prizes for perfect spelling. Mrs. Smith stopped at nothing to see that we knew our language.

All the learning in 1884–1885 was financed with a budget of $13,153.85. Most of this money went for teacher's salaries. However, some furniture was purchased. The board realized that more teachers had to be recruited, for the school population was increasing. An article in the *Dallas Morning News*, July 24, 1885, told of a high school course for teacher preparation that was going to be taught that next year. College hours were not necessary for a teaching position then — one simply had to take the teacher training course in high school, graduate, and begin teaching. This type of training was standard for many years.

Superintendent Boles proudly concluded his report in 1885 by telling of all the friends that had been made by the school personnel. Mr. Boles stated that he spent very little time in his office. He was out in the schools aiding the teachers. He was out in the community meeting the citizens. He was also pleased to announce that there had been very little corporal punishment — only two or three cases. Boles believed in firmness, kindness, and prudence, but the rod was spared.

It was disclosed that everyone lived through that first year. One teacher was ill for a week, and one student had malaria fever. They both recovered. There were a lot of measles and mumps, but there were no deaths. All in all a fine first year was had by all, and plans were made that summer of 1885 for all the activities at the school houses to be upgraded. Public education was on its way toward taking over the intellectual training of the majority of the children in Dallas.

The board shanties in which teachers and pupils were

formerly placed are giving way to magnificent and commodious brick buildings, which are the pride and ornament of
the city, and a monument to those who built them.

Those board shanties had originally been the pride because they were all the system had. But, Dallas was now becoming a big wealthy city, and the sight of those commodious
brick buildings meant progress, and generated new pride.

By 1888 Dallas had a population of about 40,000 people —
a big city. The superintendent, now Mr. J.T. Hand, stated in
his report that discipline was getting hard to maintain in such
a large city. However, because the teaching was so fine, there
was really very little friction. Morality and strength of character were taught and obviously absorbed.

There were added regulations for teachers and students in
his report. One, corporal punishment was prohibited. Two,
there were to be no medals given to students for their work,
and in turn, no teacher could accept a gift. Three, parents had
to send the children regularly to school, and if a child was ab-
sent, a written note had to be given to the principal stating the
cause for absence. Four, pupils could not leave school for outside duties. Five, during the school day, pupils were required to
abstain entirely from communication with one another by
speaking, writing, or by signs without special permission. I'm
sure a few notes were passed and were not intercepted by those
hawk-eyed teachers who according to legend had eyes in the
back of their heads.

There was a fine educational pattern flowing, and the
fourth year, 1887–1888, yielded two impressive rewards. First,
there was $544.07 left over in the school budget, which had
grown to $26,831.72 — double the amount of the 1884 budget.
*This was the first and last year that the schools of Dallas ever
had a surplus of funds at the end of the year.*

Secondly, there was a graduating class of eight lovely,
learned ladies: Nettie Bailey, Mattie Boyer, Mary Childress,
Mattie Helm, Rosa Miller, Blanche Seiden-Bitel, Vesta Stokey,
and Minnie Terry. The school board reports in the following
years continued to list the classes noting the marriages of the
girls and the careers of the men. The next year brought male
graduates. This detailed reporting went on for about ten years,
but then the system grew so large that such a personal tone
had to be abandoned.

The year 1889 was a prosperous one for the Dallas School system. Cumberland Hill School and Oak Grove School were built, both beautiful brick buildings. Superintendent Hand was instrumental in giving them names rather than numbers.

CUMBERLAND HILL SCHOOL, THE OLDEST PUBLIC SCHOOL BUILDING THAT STANDS IN DALLAS TODAY

Once upon a time there was a little boy named William P. Clements, Jr., who went to Cumberland Hill School. He loved his teachers and his school so much that he wished that someday when he was all grown up he could buy the school and stay there forever. Surely enough, when William grew up, he became the head of an oil drilling firm. He also served as the Governor of Texas, but before that, in 1970, when the Dallas Independent School District offered for sale the oldest school building still standing in Dallas, Cumberland Hill, William bid on the property, his bid was accepted, and his school, completely renovated and restored to its early grandeur, now is the home of his company, SEDCO, Inc. Bill soon outgrew his school, so the tower behind the school is also part of SEDCO. Nevertheless, he is working there happily ever after.

In 1889 Cumberland Hill School was built on a little hill slightly in the suburbs of Dallas on School Street. This street extended is now called Akard, and the new Woodall Rogers Freeway cuts by it on its western side. The school was built on a lot that was sold to the city by the Randall family, whose home had been on the hill but had burned in 1882, when they sold the property to the city for the school.

Not far from the school site was the Cumberland Hill Presbyterian Church after which the school was named. The church had a private school directed by Professor Martin, so this Presbyterian school was always referred to as the "Old Martin School." This private school was in existence from 1873–1888. Then in 1889 when the Cumberland Hill Public School was built for $20,000 by N.K. Wright and Son, Builders, the kids in the neighborhood moved to the public school and the "Old Martin School" was no more. This hill represented a very elite neighborhood, for the Randall kids went to the school with the Padgitts, the Murphys, the Burghers, the Dorseys, the Moseleys, the Tooles, the Bookhouts, the Sangers, the Crawfords, the Schneiders, and more of the wealthy society folk who lived in Dallas at that time.

In 1908 the Trinity River left its banks and flooded downtown Dallas. My mother told of the flood waters rushing into all the stores on Main Street which included her father's bakery. Her cherished piano had to be put on boxes so that it wouldn't be completely destroyed. She also remembered watching a manikin dressed in the latest style come floating out of Sanger Brothers. Because the Cumberland Hill School stood on a hill, it was above the flood waters, and the school was used as a refuge site after the devastating flood.

The Cumberland Hill neighborhood probably went through more changes than any other neighborhood in Dallas up until that time. First, living there were the very wealthy. Then some Jewish immigrants settled there. Then there was a colony of Russian people. Some Germans and Italians sprinkled themselves into the middle of it all, and finally the Mexican American families migrated to it. By 1915, there were fifteen different nationalities represented in the student body. Today going out of downtown Dallas toward the northwest one will discover that there still is an international residency in this direction, and this distinctive trait has stuck through the years. Fannin School would be one of the closest to the old Cumberland Hill going in that northwest direction, and today Fannin School opens its classrooms to many Mexican, Laosian, Vietnamese, Chinese, and other foreign-born children.

Mrs. Ned King, well-known Dallas interior decorator, taught at Cumberland Hill School in the 1950s. All the little Mexican students would stash their lunches on top of the radiators in her class. She can still remember that pungent odor of garlic floating all over the school as the hot air from the radiators blew up through the carefully wrapped tamales that were in the lunch sacks. By noon, the garlic smell was almost overwhelming. Because of all the internationals in the school there were not just lunches of tamales. There were lunches with egg rolls, sausages, spicy meatballs, and other foreign cuisines all of which had sharp poignant aromas to them. Mrs. King's classroom is now the board room of the SEDCO Corporation. She has so often wished to stop in at Governor Clements's office and ask him if ever a leftover whiff of garlic drifts by during a board meeting.

There was such a melting pot at the school, efforts always were made to teach the American way, the democratic system. For many years the students elected a student policeman to watch for the safety of the small children. Self-control was taught with self-government and self command. Dr. Justin Kimball, superintendent, in his school report in 1918 told of the success of the program. When a child was guilty of an infraction of school policy, he usually "came across" and confessed his wrongdoing.

J.E. Oehler served as principal at the school, 1933–1936. He enjoyed every moment that he was at the school and truly regretted being transferred to another school. He said that he never got to laugh as much at the other school. Working with little Mexican children and the other nationalities was so much fun. Mr. Oehler kept a note written by a devoted Mexican mother.

"Please excuse my son. He missed school yesterday because of two great events. He got a new baby brother and a new pair of shoes."

The landmark, Cumberland Hill School, with its memories, the fun, and yes, the exotic smells still stands, thanks to Bill Clements and SEDCO, Inc.

THE GROWTH CONTINUES

An amusing misprint appeared in the report of 1889. A sentence reads, "We have the very best *corpse* of teachers!" Hopefully it was a misprint. However, those teachers probably were dead at the end of the day, for the enrollment had jumped to 3,266 students, and the teacher/pupil ratio had not kept up with this increased pupil population.

And too, there were even more regulations laid upon those dedicated mentors. The teachers were told that they couldn't do anything that was forbidden to the students — no reading of newspapers, no chewing of tobacco, and no neglecting of personal appearance. The teacher's lounge hadn't been made manifest. There was yet no private lair reserved in the building for the teachers to have a good read of the daily news, a good chew of the finest tobacco, or a complete physical relief from corns and calluses and pinched flesh. There was no place to go and kick off the shoes, loosen the corset, and just let go. Fortunately, today there are terrific teachers' lounges around which schools are built.

There might have been a surplus of money the year before, but there was a shortage of funds that next year of 1889. This report offered the first voice for more pay for teachers. Superintendent Hand said,

"We hope the time will come when your (the tax payers) liberality will enable us to give them (the teachers) salaries commensurate with their abilities."

Two new things were introduced into the system — instrumental music and radiators. Mr. Will Russell and Miss Flora Russell began to teach music, and out of the fifty-three schoolrooms in Dallas, sixteen were treated to heat from a furnace. Daniel Boorstin in his book, *The Americans A Democratic Experience*, stated that the radiator was an American development. The newly created hot-air system was first installed in the Chicago schools in 1870. It was decided that if the kids in Chicago could make it with this new form of heating, then anyone could. It all seemed to work in Chicago, so Dallas kids in 1889 were given hot air from the boiler room.

The curriculum called for the scheduling of a new course — hygiene. The bones, skin, and flesh were discussed along with the circulation, breathing, digestion, and nervous systems. Students were told to sleep, exercise, bathe, and keep their feet warm. Students were cautioned not to sit in a draught, and the girls were told that any kind of tight lacing was not good. In other words, as far as the girls keeping that stylish hourglass figure was concerned, they were advised to let the sand shift naturally for the sake of health.

The wearing of corsets during the nineteenth century was always a debatable issue. This poem, published in the Houston *Morning Star*, September 17, 1839, verifies that.

> How diffident the beaux have grown,
> In fact they're perfect churls;
> Such shameful coldness now is shown.
> They never squeeze the girls.
> But the girls have devised a plan;
> In lieu of these cold elves,
> They now — oh, shame upon you men —
> With corsets, squeeze themselves.

Mrs. Camilla Rubin was teaching at Casa View Elementary School during the 1960s. She leaned over her reading circle and a little boy politely spoke,

"Mrs. Rubin, some lace from your corset is showing."

He, of course, meant her slip. She was surprised that a child of the nineteen sixties would be familiar with such an antique word as corset — the word almost faded with Scarlett O'Hara. Mrs. Rubin smiled and asked him how much was actually showing. He used his little fingers to show that about an inch had slipped down past the hem of her dress. Mrs. Rubin told the little boy's mother about it, because the veteran teacher really wondered how the child knew about corsets. The mother admitted to wearing a brace for her back which she called a corset. It had lace on it, so the little boy called everything that had lace on it a corset. A child's vocabulary always remains an interesting adventure.

THE FIRST MALE GRADUATE

There were thirteen schools in 1889, and Central High yielded yet another graduating class. This one had three men in it, the first men to graduate from the Dallas schools. One gentleman was Dick Coughanour, the son of the attorney who had come to Dallas to teach, and who had later organized the first school board. Mr. Coughanour was reaping what he had sown in his law office that day in June, 1884, when the first school board met. His son now had earned a diploma from Dallas High School.

Another gentleman in the class was Mr. Joe Bob Cave. Mrs. Joe Bob Cave, the widow of this first male graduate, (first, if the diplomas were given out in alphabetical order) told of the problem that Joe Bob brought to the teachers in charge of the graduation exercises. He was only fourteen years old when he graduated, and then at fourteen, boys were still wearing short pants. In those days, there was a puberty rite experienced. A boy became sixteen — he put on long pants — he was a man, and that was it. Joe Bob was only fourteen, so he didn't have on long pants. The teachers met to mull over the problem. Should the first male graduate walk across the stage with his knees exposed? Was this appropriate?

It was finally decided that since Joe Bob was only fourteen, it was proper for him to accept his diploma in short pants. Now, getting that diploma in short pants certainly didn't deter

Joe Bob of pursuing a manly career. He first worked for Judge W.L. Crawford, well known criminal lawyer in Dallas, as a court reporter. Then he went into the cotton business, the cattle business, and the oil business — all marks for a true Texas man. Later he married Miss Gertrude Ballard who was a Dallas school teacher, and they had two daughters, both of whom taught in the Dallas system.

In evaluating this whole situation, I think that society needs to establish a puberty rite once again, in order to cut short this prolonged youth in which young men indulge today. Sociologist Margaret Mead, always said that in strong societies, there were puberty rites. In the days of the Roman Empire, young men donned the white toga as a sign of manhood. In 1889, they put on long pants. Today, there's nothing to jar a boy into realizing that he's grown up. Today young men have to "find" themselves, and this is terribly expensive for the parents. I know, because I had a son who was hunting. I would call at the dormitory,

"Son, what are you spending all of this money on?"

"Mom, I have to find myself."

"Well, hunt fast, because we're running out of money."

My husband would yell from the background:

"Tell him I was too poor to be lost."

My husband was correct. There wasn't much money during the nineteen forties when he was growing up, even though the wartime economy had phased out the depression. There wasn't a change in pants length, but upon receiving the high school diploma, a young person knew that he was an adult and had to act accordingly. College was serious business, and during the years of World War II, entering the service was the most serious step that any young man could take.

DECISIONS, DECISIONS, DECISIONS

There was a bit of a turmoil concerning the place of this 1889 graduation, but finally the new opera house was chosen for the site of the ceremony. Judge J.C. Muse was the speaker. Annie Guyton, a student, who later became a teacher in the schools of Dallas, gave an inspiring recitation entitled, "The Man, Not the Dress." (The short pants decision might have guided her in choosing the topic.) Nevertheless, eleven girls and three men graduated that warm summer evening.

The next year brought the services of an elocutionist, Miss Grace Lambert. Now, at last, there was a professional on the scene to coach students in the interpretation and delivery of the numerous essays, poems, speeches, odes, and other recitations that were scheduled for programs and graduation exercises. Miss Lambert obviously worked all year on the selections given at the graduation programs, for those programs were extremely lengthy. It took a year to get the recitations ready, and a whole day to hear them all. But after all, with no radio, TV, movies, sporting events, there was time for proud parents to listen to the orations, poems, essays, odes, recitations,and any other oral offerings of the graduates.

Miss Lambert, being an elocutionist, probably held a B.O. degree, Bachelor of Oratory. Her educational credits were not listed in the report, but a B.O. was the accepted degree at that time. In those early speech classes Miss Lambert required each student to speak distinctly with the ever sought for "golden, rounded tones." Students were required to project and to gesture eloquently in the true Del Sartian manner. Del Sarte, a French drama teacher, worked out an exotic system of gestures and bodily movements that influenced all the drama and public speaking techniques of the day. Highly dramatic presentations were all part of the times and were all appreciated.

In June, 1891, there were three black graduates, the first in Dallas. Dr. I. V. Loud, former pastor of St. Paul United Methodist Church, was most helpful in supplying information about the education of black children in Dallas. His church, St. Paul Methodist, the oldest black church in Dallas, located across the street from the Arts Magnet School, quartered the first school for black children in Dallas. Before the public schools were opened in 1884, the only education for black children was offered in the basement of St. Paul Methodist Church. There was preaching on Sunday and teaching during the week, and the same man did it all, the Reverend Harris Swann. He not only felt called to teach the *Bible*, but he felt called to drill the Three R's into black children. There were black parents who made certain that their children got to church on Sunday for Bible study and to church during the week for book learning. This magnificent historical Methodist church stands proudly in the middle of the arts district in downtown Dallas.

There were changes in the administration of the Dallas

schools during the 1892–93 semesters. It was decided that there would be a school board member elected from each ward and that the mayor would be on the school board. This amendment came in March, 1893. That spring some more lovely young ladies came from the graduating class. Two of them were to become quite famous in Dallas for their work in education. The Valedictorian of that class was Miss Lida Hooe, who became supervisor of art in the Dallas schools in 1904. The Salutatorian, Miss Edna Rowe, was a teacher for fifty-four years in the district. Dr. Justin Kimball, who served as Superintendent of schools in Dallas from 1914–1924, declared that Miss Rowe was the most brilliant woman he had ever met.

"She had the brains of a man." Dr. Kimball had some rather chauvanistic leanings as we will see in later chapters of this book.

Regardless, Miss Rowe was one of the most outstanding teachers in Dallas, and hundreds of students will readily verify that fact. Mr. Stanley Marcus praised her abilities. Mr. Ely Straus, another Dallas businessman, stated that he sailed through English at The University of Texas, because he had had Miss Rowe at Forest Avenue High. A school in east Dallas bears her name, and a rare book collection at the Dallas Public Library honors her achievements in the field of education.

TEN YEARS OF PUBLIC EDUCATION IN DALLAS

"A people's patriotism is measured by their intelligence and the intelligence of the masses is measured by the efficiency of their public schools."

This statement was made by J.M. Howell, president of the school board in 1894. The schools had been open for ten years, there were eighty-seven graduates, the enrollment was increasing, and there were new and greater opportunities for learning. By this time there were three courses of study available at Central High. There was the classical course. This prepared one for the finest liberal arts college. There was the scientific course. This prepared one for the technical and scientific course of study in college. Then there was the English course. This prepared one for teaching. All three courses required that the student take three years of Latin, four years of English, and courses in algebra, geometry, trigonometry, chemistry, astronomy, physics, political economy, history, botany, zoology, and government. The classical course really differed in only one way — four years of Latin were required instead of three.

The beginning of a sliding pay scale was a new venture in arranging for teacher salaries that year.

                1 year experience — $45 a month
                2 years experience — $50 a month
                3 years experience — $55 a month
                4 years experience — $60 a month
                5 years experience — $65 a month (Top salary)

The principals were paid just a bit more. These salaries were low even for that day.

The old Central High School building needed to be replaced, and the principal, Mr. William Lipscomb, was working toward its replacement. Meanwhile another building was under construction. The Dallas council had called for the building of a black high school to be named Booker T. Washington. When this building was completed it was identified as the finest high school in the Southwest for black students. That original building now houses the Arts Magnet School.

The Superintendent of Schools, Mr. J.L. Long, proudly announced that there were 5,137 students enrolled in the system. He also announced his schedule of activities. He was in his office each afternoon from 3:30 to 4:30 P.M. He also had office hours from 2:30 to 5:30 P.M. on Saturdays. The rest of his time was spent in the schools helping the teachers.

The superintendent instructed the teachers to make extra reading assignments. He felt that the teachers must "excite the students into such a disposition" of wanting to read. He said that the upper elementary grades should be reading the works of Hans Christian Anderson, the Grimm Brothers, *Arabian Nights, Robinson Crusoe,* and the Sir Walter Scott poems and ballads. Superintendent Long was himself excited over the fact that each of the sixteen schools had a library. He listed three reasons why he thought that there should be school libraries. One, there was a strong relation of the teacher to the child's mental and moral development. Reading made this relation even stronger. Two, there was a meager supply of appropriate literature to be found in the homes of some of the children. A library at school for them was a necessity. Three, the library was the most powerful agency in the world. J.L. Long felt that there should be a public library in the city of Dallas as well as the school libraries. He was instrumental in getting one.

THE SECOND DECADE

"Learning maketh young men temperate, is the comfort of old age, standing for wealth with poverty, and serving as an ornament to riches."

Cicero wrote that for school teachers whose learning had to stand in for the wealth that they would never experience. That sliding pay scale offered in 1894 did raise the spirits and the pay checks some, but really not enough. For the teachers had taken a cut in pay in 1893, the year of recession, and all that the scale really did was to bring their salaries up to what they had been in 1892. Still, these called servants of education felt that they fared better that year. In fact, the whole system began the second decade of its existence with an upswing. There was a farsighted school board president in 1895, F.M. Ervay:

> We do not wish to disparage the private educational institutions of other states; but it is the duty of our public school boards to place the public free school system upon an equality with the very best there is in the republic.

What he really meant was that the Galveston and Houston public school systems were doing more building and more hiring of teachers than Dallas was, so the Dallasites had to get busy, meet, and beat such growth. Ervay felt that the property owners would want to up those taxes, so more could be done for public education. He hustled in two new teacher specialists, G.W. Ware for penmanship and art and Anna Goslin for music. These two special teachers were a must if Dallas schools were going to keep up with educational trends in the country.

A TEACHER INSTITUTE, DALLAS, 1898

A teacher institute was held in Dallas in 1898, and the major portion of the meeting was devoted to the importance of teaching geography. As an elementary school student I always wondered why we spent so much time on geography, but I never asked because I was terrified of my geography teacher, Mrs. Minnie Bone. We just learned what she taught without question. Minnie Bone was famous for her maps that hung all around the room on rollers. She'd jerk those maps down with gusto, and we children would sit straight up and learn where everything was — cities, mountains, rivers, oceans, streams, gullies, caves, molehills. Nothing was too remote or too small for Mrs. Bone and her maps. Years later at North Texas State University, I was appearing in a Noel Coward play. I entered into a scene and one of the characters in the play asked me where I had been. My line was,

"I've been to Kuala Lumpur, where hardly anyone ever goes." A cast member stopped the rehearsal to ask where Kuala Lumpur was.

"It's in Malaysia. And why do I know? Because with Minnie Bone in the fifth grade, we went everywhere including those places 'where hardly anyone ever goes!' "

We kids weren't the only people terrified of Mrs. Bone. Our parents were scared of her too. When I came home and announced to my father that Mrs. Bone was selling World Books and that she thought I needed a set, my father immediately put in an order for the books, with bookcase and study guide, because he didn't wish to tangle with Mrs. Bone. She held the respect of parents and children in the entire Robert E. Lee School district. Amid my elementary school memorabilia I found these lyrics that I wrote in the fifth grade, and this was quite a tribute to that grand lady of geography.

> My country tis of thee,
> I must learn geography
> If I should roam.
> Watch all those rivers flow
> See where they're bound to go.
> Their current I will know,
> Hail, Minnie Bone!

Superintendent J.L. Long, wrote about the 1898 teacher institute in great detail. He stated that the teachers felt that geography was the basis of all subjects — all science. In geography a student learned the culture of man, the attitudes and feelings of man, and the universal laws controlling the earth. Knowing all this would bring a student "into the discernment of God." Finding God was an important part of the curriculum back then.

Also, Geography was considered a practical subject. The

lines and river directions determined the climate of a place. The climate determined the occupations and manner and customs of the people; knowing all this would lead a child to the understanding of all people.

The teachers agreed that literature and geography would be studied together. This was a very practical approach. Literature would become more meaningful and more interesting to the students. Mr. Long also reminded the teachers that the subjects must be kept alive. "The children will be naturally curious, unless their curiosity is stamped out by a distasteful and incompetent teacher."

The superintendent recorded the exact words from the various teachers and principals in attendance at the institute. Leila P. Cowart, principal, stated that she was "never very successful in teaching the change of seasons." She also stated that she always taught map drawing. This encouraged preciseness and neatness. Miss Cowart went on to state that she taught with the book open. "A teacher should omit questions referring to obscure or unimportant places." (She and Minnie Bone would harbor some differences over that statement.)

Mr. Long stated that "there was a most interesting discussion along here, in the midst of which a very enjoyable tilt between Miss Cowart and Mr. William Lipscomb, high school principal, took place." (The superintendent went on to say that no effort would be made to describe this tilt. "It would be like attempting to report a sigh, an atmosphere, a ripple of laughter, or a flood of sunlight.")

It's hard to believe that those words of poetic excellence came out of a school board report. J.L. Long gave those reports a definite touch of class.

The final session of the institute concluded with everyone agreeing that the students needed to study geography so that they could see human relationships. This study had practical value. Now, this thought was to be the last for the day, and the institute was to close. However, Mrs. T.M. Simpson, teacher at Columbian Elementary School, wanted to make sure that everyone understood the meaning of "practical value." She opened a whole new can of worms, and the teachers had to stay an extra hour in order to discuss this nebulous question. She went on to say that it was most important to cultivate a love for the beautiful. Education was to give pleasure. A rebuttal came from Mr. Harvey Armstrong, whose job title was High School Assistant, not in charge of a department. He stated that a "pupil should become self sustaining before he is entitled to the luxuries of life."

Mr. Lipcomb retorted that he did not believe that "people had to be rich before they could enjoy the luxuries of life." As a true educator he went on to state that "correct information removes prejudice, broadens character, begets interests and develops tolerance, sympathy, and brotherly love." In education, the money made must not be considered — only the love given.

The meeting went on with more discussion. It was decided that a teacher who only tested for knowledge — failed. Correct thought would lead a pupil to correct reasoning. Only with accurate reasoning powers would he succeed. Mr. Long finally concluded the institute with this statement, "Teaching is like building a wall. The bricks must be polished so that they will fit together in a solid wall of life."

As a former high school teacher, reading of this institute, I thought of three things. First, I realized that faculty meetings and institutes have always been the same. They're all very idealistic, and they would all be at least one hour shorter, if someone didn't bring up something just as everyone was getting ready to leave.

Secondly, I realized how much a touch of geography would have added to my American literature classes. *The Song of Hiawatha* was required reading. Combining the reading of that poem with a geography lesson would have offered a truly exciting study. We wouldn't have stopped with the reading of the "shores of Gitche Gumee." We would have studied the current of the river. Those river currents just might have been the cause of Hiawatha's poor relationship with his father, the West Wind. Perhaps his father should have blown from the East. And too, all those warm feelings that Hiawatha had for Minnehaha, could have been helped by the climate. I can see all sorts of possibilities that would have been revealed if a deeper study of geography had accompanied the reading of that poem.

Thirdly, I stopped to evaluate my teaching. Did I really polish bricks? Did I keep my classes alive? I certainly tried to by answering each poignant and penetrating question that a student would ask with a truthful and stimulating answer. In Senior English, several times a week, a student would ask,

"Why do we have to read this Shakespeare junk?" I always answered in a tasteful and competent way. "Because the school system pays me to teach this course of study to the students of the district. You're a student of the district, so learn it."

This answer and the fact that by the end of the day some of Hamlet's madness had set into my personality, always seemed to satisfy their inquisitive minds.

Actually, the last senior English class that I ever taught was really kept alive by the fact that I almost had a baby in the classroom. The seniors gave me a baby shower and one of the quick-witted and long-sighted students pointed out that all the baby cloths were yellow so that I could have a boy or a girl. Fortunately, Jill, the daughter who was born, was a pretty baby who was readily identified by the fawning public as a girl, even though her wardrobe was dominated by yellow.

AS THE CENTURY TURNS

The course of study for that year, 1898, was recorded at the end of the written report. It remained much the same except there was a course in nature study added in the first grade. This study would have two lessons each week; the seasons would be studied. The children would study nature's way of preparing for winter. These questions would be answered:

"Why do the leaves fall? Why do some trees remain green? Why does the water freeze?"

The grande dame of education at that time, Leila Cowart, had mentioned at the teacher institute of the trouble she had in teaching the seasons. To a layman, not in the educational field, the teaching of seasons would appear to be a fairly simple thing — so simple one wondered it "taught" in the first place. Not so. Margaret O'Neill, a master teacher for thirty-eight years in the Dallas schools told of having trouble teaching the seasons to her elementary school class at Thomas W. Field School. When she thought that everyone understood about winter, spring, summer, and fall, a hand shot into the air.

"I know the four seasons. There's deer, quail, dove, and oh, yes, rabbit." Mrs. O'Neill took a deep breath and started all over in the study.

The report for 1898 was completed with two reminders. Calisthenics were to continue twice a day, and every student must commit to memory twenty-five lines of poetry each week.

The turn of the century came and with it such a vast increase of students. The system started out with (eventually) 1,455 students, twenty-three teachers, and property valued at $32,411. Now, in 1900, there were 6,515 students, 124 teachers, and property valued at $293,395. The secretary of the school board, T.G. Terry, proudly reported the figures.

The 1900 report began with these words of J.L. Long: "The community that has placed knowledge within the reach of all its members is civilized."

The kids were pretty civilized, because there was very little corporal punishment reported. Teachers all worked toward less truancy and better cooperation between school and home. Knowledge was within the reach of the children of Dallas, a large city of 55,000 people.

Three changes were spotlighted in the report. First, there was now a library in every school. There wasn't a librarian on the scene yet, but the books were available for the students. The principal served his school as librarian.

Secondly, the students were allowed to leave the schoolgrounds to go to lunch. There was always a scheduled recess period for lunch, but the kids ate in the classrooms. Now, they could eat out which was better for the teachers. A ballot was sent to the parents who were to determine whether the free period would be thirty minutes or one hour. The parents naturally voted for the thirty minute period. The less time that the students had outside the school, the better.

Thirdly, there was a mothers club formed, and Mrs. George B. Dealey was president. It was called the Dallas Public School Art League.

The routine at the high school was just clicking along with Mr. J. Morgan, principal. However, he looked around at the high school and saw that it needed much repair. There had not been a tax levied since 1890, so money was running short. He approached the School Board for more tax money, and got it. A ten cent tax for every $100 worth of property was levied for education, and a five cent tax on every $400 worth of property was levied for the care of the school buildings.

The chemistry lab at the high school was a great source of pride. The students in class were able to successfully experiment in wireless telegraphy, in the observance of temperature, and in the study of atmospheric pressure and air currents. This lab at the high school was the closest thing to a weather bureau that the citizens of Dallas had, for a weather bureau had not been set up yet in Dallas. However, it was soon to be.

The first weather man in Dallas was Dr. Joseph L. Cline, who told his story in his book, *When The Heavens Frowned*. Dr. Cline graduated from a small college in Tennessee and then joined his brother in Galveston, Texas. There he worked for the weather bureau and in 1900 predicted the hurricane that was going to take thousands of lives, almost his own. He so accurately predicted this disaster that after the devastating hurricane he was sent to the U.S. Weather Bureau in Puerto Rico. Then he was sent to Corpus Christi, and then finally he was sent to Dallas to establish the first weather bureau station here. This station was in the old Dallas Cotton Exchange building on Akard. It was later moved to the new exchange on St. Paul and remained there until it was consolidated with the Love Field Airway Service. Dr. Cline always helped the students at the high school.

Dr. Cline was the father of Durwood Cline, Oak Cliff High graduate, who opened a music store in the 1920s on Elm Street. Durwood also conducted one of the most popular dance bands that played in and around Dallas for over fifty years.

PENMANSHIP

A report from the writing and drawing supervisor, Mr. G.W. Ware was included in the 1900 report. He pointed out that vertical writing was growing in favor more and more with the teachers. Mr. Ware in his report cited that "... they laughed at Christ, they poked fun at Columbus, they teased Fulton, and now the general public is condemning vertical writing." However, he felt that it would eventually be accepted.

Mr. Ware went on to point out that five hundred years ago people felt that education was too dangerous for all to have. Four hundred years ago a few dreamers like Erasmus were around pushing for more education. The art of printing was created three hundred years ago. This was a boost to learning. Two hundred years ago Locke got things rolling. Then one hundred years ago there was some public education enjoyed and appreciated. Drawing was taught only to the especially talented fifty years ago. Twenty-five years ago drawing entered some of the public schools. But today, 1900, all the elementary children enjoy art classes.

"Tomorrow, there will be art classes in every school." Then Mr. Ware quoted Horace Mann, famed educator.

> With no other guide than a mere inspection of the copy books of the pupils, I could tell whether drawing was taught in the schools or not; so uniformly superior was the handwriting in the schools where drawing was taught in connection with it. On seeing this, I was reminded of that saying of Pestolozzi — 'that without drawing there can be no writing.'

LITERATURE

"A liking for good literature and an appreciation of true art is the best possible safeguard young people can have against low forms of amusements. Good literature is a source of pleasure and an influence for good."

The superintendent approved the reading list for the children in the primary grades on up through high school. He suggested that they read stories dealing with showing kindness to animals. Nature study books were on the list. The older children were to read *Evangeline, Ivanhoe, Merchant Of Venice,* and *Enoch Arden.* The high school crowd was to read many works of Longfellow, Whittier, Hawthorne, Bryant, Poe, and Lanier. In order to graduate, a student had to read and study the meaning of the *Ancient Mariner, The Tempest, Macbeth,* and *Paradise Lost.* Those in the Latin classes had the advantages of still reading and studying *Ceasar,* and the works of Cicero and Virgil.

MUSIC

The music teachers continued teaching their special courses pointing out that "a song will always fill the heart of a child."

Music would always be needed. The basic subjects taught "to know;" the music courses taught "to do." *Knowing* was essential; *doing* was important too.

MATH

In 1900 the math department in the high school expanded to include one course on a college level. Those students taking this course were going to engineering school, so they would be well prepared for this technical scientific course.

1900–1901

The twentieth century had arrived and the students of Dallas were ready for the changes that it was going to bring. The spirit of individualism reigned, there was general prosperity, and a feeling of expectancy was in the air.

William McKinley ran for president and won. His running mate, Theodore (Teddy) Roosevelt, considered the job of vice-president as a road to nowhere. However, an assassin's bullet claimed President McKinley, and Teddy was in the White House. President Roosevelt attended a reunion of his Rough Riders in San Antonio and on his way back to Washington, he stopped off in Dallas. School turned out for him, and the kids all went to the parade in his honor. My mother was there in the crowd of children, and she told all about it — several hundred times. It would be impossible for me to forget the story.

Chapter Two

The Turn
Of The Century

On a spring day, 1905, Leila Patience Cowart marched her students from the Columbian Elementary School, which was on Akard Street, where the Convention Center stands today, down to Main Street, where they waited patiently at the curb for President Theodore Roosevelt to ride by in a horse-drawn buggy. Every child was clutching a bouquet of flowers which he or she had purchased at the school for ten cents. The children had been instructed to toss the flowers gently at Teddy as he passed by. My mother was in the crowd and she recalled how the girls carefully directed the flowers to the smiling, waving president. The boys rolled the flowers into balls and threw them overhanded. The rolled flowers were harmless missiles, but Miss Cowart was outraged over this action. The boys stayed in that day after school and got a proper talking to. It was always dangerous to ruffle Miss Cowart.

Leila Cowart was principal of Columbian School, the school named after Christopher Columbus. She ruled like a queen from that first school day in 1884, and her regality impressed the teachers and the students. She never married. "It's vulgar for all the women of a family to get married. In every common family, you'll find all the women married."

She lived with her Confederate brother, his family, and another unmarried sister. This sister, Miss Lora Cowart, had a private school for girls in Dallas where she taught all the Southern refinements. With two unmarried girls, this family had a double helping of class.

Every morning Miss Cowart arrived in her buggy drawn by her horse, Patsy, assisted by her gardener, Mr. Creel. The children gathered to pet Patsy, but not for long, because as Miss Cowart alighted from the buggy, the children rushed into place. The girls lined up on one side of the walk, and the boys lined up on the other. Miss Cowart passed between them and the children bowed as she passed.

The teachers were all at the door to greet their principal each morning. The towering Miss Cowart strolled in like a royal princess. No one ever complained at her school. One of the Cowart platitudes set the tone, "You must not complain. Say you are well or all is well with you. You cannot please by piping on that minor chord of disease."

The teachers and the students followed Miss Cowart into the assembly room each morning, so that they could all "breathe." She raised the windows regardless of the temperature outside and made everyone breathe. They would vigorously inhale and exhale for about five minutes, or until Miss Cowart decided that their lungs held only the freshest of air. Then she would lead the group in song. Every morning, they began the singing time with the hymn, "Come Thou Almighty King." This would have been all right — except that three-fourths of the children were Jewish. Dallas had an unusually large Jewish population living in the downtown area. The parents of these children were merchants, and some of the families lived above their stores. Others lived nearby. Columbian was the closest elementary school to town, so the Linz, Titche, Harris, Kahn, Marcus, and Dreyfuss children were all there. Not one would refrain from singing, "Come Thou Almighty King." Miss Cowart was a stern taskmistress; therefore, it was safer to sing of the Lord's coming than it was to cross Miss Cowart. The Jewish parents didn't complain about their children singing a Christian hymn, because these parents were also terrified of Miss Cowart.

Still in assembly the children and teachers pledged allegiance to the flag and sang, "My Country 'Tis Of Thee." Then everyone marched to their classes for reading, numbers, and penmanship. Reading was out loud. Articulation, enunciation, pronunciation remained paramount in importance. Everyone was urged to have a good tone, clear and full, and the teacher was told to help her children avoid drawling and speaking in a monotone. "Read with expression," was the constant command.

Nothing is more boring than having to listen to a kid read in a monotone. Miss Lottie Burr, a funny lady who taught and entertained students for years in the Dallas schools, always said that the best way to get rid of a visiting parent or school official was to have the worst reader in the class get up and read a part of the Constitution. It was amazing how quickly that parent or school official would move on to visit another class or suddenly remember a pressing appointment. Listening to a kid haltingly read in a monotone is a terrible experience. Teachers of reading struggle against this practice.

At noon Miss Cowart would dismiss the children for lunch and recess. One of the favorite play areas was the Confederate Cemetery across the street from the school. (This is the Confederate Cemetery that is in front of the Convention Center.) Before the recess bell had ceased ringing, the kids were bounding over the school yard, across the street, and into the graveyard. However, as soon as they arrived at the cemetery for a good game of tombstone hopping, a window at the school would fly up, the head and shoulders of Miss Cowart would lunge out of it, the lady's big rolling voice demanding,

"Get back into the school yard immediately." With no hesitation, every child came back, and certainly there were no stragglers in the crowd. One might hear a kid say under his breath, "One of these days, we're going to get to stay and have a good time in the cemetery."

Every Friday afternoon from 2:30 to 3:30 P.M. was speech day. The students who were studying elocution at one of the private schools in Dallas were always considered the bold ones. They would give readings with enthusiasm and expression, laden with multiple gestures. With a toss of her braids, the most precocious and sophisticated little girl in the class would delight her classmates with a reading such as this one.

> You must wake me early, mother,
> You must wake me early, mother,

> You must wake me early, mother,
> For I will be queen of the May.

The repetition was good for the study of vocal variety.

Everyone recited on Friday. There could be no shyness. Oral recitation was expected, and if the rather slight, timid, not so sharp little boy did not wish to recite, he really could not do much about it. He had to get up and do his best.

The teachers of the twentieth century were greatly affected by the laboratory school set up at the University of Chicago by John Dewey. Dewey wanted to train students for useful living. Self-expression, cooperation, activity, experimentation, construction, play and contact with nature became the watchwords of his new school. The early Dallas educators studied John Dewey and used some of his educational theories. The children were urged to describe verbally the things they saw. They were asked to explain their feelings. The pupils at Columbian really never had any trouble finding self-expression, cooperation, activity, experimentation, construction, play and contact with nature, because they lived downtown, and at the turn of the century there was plenty to see and experience in downtown Dallas.

My mother was born in 1894 and reared on Main Street in Dallas, and she never ran out of stories about the happenings that took place in front of her father's West End Bakery. Genealogists always find that in every family, there is at least one who swears that the family property used to be where *now* the busiest intersection in the city can be found. This was surely true of my family. The John Kennedy Memorial stands where my grandfather's bakery once stood. Mother could never remember exactly when my grandfather sold the rich piece of land, but sell it he did. We have none of the wealth from the sale, only the memories of the street.

The children who lived on Main Street received a liberal education at Columbian School and many learning experiences from the street. They learned to tell time from the clock in the tower of the Courthouse, known always as Old Red. The tower with the clock had to be removed some years ago when the old red building got top-heavy — the tower was putting structural stress on the building.

There was plenty of self-expression for the kids at Columbian School, a la John Dewey, when on their way to school they saw E.H.R. Green, Hetty Green's son, drive the very first automobile in Dallas. He didn't drive it himself. He had a chauffeur, Jess Illingsworth, who was a race car driver and an automobile enthusiast. Some children went down to the depot and watched a crew unload the mysterious four cylinder buggy off the train from St. Louis. Then they watched Jess help the large and smiling Ned Green into the car for the drive down Main Street.

Ned Green never let the children ride with him, but Mr. John Schuett, the businessman who had the *second* car in Dallas, took the kids for rides. My mother remembered the car vase in the Schuett car. There hanging between the side front and back windows was a china vase for flowers. Schuett's car was electric, and it went twenty miles an hour down Main Street. It didn't have what children might look for today in a car — radio, tape deck, stereo speakers. But who needed those things when one had a car vase full of fresh flowers.

The children who lived downtown experienced automatic temperance lessons. There were at least five saloons on every block. The wealthy and elite who indulged themselves a little too much, were allowed to "sleep it off" in the back rooms of the saloons. However, the poor drunk who became unruly and didn't have any more money for drink was thrown out on the street where he would lie sprawled until the "hoodlum wagon" came by and hauled him off to the jail house. All this excitement was witnessed sometimes daily by the sparkling eyes of the downtown students.

The last lynching that was ever to take place in Dallas happened one afternoon when the children were returning from school. A black man had been arrested for molesting a child. The townsfolk didn't wait for his trial, but broke into his cell, threw the accused victim out of the courthouse second-story window, dragged his lifeless body down Main Street, and hung the body on the Elks Arch, corner of Main and Akard. This was in 1910. Obviously, there was plenty of action for Show and Tell in Dallas at the turn of the century.

John Dewey also said that the teachers should make the most of holidays. The learning of the calendar and of special days was an important experience. Miss Cowart agreed wholeheartedly on this point. She really went in for the Maypole Celebration. Every child in the school appeared at some time on stage during the production. My mother was in the middle of it all. The celebration in 1902 must have been an important occasion because a picture was made of my mother and her brother in costume after the production. The younger girls played the parts of garden flowers with the blondes being lilies and the brunettes roses. Judging from my mother's coloring and costume, she was lily material. The older girls drifted through the flowers with sprinkling cans watering the "garden" of students. My mother's brother was given a major role in the nursery rhyme dramatization. He was Jack Sprat, and my mother remembered well his rather plump "wife."

Pageants were beautifully organized and perfected at the school, because Miss Cowart directed. She did the whole thing with numbers. A child was given a number and stood on the corresponding number written on the floor of the stage. The directing was rather mechanical, but the children never questioned where they were to go. They went to their numbers. Miss Cowart told them to see the number using only the corner of the eye.

"Don't look down," she'd command in her authoritarian voice.

After the Maypole production, many of the children went to the ice cream parlor across from the school for a soda. The girls sat on the curled wrought iron chairs like little ladies sipping their drinks. They were horrified when the boys made awful noises by sucking violently on their soda straws. This lack of refinement was most distressing to the girls who were still delightfully dressed as flowers.

Mr. Dewey didn't stress memory work as Miss Cowart did. There were memory gems each week. A student committed to memory at least twenty-nine lines of a good poetical or patriotic selection. Patriotism was a prime topic in all schools. There was a sociological reason for this. The American people were in the midst of a growing spirit of nationalism. Public education was a tool of the national state. People began to have the power of reading, writing, and speaking. Most believed that the crucial factor in assuring the use of this power for the benefit of the state came through patriotic education. This was a part of that broad western movement of nationalism, and Dallas was in that movement. In fact, as well as being nationalistic, Dallas was known as the city whose population never ceased to praise itself. Dallas people believed in Dallas. It was as early as 1873 that the *Fort Worth Democrat* complained that the first thing the children east of the Trinity were taught to speak was, "Hurrah for Dallas," and under the tutorage of Miss Leila Cowart, they spoke it in golden, rounded, tones.

A PARADE OF GRADUATES

Horace Mann served in Massachusetts four years as a state representative and then four years as a state senator. In 1837 he was appointed secretary of the state board of education and labored for the rest of his life to improve the public schools, to increase teacher's salaries, and to set up teacher training schools. One day Mr. Mann was viewing a school and said,

"It does seem that these massive buildings, with their beauty of design and their elegance of appointment, represent a great outlay of thought, of labor and of money for the education of the youth of the country, but the saving of only one boy would be an ample return on the investment."

A listener asked,

"Mr. Mann, do you not think you made that statement rather strong?" Mr. Mann replied,

"Not if it were my boy."

It's great to save one boy, but a school system will always be judged by the number of successful graduates which it produces. Dallas High School kept up with its graduates for ten years, proudly reporting each year in the annual school report the whereabouts and the activities of their successful grads. An alumni association, the first of its kind in Dallas, was organized in December, 1897, with Frank J. Hall as president. Frank Hall, class of 1893, was the first graduate to become a doctor. He later served as the vice-president of the Board of Education in Dallas.

One of the outstanding and early presidents of the alumni association was Mr. Eugene Locke, Sr., class of 1902. Mr. Locke after graduation went to law school, became an attorney, and married Marie Murphy, whose father J.P. Murphy owned and directed the first big real estate company in Dallas, Murphy and Bolanz. Eugene Locke was one of the charter members of the Dallas Foundation. He with George Dealey and Edwin Kiest, drew up the first flexible community trust to be created in Texas. He also served on the board of directors of Equitable Life. As chief justice of the Texas Supreme Court under Governor W. Lee O'Daniel he was known as a "seeker of justice, a man of good will with rightful intentions and responsible of all matters of life."

He had a son, Eugene Locke, Jr., who graduated from North Dallas High in 1934. Eugene Jr., like his father, was an attorney. He ran for governor of Texas but lost. Later he served as U.S. Ambassador to Pakistan and Deputy Ambassador to South Vietnam. He was holder of the Freedom Medal.

Eugene Locke, Sr., was not the first Dallas grad to become an attorney. W. Sherwood Bramleitt, class of 1891, was the first attorney. The first graduate to teach school in Dallas was Mrs. M.S. Sine (nee Helm) who graduated in 1887. She taught at Cumberland Hill Elementary School. Mrs. Jules Roberts (nee Bryan), an 1888 graduate, became the first vocal teacher. The Lawther brothers, William and Raymond, who graduated in 1896 and 1898 respectively, opened a feed store and made a great deal of money.

Another graduate who became an attorney was Lucius Quintus Cincinnatus Lamar, III, class of 1899. This young man was named for his grandfather, the brilliant, fiery, influential Mississippi senator, L.Q.C. Lamar, I. President John Kennedy included the gallant senator in his book, *Profiles Of Courage*. Kennedy told of the day in 1874 when the freshman congressman Lamar, from Mississippi, spoke ever so simply yet ever so clearly to touch the hearts of every listener as he pleaded for amity and justice between the North and the South. The U.S. Congress was still torn assunder by the remembrances of the war, and with this one unforgettable speech, L.Q.C. Lamar reached some hearts and changed some attitudes of both Southerners and Northerners when he quoted his arch enemy, Charles Sumner of Massachusetts.

"My Countrymen, know one another, and you will love one another."

Somehow after that day in 1874, the iron walls and the bitter fences that were still standing between the South and North began to melt and fall.

The father of Lucius Quintus Cincinnatus Lamar, III, the Dallas graduate, died, and his widowed mother married Dallas Judge W.L. Crawford, an unforgettable criminal lawyer. Judge

Crawford, known for his tears, was able to cry on cue, and with his persuasive tears he was able to turn any jury into a ball of putty ready for his molding. Mrs. Crawford became the first lady of art in Dallas. She turned the Ross Avenue Crawford home into an private art gallery, and she introduced the first impressive art to Dallas society.

There were other graduates who went on to accomplish great things. Frank B. Godley from the class of 1900 went to the U.S. Naval Academy. Roy P. Howell, also of the 1900 class, became the typical Texas rancher in Weatherford, Texas. Miss Minnie Lichtenstein, class of 1901, married Herbert Marcus, who founded the renowned Neiman Marcus Store. He became the nation's leading merchant, and now his son and grandsons are minding that store quite well.

The black schools had their share of brilliant graduates who went on to fine futures. The first black graduate to become a doctor was John W. Reed. He graduated in 1892, went on to medical school, and settled in Denver, Colorado, to practice medicine. Mrs. E.O. Lindley, (nee Hall), taught at Booker T. Washington High. She graduated in 1892 and stayed to teach at her alma mater. Ammon S. Wells, class of 1895, was the first black lawyer who was a graduate of a Dallas school, and Charles L. Morgan, class of 1897, was the first graduate to become an accountant.

The citizens were so impressed with their graduates that they stayed right behind the public schools, watched their growth and determined some places where the schools needed improvement. The 55,000 people living in Dallas in 1902 had to pay more taxes, but paying these taxes was considered the duty and the privilege of any citizen who had the opportunity to live in a large and exciting city like Dallas. Citizens decided that they wanted their schools to be numerous and small. A small school would serve an immediate neighborhood, and the educational leaders found that if a neighborhood spirit developed within each school, there were no severe discipline problems.

For the first time in 1902, boundary lines were set that would determine the population of each school. Until that year, a student went to whatever school he wished to attend. Usually he chose the one nearest to him, but not always. It was discovered that if a child went to a school and in going had to pass another school on his way, trouble would erupt. Therefore, thinking again toward developing a closely knit neighborhood spirit which would offset many discipline problems, the school board set boundary lines, and each child was required to attend the school in his district.

The major problems that the principal had with the children still dealt with tardiness and truancy. Superintendent J.L. Long noticed that the attendance tied in closely with the cotton crops. When the crops were good, there was a drop in enrollment of both white and black students. When the crops were good, the black students dropped out to work. The white people made more money and could send their children to private schools. Even though there were successful graduates all around to prove the worth of public education, private education was a status symbol to some families.

Those successful graduates caused more educational backing, for in 1902, a patron society was formed. These patrons were very interested in the examinations and evaluations of the students. Teachers were encouraged to give lots of tests. After all — the students were going to have to take college entrance tests and civil service tests, so it was best that they become acquainted with the testing process. Besides, a good test is a good review of the subject matter, so testing was definitely encouraged.

The patrons were concerned about the health of the students. They arranged for an annual eye examination for each child. However, primarily they were interested in the Dallas High School building. The building was purchased in 1884, and now in 1906, the structure was unsuitable for high school students. It wasn't large enough to hold all the students comfortably, the stairways were objectionable, the halls were long, dark, narrow, cold and uninviting. The classrooms were too far apart. In other words, it was time for a new school, and the school patrons felt that they could easily persuade the school board to assess taxes for the next school building. The tax burden would be light if one's home was assessed at $1,000. Then the $9 a year tax assessment could be afforded by most home owners. The desired new high school building was built.

PUBLIC SCHOOLS — PREP SCHOOLS, TRAINING SCHOOLS

Today people are very concerned about the quality of education that the students are getting in the public schools.

"Much more reading and communicative skills should be mastered," was one of the demands made by Ross Perot, the world renowned Dallas businessman who has taken a personal interest in public education. Like interested citizens everywhere, Mr. Perot is disturbed by the low achievement scores that are made by the students in Dallas. Actually, all over the United States test scores reveal public schools are not turning out well-educated people. However, if Mr. Perot were to look into the curriculum of the schools, the achievement records of the students, and the teaching skills displayed by the teachers, at the turn of the century, he would be extremely impressed. Without second thoughts, aggressive, successful, and intelligent leaders and achievers of the Dallas community entrusted their children to the public schools because these schools were like superior prep schools and academies — ideal for those students going on to college. Also they were fine training schools for those who were going from high school into the skilled labor force. However, regardless, of which road a student took, every student had to learn to read well and to communicate effectively or he could not graduate.

There were literary societies and debating societies in the Dallas schools patterned after the Greek literary societies and the Hasty Pudding Debate societies of the eastern universities. These societies were maintained in connection with the regular school work. The teachers taught the students to read, and the literary and debate societies gave the students the opportunity to use the reading and speaking skills. As always, learning was fine, achievement was satisfying, but using the secured knowledge made the knowledge exciting.

The first debate recorded in the Dallas schools was on this topic: Resolved, that there should be municipal ownership of public utilities. Eugene Locke, Sr. was on the team and held to the affirmative side of the question. Mr. Locke was the valedictorian, June, 1900. At the graduation exercises he recited two essays that he had written, "The Art of Seeing Things" and "Live to Do and Not to Dream." He was trained to speak fluently, because Dallas pupils had constant and systematic drill in declamation, recitation, reading, composition, debate, original oratory, and such other appropriate exercises that would contribute toward a complete mastery of the English language. It was also the concern of the English teacher to add ease and dignity to the pupils' general bearing and to promote the development of the tastes and accomplishments of a cultivated and highly educated people.

In October, 1901, there was a debate held that used a topic that had all America talking. Booker T. Washington had dined at the Presidential mansion on October 16, 1901, and in spite of efforts to avoid publicity for the affair, Washington's name was printed on the list of official callers for that day. A Theodore Roosevelt biography recorded,

"Southern whites reacted violently to the news. They accused the president of encouraging dangerous concepts of racial and social equality. Their protests led friends of the Negro into a spirited defense of the incident."

So, it was a daring act of the debate coach at Dallas High to offer this debate that fall: Resolved, President Roosevelt used very poor taste in inviting Booker T. Washington to dine at the White House. Because of the Southern gentility which existed so strongly in the people of Dallas at that time, it was surprising to note that the topic was even considered to have had a negative side. Well-remembered Dallasite, E.O. Tenison, a student then in the high school, was part of that debate squad. Reports do not show on which side he debated, but it is interesting to read from Ted Dealey's book, *Diaper Days In Dallas*, that Ed Tenison "always came to school in a two-horse surrey driven by a negro." One might draw his own conclusion. Nevertheless, the debate was held without any incident at the school. Actually, there was very little student unrest at any school at any time, for at the beginning of each semester *all* of the students in the Dallas schools would sign an oath of perfect conduct. The oaths were usually kept.

One of the early literary societies was called A.D.A. The students met after school for debates and literary discussions. There was fun too on the agenda, because on October 15, 1904, the kids met to debate: Resolved, that United States senators should be elected by direct vote of the people. The minutes of the meeting note that after the debate, they hastily rushed off to the fairgrounds to see the fireworks display. On October 29, the membership had a Halloween party at Judge Cockrell's home, and these costumes were seen: Queen of Hearts, Little Lord Fauntleroy, Martha Washington, Happy Hooligan, Foxy Grandpa, and Uncle Sam.

In November of 1904, the debate squad planned a trip to Weatherford, Texas, to debate with the Demosthnenic Debating Society of Weatherford High. There was a great interest in this first out-of-town debate, and Mr. Charles Tomkies, the coach, gave his students all the coaching needed for success. These literary societies and debating clubs were all over the country, even in the small hamlet of Weatherford, for the nation was striving to become a totally literate country with everyone gaining a fine background in the English language.

Later that same year, another literary and debating society was organized, the Phi Kappa Fraternity. One of their first topics to debate was: Resolved, that every citizen of Dallas should vote *for* the bond issue on November 14. They conquered other subjects too, such as: Resolved, that the people should uphold the President in his fight for railroad rate regulation and: Resolved, that prohibition is the best method of solving the liquor situation. Both of the societies were directed by Mr. Tomkies. Principal Morgan mentioned that all debating practiced by the A.D.A. was modeled after the United States Congress and the Phi Kappa debates were modeled after the British Parliament. Therefore, the students were trained in both styles of debating.

In 1906, the Phi Kappas sponsored a debate: Resolved, that football is beneficial to universities. Tickets were sold for the event, and the proceeds went to the football team at the school. The whole student body attended and showed much enthusiasm for the event.

When the new school was built on Bryan in 1907, another literary society was organized, the Theta Delta Phi. This group gave a peace program on May 18, 1908, commemorating the anniversary of the first meeting of the Hague conference. The principal mentioned that the new building was so much more suitable for debates and other literary society programs. However, the societies were not only debating in the auditorium. By this time, they had enthusiastically branched out into the community. A special program was held at the library on the

100th anniversary of General Robert E. Lee's birthday, and a handsome oil painting of General Lee was presented to the school.

The intellectual attitude drifted into the high schools of the early 1900s, because as I stated at the beginning of this chapter, the schools were not totally divorced from the attitudes of the private academies. Even though the schools were free and public, there existed an intellectual snobbishness, and the clubs were formed to display it. There was the Johnsonian Club, that claimed Samuel Johnson, the poet, essayist, moralist, and major literary figure of the eighteenth century, as their leader. The purpose of the club was set down in the constitution, and I dare say that some college students today would have trouble understanding the whole purpose of the club.

> We wish to state our intention in as predicatory a manner as possible. The epitome of our cogitations is that we may, by study, eventually acquire the same ability to produce agglutination of thought, and conclude our compositions with the same fortunate epiphonemas which characterized the writings of the constituents of the original organization.

This original organization of which the club spoke was composed of the intellectuals who clustered about Samuel Johnson, including James Boswell, Edmund Burke, David Garrick, Oliver Goldsmith, and Bennet Langton.

The deep study of history was not neglected by these literary societies. "In history we rival Ridpath in the profundity of our knowledge, and surpass Hume and Gibbon and Gardner a triple century, while we rival Cicero in displaying it." The constitution of the club revealed that the teacher, Miss Sophia Pappenhagen, was helping students to learn, understand, and interpret history.

Miss Pappenhagen's dearest friend and companion was Ruth DeCapree. She too headed a literary society, The Ruth Club, named for her. She was the critic of the club, the name given to the sponsor, and she too guided her students down a most literary and scholarly path.

These organizations were all for the boys. However, the girls created a literary society, November 19,1909, the Philomathean Literary Society. The principal was all in favor of this, because he stated in the yearbook, "Cultural and social train-ing will bring advantages to the girls."

The Gamma Lambda Literary Society promoted the idea that ladies were more charming if they spoke well. The girls studied the speeches of the great orators. They learned these speeches by memory and recited them at the meetings. The girls also learned parliamentary procedure.

Delta Lambda was organized for the girls by Edna Rowe, who at that time was teaching at Central High. The program given by this literary sorority and most remembered by stu-dents was one that Miss Rowe prepared on James Whitcomb Riley. She trained several girls to recite the Riley poems in the well-known dialect in which the Riley poems were written.

The Jesters were organized a little later. This was a soci-ety of men like the Johnsonians — an ultra witty, jolly, literary crowd. Papers were read and mock trials and debates were held. The club was formed with the idea of social enjoyment in view, but the members soon found that their keenest enjoy-ment lay in things that instructed while they amused. Mr. Mil-lington, the English teacher who sponsored the club, touted, "Get the big ideas in view and never let your eyes wander from them."

The Forensic Society was organized, April 18, 1911, by Miss Rowe. This was the first society that was coeducational. This was a milestone because girls were just not considered a part of the male dominated debate scene. Miss Rowe pointed this out to her newly organized club. The men and women held to these vows:

1. To improve ourselves in the use of good English both oral and written expression.

2. To overcome our timidity or self-consciousness, so that we can express our ideas clearly to a group of people, for this accomplishment will be of great value to us in our future life.

3. To learn self-control so that in the contest of life we shall not give our antagonists the advantage by getting ex-cited.

4. To learn to speak quickly, to be attentive, alert, and to use every word to the best advantage.

5. To be able to accept defeat gracefully, since we cannot always come out victorious.

6. To understand parliamentary law.

7. To strengthen our school and give every member who has ambition a chance so that in the future we may have the pleasure of pointing to some great statement or orator and say — he had his first training in the Forensic Society of Dallas High School.

These promises were fulfilled, for many of Dallas's leading businessmen claimed that Miss Edna Rowe inspired them to accomplish things that otherwise they would not have accomplished.

The students were not satisfied with only literary societies, so in 1912, they organized themselves into a congress. This congress was quite active. The representatives of the congress challenged debaters from Phi Kappa. They debated child labor laws, abolishment of capital punishment, and the state interscholastic league topic that year: Resolved, that the initiative and referendum should be made a part of the organic law of our state government.

As other high schools entered the Dallas system, they immediately organized literary and debating societies. The debaters at Dallas High didn't have to go to Weatherford, Texas, to debate or anywhere else. There was competition much closer, for Oak Cliff High School was annexed in 1904, with W.H. Adamson as principal. The Polimic Society was organized first with debate as the main function. In 1913, when Oak Cliff High moved into the building that it now occupies, a teacher arrived on the scene who was to have quite a bit of influence on the whole school for many years to come. Even today her influence is felt at the school. This was Elizabeth W. Baker. Miss Baker inherited quite a bit of money unbeknownst to most people, and after her tragic death in an automobile accident, her will stated that all of her money and property was to go to Adamson High School. Large scholarships are given each year to worthy students at Adamson from the monies in the Elizabeth W. Baker Scholarship Fund.

When she was teaching at Adamson, Miss Baker organized the Adamson Literary Society. The detailed minutes of that first meeting ended with this statement. "Everyone took an active part except one, and he was sick."

Miss Baker held to the Aristotelian Doctrine when she taught speech: A good speaker is a good man. On Friday, May

9, 1913, she established the Anti-Tobacco League. This club was formed to aid its members in public speaking, however, they were to speak only against tobacco. As Aristotle held to the fact that a good speaker was a good man, Miss Baker held to the fact that a good speaker did not use tobacco. She told her students that the smaller boys usually began to use tobacco because they thought it was manly. Therefore, she organized the manly crowd into a club and urged them to be good examples. Miss Baker was called an advisor of this club. Every member took the pledge: "No tobacco until twenty-one." In other words,

"If you spoke, you could not smoke." This remains terrific advice for any speaker, since the use of tobacco does tax the vocal chords so horribly.

Two other literary societies were established at Oak Cliff High. Mr. E.H. Wray was critic for the Phi Delta Society, a debate society which also studied literature. At the first meeting, two declamations were given, and work on the state interscholastic league topic was begun. The topic that year was Resolved, that the women of Texas should be granted the ballot.

There was another literary club at Oak Cliff High which was dedicated to poetry reading. Mr. Charles L. Syron was the critic for this club, the Alborado Society.

> Among the world's poets
> Tributes are paid to Lord Byron,
> Among the society critics
> We pay ours to Mr. Syron.

In one of the earliest programs, poetry was read by Miss Pearl Wallace. She was to become Mrs. Pearl Wallace Chappell, a leading expression and speech teacher and also a little theatre director. She opened the Dallas Academy of Speech and Drama in downtown Dallas. Later she moved her studio to Cole Avenue where she taught until her death in 1969. The barn in the back of her home on Cole Avenue was used for her classes and for a rehearsal hall for various community theatre groups.

One of her most successful theatrical ventures was the presentation of the Chappell Strolling Players. These players were appropriately costumed and presented *commedia dell'arte* at shopping centers and community halls for passing theatre patrons to enjoy.

She was also famous for the Laurel Land Easter Sunrise Pageant, which she wrote and which she directed for a number of years. Thousands of people each year came to Laurel Land Cemetery as early as two or three o'clock on Easter Morning, in order to get a front row seat for the annual sunrise pageant. This extraodinary production, which depicted the last week of Christ's life, was written for a "cast of thousands." It was quite an undertaking to cast, direct, costume, and produce the enormous production. When Mrs. Chappell could no longer do this, I was asked to take over. I was in charge of the pageant for nine years, and I found that it was very difficult to present, but most inspiring to see.

On March 8, 1917, one hundred and twenty-five people came together in the Adamson High School auditorium to hear a program created by the Phi Delta Literary Society. In the opening address a student told how to be prepared for life. A debate followed. The topic was: Resolved, that the United States should place an embargo on munitions of war to the belligerent nations of Europe. The debate was heard with intense interest, because it was just days later that German submarines torpedoed three U.S. ships, and four weeks later, on April 2, President Wilson asked Congress to declare war on Germany "to make the world safe for democracy."

There was a congress established at Oak Cliff High. They modeled their constitution after the one of the United States. Their calendar contained both national and international subjects. They also included some school subjects.

1. Extension of suffrage to the girls at Adamson.
2. Bond for an extension of Union Station in Dallas.
3. The establishment of a campus patrol at Adamson.

Miss Baker kept working toward influencing the younger boys for the good. Principal Adamson gave a big shot in the arm to the debating society when he offered money to the winners. Prize money certainly brought about added enthusiasm. Seven dollars and fifty cents went to the first place winner, and two dollars and fifty cents went to the second place winner. The contest was held at Cliff Temple Baptist Church.

Meanwhile, at Dallas High School, debates were still arranged. In 1913, there was a public debate with Terrill School. Terrill was an outstanding private academy for boys. The school was founded in 1906 by Menter B. Terrill, who before coming to Dallas had been the president of Denton Normal, now North Texas State University. The Phi Kappas from Dallas High proposed the public debate and speaking contest. One of the fathers of a boy on the Dallas High squad, Louis Hexter, arranged for a special Louis Hexter medal to be given for orations. Hexter today remains a prominent name in the Dallas business world.

Recognition from all over the state came to one of the debate teams in 1914, when this Dallas team went to debate in Austin in the State University Interscholastic League contest for the first time. The teacher, Charles Tomkies, coached more winning teams than any one in the state that year. Dallas won the district by defeating the teams from Tarrant County, Cleburne, Waxahachie, Denton, and Springtown. In Austin that year, the Dallas team came in second losing only to an Austin school. Nevertheless, the students returned in grand spirit, and a mock debate was held in their honor on their return. The topic was: Resolved, that land is more necessary than water.

Because Mr. Tomkies's debaters were doing such outstanding work, Mayor Wozencraft offered a cup to the best team in 1917. Mayor Wozencraft was known as the "boy" mayor of Dallas, because he was so very young when he served in such a prestigious position. He had graduated from Dallas High himself only a few years before where he was a winner in debate and also in football. That first Wozencraft cup was won by the Phi Kappa team. After the debate: Resolved, that a constitutional tax of one mill, equally apportioned, should be levied for the support of the state institutions of higher education and that supplementary appropriations by the legislature should be prohibited, Louis Hexter spoke on "National Hysteria." He closed his oration with a prayer for Europe and for peace. However, war was inevitable.

Just before the United States entered the war in 1917, Forest Avenue High School opened. People were moving to the south side of town. Many of the wealthy Jewish families were moving on Forest Avenue. So this shift in population demanded a new school. The facility cost three hundred thousand dollars, and in it was an auditorium, the largest and most thoroughly equipped school auditorium in the South. It seated twelve hundred people in opera seats of mahogany. It even had draperies. It also had two large concrete lions on the front steps — the first school ever to have its mascot artistically and strategically placed in constant view. Today, Forest Avenue has been renamed Martin Luther King Boulevard and the school is named James Madison High.

Two of the teachers, Miss Rowe and Mr. Tomkies, who had put much strength into the literary societies at Dallas High, were moved to Forest. Mr. Tomkies, with a nucleus from the Phi Kappas who had transferred from Dallas High to Forest, organized the Hamilton Literary Society for debating. Of course, with this core group, Forest was equipped and ready to start intercity debates immediately with Oak Cliff High and Dallas High. On March 23, 1917, the teams got together to debate: Resolved, that the labor unions, as they are now organized, are sound in principle and deserve the support of public opinion.

The senate was organized by the interested students at Forest with E.B. Comstock and Wiley Parker serving as sponsors. The great orator, Henry Clay of Kentucky, was the inspiration for this group.

Forest Avenue High in 1917 sponsored the first Interscholastic League meet in Dallas. The literary societies continued to debate current topics. Mr. Stanley Marcus was on the debate squad at Forest, and in his book, *Minding The Store*, he mentioned the vast amount of knowledge he acquired from his involvement in the literary societies.

In 1919, Miss Myra Brown arrived and organized the Standard Debating Society. She pointed out that the society stood for work. She recognized that the words of man were never perfect, but young people still needed to seek perfection. The work and the attaining of perfection were held together by fellowship.

At Dallas High the Wozencraft Award was still coveted. George Dealey, publisher of the *Dallas Morning News*, also gave a medal to the best individual speaker of the year. These public debates continued to draw large crowds. There was an added treat in that the Philharmonic Orchestra of Dallas High often furnished numerous renditions of popular and classical music preceding the debates.

Literary pursuit continued in the high schools that were going to open as Dallas continued to grow. What the students did not get in the classrooms, they found in the literary socie-ties. Chaucer, Spencer, Shakespeare, Bacon, Milton, Burns, Wordsworth, Dickens, Thackeray, Byron, Shelley, and Keats were intensely studied in the classes, and the students were given further study in the literary societies that met after school. It was always an honor to belong to one of the scholarly groups. There was nothing sissy about it at all. The scholar was accepted and admired.

Chapter Three

Great Advancements

Dr. Justin Ford Kimball was called the builder of schools, the founder of health plans, the instigator of new school programs, but to us school kids who rode the Vickery bus to transfer to the Crosstown streetcar (so that we could get to Alex W. Spence Junior High) he was that nice man who got on the bus at Vickery and MacMillan and rode on downtown. We didn't know about all the great things that he was going to do or had done. We just knew that he was somebody special, because all the gentlemen riding on the bus would greet him with a hearty,

"Good morning, Dr. Kimball. You're looking fine, Dr. Kimball."

He always seemed more interested in us kids than anyone else. His friendliness impressed me. Dr. Kimball was the superintendent of schools from 1914–1928. That didn't impress me, because I was an immature junior high person, an unsophisticated 1944 type, and it would have taken Roy Rogers, Trigger, plus Dale, and Van Johnson and June Allyson to get my attention. But all the students on the bus liked Dr. Kimball, because we knew he was genuinely interested in us, and he seemed interested in our school and teachers.

I not only got to see him on the bus, but I saw him at all my piano recitals. He lived on Vickery Boulevard just down the street from Ludie Rae Gardner, who taught piano to all the children in that neighborhood. Dr. Kimball's niece took lessons with me, and so her famous uncle attended all the recitals. Sometimes he would ask us all up to the big two-story house for refreshments after the recital. *This* impressed me, not the fact that Dr. Kimball was a Dallas leader.

Born in Huntsville, Texas, into a family with a long line of ministers, teachers, and scholars, Justin Kimball was expected to excel in school, and this he did. When only ten years old he was the master of the Hebrew and Greek languages. At nineteen he was a graduate of Lebanon College in Louisiana. He went on to receive a Bachelor of Law Degree from the University of Michigan. In 1899 he received a Master of Arts from Baylor University, and later in 1920, Baylor awarded him the degree of Doctor of Law. All these honors were earned by a farm boy from Huntsville, Texas, who came from a family of achievers and who definitely fitted into that family pattern.

He started teaching in a one-room schoolhouse in Navasota, Texas, but he soon became principal of the high school. Then in 1901, he became Superintendent of Schools in Temple, Texas. Later he decided to retire from education to practice law in Waco. However, always an educator at heart, he was soon back in Temple as Superintendent of Schools until 1914, when he came to Dallas to assume the superintendency here.

The year 1914 was a disastrous one for the cotton business. There was a war brewing in Europe. This uneasy world condition caused cotton prices to drop to four cents a pound. King Cotton was having trouble holding on to the throne, and because cotton determined the condition of much of the Texas economy, the "Buy a Bale" campaign was launched to save the cotton industry. On top of all this there were changes coming in all industry, more people were moving into the cities, and money was scarce.

It was this year, 1914, that Dr. Justin Kimball arrived in Dallas to be Superintendent of Schools. He was the man of the hour, and the school man for the next ten years. Those years brought more change to our country, and thus to the schools, than ever experienced before. Besides the economic failures, the coming of war, the shift in population from farm to city, there was a change in the educational philosophy, and Justin Kimball was to weather it all quite well. He was a good school man who appreciated the power of knowledge and who appreciated those teachers who shared their knowledge with the deserving students they taught.

Dr. Kimball took one action which helped his teachers and brought him national fame and the gratitude of millions. In those hard economic times he worked out a plan for his teachers to draw funds when they were not working because of illness. He set up a fund for their hospital bills by collecting fifty cents a month from each teacher. He worked this plan into a prepaid hospitalization plan with Baylor Hospital — calling it the Baylor Plan. This concept of prepaid health care caught on and similar plans were initiated by other groups. The first commercial company to offer prepaid hospitalization to its employees was the *Dallas Morning News.* Later in 1933, at St. Paul, Minnesota, a group there started such a plan and used the Geneva Blue Cross, an international symbol for help, as a symbol for the plan. This caught on, and by 1939, the Blue Cross hospitalization plan was advertised all over the country. Blue Shield, with its added benefits, came from the California Physicians Service. But Blue Cross was founded in Dallas by Dr. Kimball, and he did this for his beloved teachers and not for fame or profit.

When Dr. Kimball arrived in Dallas he decided first to raise teacher qualifications. He looked at the crop of fine teachers that he already had, planned to make them finer, and he planned to bring in the very best of new teachers. Therefore, a ruling on teacher qualification was passed. A new teacher had to have a college degree in order to teach in Dallas. Until 1915, the teacher training course taken in the high school had been enough, but a college degree was required after that year. Dr. Kimball, a loving and understanding administrator, told his current teachers that they would eventually be required to have degrees but certainly not immediately. Going to school each summer was obviously one way by which they could acquire their degrees. Night courses were available and so were the funds to pay for the tuition. Dr. Kimball urged the teachers not to take any courses that wouldn't count toward their needed degrees, and he promised financial reward for them when they became college educated teachers. He really never gave a completion deadline to the experienced teachers who had been serving so faithfully through the years. He just assumed that they were working toward degrees, and actually all of them were.

Because the schools were showing such great growth, the platoon system was introduced into the schools by Dr. Kimball. More kids could be taught more effectively in less time with less teachers. There was an art teacher, a music teacher, a gym teacher, and eventually an auditorium teacher (speech arts) at each school. These specialists would have the students several hours a week — thus freeing the homeroom teachers to teach reading, math, and science to the other groups who were not in the special classes. It all worked well.

Dr. Kimball's display of thrift showed everywhere. He watched and accounted for every penny. He squeezed something out of everything.

> Old refrigerator at high school — $7
> Bench at Bowie School — $33.75
> Old desk at Douglass School — $29.00
> Salvage at Oak Grove School — $3.26
> Junk — $1.55
> Old slate at shop — $7.50
> Glass at warehouse — $76.00

Still, under the watchful, thrifty eye of Justin Kimball, there was an overdraft of $8,293.64 that first year of his administration. However, the property value of the schools was $1,908,947.39. So, the Dallas schools could be now called a million dollar operation.

After Dr. Kimbell had been superintendent for one year, he called Mr. E.D. Jennings from The University of Texas to evaluate the Dallas schools. Mr. Jennings, in checking the efficiency of the educational system in Dallas, first took an overall look and made several suggestions.

"It is not sufficient that the supervisor should take the message to Garcia. It is equally as important that they (the teachers) see that Garcia (Dr. Kimball) gets the message."

This was a check and balance system between supervisors and teachers. First, Mr. Jennings insisted on more supplementary reading. A student should read at least twelve to fifteen books extra each semester. Secondly, he advised that there be a standardized grading program. The grading had been different for each school, and he pointed out that "this begets more misunderstanding and heart burning among parents and pupils." But, standardized testing was a difficult order to carry out.

Mr. Jennings then went into the schools. "In the beginning of my visits I found a nervous feeling on the part of the teachers. however, as the time went by, I felt that I was in the hands of friends."

An evaluation had never taken place before by an outsider. Dr. Kimball visited the classrooms regularly, but never had the teachers been checked by someone with a masters degree from The University of Texas. What did he know about the schools in Dallas? Those teachers were very human. They were going to suspect any outsider, until he proved himself an interested and sensitive party to their cause.

In order to bring a complete report, Mr. Jennings first checked the school rooms themselves to see that they were conducive to learning. Then he looked at the teacher as an executor and a manager. Then he observed the teacher as an instructor. Did the teacher suit the subject matter to the students in such a way as to inspire the students? Everything was rated as excellent, good, fair, poor, or valueless.

The room got an excellent rating if it was ventilated with "invigorating air." The furniture needed to be in order. Plants got extra points. The room was given a low rating if there was a "peculiar smell in it." Without air conditioning or fans, in a room full of sweaty little kids, keeping an invigorating air was a full time task in itself. And too, in the winter time, a child might come to school with a bag of asafetida around his neck to ward off cold germs. Those bags certainly could set up an unusual scent. Mr. Jennings was asking too much when he insisted that the teachers get rid of peculiar smells. He had forgotten the fact that children always have unique odors about them.

A Dallas teacher, a maiden lady, sent a little boy home one day because he smelled. The little boy came back (still smelling) with a note in his hand. "I sent my son to school for you to teach, not to smell. Besides, my son does not stink. He smells like his father. He smells like a man. You're an old maid, and you don't even know what a man smells like."

The evaluation called for the teacher's personality to be

under study. "The ladies should be beautiful and properly and attractively dressed for the occasion." The teacher needed a modulated voice. She was marked down if she "was ugly, sickly, or had an antagonistic voice."

Mr. Jennings looked for good teacher/pupil relationships. The teacher had to be cooperative, sympathetic, friendly, and courteous. There had to be an obvious skill in management. If the teacher was well trained and selfgoverned, then that teacher was an excellent role model. The evaluator also looked for the teacher's skill in directing the pupil's study. Was the class ever idle? Was the new work connected with the old? Was the teacher still screaming out assignments and information after the bell had rung.

Children wait for the bell like nervous race horses. When a teacher's timing is off, she can be found screaming, "Wait! Wait! Stop! I haven't told you about tomorrow! " Unfortunately kids won't wait — especially for an assignment. Once the bell has rung, they're off and running.

The report checked the values in the teaching methods that were used. Was the subject matter fitting to the mental age? Was the child learning anything? What about written outside work?

The last thing on which Mr. Jennings reported dealt with the student's appreciation of the subject matter. Was the class awake? Boredom is always a hazard in the classroom, because some of the most brilliant teachers are the world's dullest lecturers.

I had a government teacher who was so boring we students all stuck pencils and blunt instruments into our arms and legs in order to stay awake. Still nothing we did could penetrate our brains or bring us to a level of consciousness so that we could absorb any of the gentleman's vast knowledge. This was a sad situation, and unfortunately it is quite prevalent in the schools.

Dr. Kimball, being a just and democratic administrator, gave the teachers an opportunity to evaluate Mr. Jennings. Their answers were obvious to anyone who has ever been in the field of education. They asked how anyone could really measure in figures the intangible? How could one measure learning with such varied subjects? Every child was so different. The teachers noted that one never performed well under observation, and besides, Mr. Jennings didn't stay long enough in the classrooms to really find out anything.

Nevertheless, from this evaluation and from Dr. Kimball came some regulations that dominated the educational process in the Dallas schools for many years.

The aim of the elementary school was to teach first a love of life. Learning could only take place when the student had a love of self. With self confidence, a child could adjust to the physical and mental environments. The French philosopher, Rousseau, was considered correct in his theory of the *tabula rasa*. Rousseau felt that every child was born with a clean slate. The world wrote upon it. All was learned. Rousseau stood as the voice of the common man during the eighteenth century when France was readying itself for a revolution. He was very sensitive to all class distinctions and was demanding a leveling at a time when the monarchy was holding tight rein on the people. His theory was accepted by the Dallas schools in 1915.

Manual training was added to the elementary school curriculum. The manual arts awakened the subnormal children and the same training quickened the normal. The girls were offered home economics. Dr. Kimball felt the schools of the south did not teach enough "bread and meat." Many students were forced to leave school after the elementary years for financial reasons. They needed to go out with a way to make a living.

The most important subject was to remain as always — reading. The children were constantly to be improving their reading skills, their recitation, and their spelling.

"The one who reads widely is at home anywhere," stated Dr. Kimball.

It is through reading that a child is able to think the best thoughts in the world. "The past is familiar to him and the present is a part of him. Reading makes a full man. Conversation makes a ready man."

In teaching arithmetic it was advised to use real and local stories in the problems to be solved. Then the whole process would appear more necessary. The math teachers were to use Dr. Kimball's book, *Teaching Mathematics*.

The high school teacher was told to teach and not just give lessons. "Civilization rests on strong instincts and imitation. Science rests on curiosity. The teacher who most effectively and systematically stimulates curiosity is the best instructor.

The teacher who constantly tempts the imagination is the best possible trainer of children. The teacher who combines *both* is a joy and a blessing to the students who call him or her teacher."

The course of study for the high school included the following subjects:

> English: Composition and the reading of Hawthorne, *Macbeth,* , Milton, *Julius Ceasar, Idlys Of The King,* and *Tale Of Two Cities.*
> History: Ancient, Medieval, English, and American.
> Latin: Declension of verbs and the reading of Caesar, Cicero, and Virgil.
> Math: Algebra, geometry, solid geometry, and trigonometry.

Aside from these studies there were courses in commercial law, bookkeeping, shorthand and typing, chemistry, physics, botany, and zoology. During the first semester the girls in domestic science were to make an apron, a corset cover, and a nightgown. During the second semester they were to make *drawers* with lace. (The wife of England's King George III, Queen Charlotte, created and designed lady's underpants. Until Charlotte introduced this type of underwear, it was a bit breezy under those hoop skirts. Because she "drew on" these pants, she called them "drawers." This was a regal word in its beginning. Now it is used in a comic, rural sense. However, in 1915, it was an acceptable term, or Dr. Kimball would never have used it.)

In the drawing and design classes there was work in freehand, practical, watercolor, leather (bookbinding) and clay. An art history course was offered. Manual training included mechanical drawing, woodworking, cabinetmaking, machine work and drill press.

In order for all this learning to occur, the salaries of the teachers increased some. The principals received $1,000 to $1,800 a year. The high school teachers also received $1,000 to $1,800 a year. The elementary teachers received from $495 to $810 a year.

Mrs. Madge Beachum, who taught in the elementary schools at this time told of the furor that evolved over the fact that the elementary teachers were not paid as much as the high school teachers. Mrs. Beachum stated that it came down to this question.

"When one builds a house does one spend more on the roof or on the foundation. The thought applies to building a child. Do you spend more on the foundation (elementary teachers) or the roof (high school teachers)? " The argument was never resolved until later years when teachers' salaries were scaled according to the amount of their education and the amount of their experience.

A HANDBOOK FOR TEACHERS

In 1918, Dr. Justin Kimball published a *Handbook For Teachers* which listed ninety-seven suggestions for good teaching. The book almost reads like the Beatitudes in the Gospel of Matthew — "blessed is the teacher who . . ."

In the foreword of the handbook, Dr. Kimball recalled his grandmother's recipe book containing over five hundred recipes. Grandmother wasn't about to follow all the recipes perfectly, she wasn't able to cook them all, but what a pleasure she derived from trying. The cookbook was not only a guide to good cooking and a fine reference book, but also a book of faith and ideas. The superintendent wished the teachers to think of his handbook in terms of Grandmother's cookbook. It was not possible to cook them all, but a teacher could surely try. The book was to remain a constant guide.

All of the suggestions are not listed here, because their listing is a book in itself. However, to get a flavor of the times and a taste of the personality of Dr. Kimball, I will record a choice few. They're still good recipes — times change, but the needs of students and teachers do not. It's unlikely that a good cook would destroy his or her first cookbook, so the question could be asked — just how out of date is the following counsel?

"Destructive criticism is something that no teacher will want to make. In fact, destructive criticism is something that one does not make at all.

"The superintendent will be available for teacher conferences from three to five, weekdays and from eleven to twelve on Saturdays. New teachers are to come and talk with the superintendent."

If a teacher doesn't know something, he should ask. Principals get paid to answer questions. Also, do not be afraid to ask questions of fellow teachers. It is better to ask a question than to make a mistake.

(Dr. Kimball pointed out that "our tenderest spot is our vanity.")

Programs and seating plans should be conspicuously posted in the room. Many teachers have ingenious devices to do this such as framed bulletin boards. Do ask the manual training boys to make you a bulletin board. An old principal whom the Great Teacher has long ago promoted to the better world used to say: 'When you find a teacher who is frequently off her program, you either get a new program or a new teacher or both.' To follow a different program than the one posted is inexcusable.
Passages must be free of loose desks and other obstructions.

(The desks in those days were screwed to the floor.)

Teachers not only are hired for brains, but also for patience, sympathy, cheerfulness, encouragement, confidence, and inspiration. A scolding, nagging, gossip who may know the dictionary in its entirety is as proper a candidate for dismissal from a teacher's position as is the most pronounced illiterate.

Test at the first of the term. Test at the end. Compare the scores. There should be marked improvement.

One teacher did not progress. She had gotten too used to herself. Her particular way of greeting children, of filling the day was monotonous, uninspiring, and dull. Unless one has a healthy suspicion that one needs improvement one gets used to one's self and remains dead too long before burial. An old lawyer tells young ones that if they lose nervousness before a jury it is a bad sign. They ought to be anxious enough to succeed, so that they are nervous. Good actors have a little stage fright always. The lover whose proposal has no nervousness in it, is not likely to succeed.

(The great educator exposed his romantic side in that one.)

This is a public school. The teacher who takes the trouble to write to the principal what some visitor said and who said it, does a service of value.

Help the parent when he comes to visit. Don't let him go away mad!

Tired teachers beware!

(Today's burnout.)

So long as the country lets teachers work at starvation wages, their complaints seem natural. But complaining can become a habit. A worried teacher, a tired teacher, is self-poisoned by bodily fluids. Only fresh air, rest and recreation will remove the poison. Talking about it and bemoaning the situation makes it worse. Relax and watch your worries and troublesome problems vanish.

Neglected cases of Lagrippe [flu] in the spring has been the cause of the physical breakdown of more teachers in Dallas than all other cases combined. Watch the spring cold for your life!

Writing a word forty times because it was misspelled is folly!

It is a sad day when a child discovers that a teacher isn't perfect and worthy of his whole faith. Public controversies over the school are so unfortunate. The child hears some teacher attacked and his confidence which is his breath of life is shaken or impaired.

(Today, it is hard for anyone to hang on to a fine role model, since the media is able to expose all activities of an individual whether the activities are moral or immoral, legitimate or illegitimate, acceptable or unacceptable.)

Also the faith of the child in the goodness of the teacher is broken when the teacher reacts in anger. The teacher who goes about rapping knuckles sets up distrust in the students.

The teacher who speaks in sarcasm is a traitor. The teacher who reads into the actions of the child images of which the child is incapable is a public enemy, a social outlaw.

The spirit of revenge is unpardonable against the holy spirit of teaching.

The highest criterion in school questions is the welfare of the child.

The valuable books are the planning book and the progress book.

Corporal punishment is primitive. Don't do it in anger. Put off punishing for a day. Corporal punishment is usually used because there is no imagination in punishment. Fit the punishment to the crime. The sight of switches is detrimental to the finer things of the school.

(The most imaginative punishment that I discovered in all of my research for this book was rendered by Dr. W.T. White, when he was principal of Sunset High School. Dr. White dealt almost daily with a boy who was a show-off. This student made certain that he was seen by teacher and students at all times. The teachers would endure his exhibitions for so long, and then he would be sent to the principal. Dr. White, not needing to turn to the primitive punishment because of his keen imagination, locked the boy in the school trophy case in the front hall for the day. There this show-off could be viewed all day long by students and teachers and not bring trouble to any classes. After spending a day in the trophy case, the boy never disturbed again. Some psychologists and psychiatrists would gasp in horror of such a thing, claiming that this action could destroy the boy's psyche. But, Dr. White knew his students too well to ever harm their personalities. This boy grew up to be a fine citizen who never forgot the day he spent in the Sunset High School trophy case. As Dr. Kimball attested, it only took a little imagination.)

Be sociable. A new teacher must be friendly and the old teacher will be happy to help in adjustment.

Drill for accuracy in arithmetic. Practice the habit of accuracy. Speed will come.

Care for all materials — scissors, pencils, paper, paste, ink, and drawing paper.

Decorate the room. There must be the element of decoration in the room. Dull rooms can be made happy places with decor.

Public opinion is powerful. Assist in enforcing a high standard of life.

There should be no slang spoken by the teacher. Slang lowers the tone of the teaching. Using slang is most harmful in the schools where the children come from homes where there is meager use of the English language. Use the cleanest, clearest, choisest English of all.

If you slap the face of a child once, pray God to forgive you for bad temper and worse manners. If you do it twice, resign.

It is our patriotic duty to use the war [World War I] to gain patriotic impulses from the students.

The purpose of fire drills is to discipline the children to good behavior. Speed is not important. The danger lies in panic, not fire.

By the end of the third year the child should be able to

read anything in which he is interested, spell the words that he uses, and know how to add, subtract, divide, and multiply.

A poor reading class is inexcusable in any grade. Skill in reading comes from reading interesting materials, not from drill. By the end of the third year the child should not be reading haltingly or stumblingly or painfully.

(Dr. Kimball here was being too idealistic. I taught classes in college where students halted, stumbled, and moaned when they read. Mrs. W.D. Greer, librarian at Gabe P. Allen School, was told in her college courses when she was preparing to be a librarian, that the secret in getting children to read was to get the right book to the right child at the right time. This worked for her when she was dealing with a child in the fifth grade who just couldn't read. She was discouraged about this child's inability to read, so she offered him a book on Babe Ruth. There's not a kid alive who doesn't love baseball. After weeks of struggling with each word in the book, the little boy finished it and marched proudly up to the thoughtful librarian and offered her the book. "If you haven't read any good books lately, here's a great one. You really ought to read it.")

In the fourth year, offer fractions.

The seventh grade is the era of adolescence. If the teacher does not make the child handle and rethink in new combinations what he has learned and knows, then the child has missed his most valuable birthright.

Excessive talking by a teacher is prima facie evidence of poor teaching.

Courtesy pays large dividends.

The teaching hour is like the hour of battle to the soldier, the sermon hour to the preacher, the sick room to the physician, and the harvest to the farmer.

Hospitality is one of the finest human virtues.

A soft answer turneth away wrath, but grievous words stir up anger.

(Dr. Kimball for many years taught a men's Bible class at First Baptist Church, Dallas. His Bible knowledge and faith always poured over into his school policies.)

A principal is careful in thought and sound in judgment. When a teacher says, 'Will you back me up on this?' the principal without hesitation will answer, 'Yes, if what you do is backable! '

(The great educator coined a word for immediate use.)

Good housekeeping in school begins at the teacher's desk.

We must never forget that schools exist for the welfare of the children, not for the benefit of the teachers.

The Great Teacher said, 'The poor ye have with ye always.' The weak student you will have with you always.

The temperature should be kept between sixty-eight and seventy-two degrees. If you're cold then wear more clothes. It's dangerous to be too warm. It's better to be cold.

Interrupting another teacher is thoughtless and selfish.

The school telephone should not be used during school hours. Patience and tact must be used in receiving complaints and grievances that come over the telephone. It is hard to make a friend over the telephone. It is easy to lose one.

Beauty costs no more than ugliness and squalor.

Keeping a child in at recess is only good for pupils who cannot get along with other pupils on the school ground.

Flowers and plants in the room are splendid and worthwhile.

Reading papers written by students exhausts the mentality of teachers quicker than any other work I know. The first four or five papers are educative. The rest are stupefying. By marking papers the teachers become utterly fagged out by the dreadful grind. Let the students sometimes grade each other's papers.

The teacher's rest room is a place to rest. There should be no school talk. Spend the hour in complete repose and relaxation with eyes closed, resting prone and relaxed on the couch thinking of nothing. If you can't do this, don't get in the way of those who can.

Teach etiquette of the flag. Know words of patriotic songs. The war [World War I] has furnished us with lessons on ethical ideals and aspirations. American boys will now talk seriously on topics that a few years ago they would have thought sissy.

Teaching is dreadfully trying on little, selfish, contentious souls and on old maids of either sex, whether married or single. But it is a tower of strength for the generous of heart and brain.

The Dallas school teachers and administration body will not be happy until all children are educated!

Some of the language in these suggestions is a bit archaic, but the thoughts remain timely because the thoughts were those of a gentleman who considered first the well-being of the schoolchildren of Dallas, who loved his teachers and administrators, and who was well grounded in God's eternal commandments.

AN UNUSUAL TEXTBOOK

Dr. Kimball wrote a text book entitled, *Our City, Dallas*. "This book is dedicated to the boys and the girls of the Dallas Public Schools who shall make or unmake the Dallas of tomorrow in the hope and faith that all shall render service, high and heroic if need be to the city that we love."

The book, *Our City, Dallas*, published in 1927, was written by Justin Kimball when he was no longer superintendent of schools but was serving as president of Baylor Medical School. His heart still remained with the students of Dallas.

The book contained not only the history of Dallas up until 1927, but it also explained the immediate problems in Dallas and the solutions to those problems that could be considered. It was a history book, but it also served as a guide to further growth of the city. It was similar to our *Goals For Dallas*. However, Dr. Kimball's book was written to be used as a textbook, because it contained a study guide for the teachers as they taught the book in their social studies classes.

The book was a timely piece, because in 1927 Dallas experienced a growth spurt that continued into a steady stream of increased population. The 1927 *Forest Avenue Annual* put it this way,

> Dallas has some reputation,
> That's not all, don't you see,
> It's that growing population
> But it ain't what it's gonna be.

The Kessler Plan for Dallas was first discussed in the book. The Kessler Plan presented a design that the city was to use as its major strategy for future growth. The teaching guide to this chapter stated:

> The essential feature in teaching this chapter is to impress upon the child the fact that Mr. Kessler made a plan for the city as a whole — that it was one plan for the city as a

unit, and at the same time gave us a plan that touches every part of the city. For this reason one of the questions in every class should be, 'What part of the Kessler Plan touches our school district and our part of the city?' Another should be, 'What features of the Kessler Plan bind our part of the city into the city as a whole?' Teachers should make liberal use of the maps and diagrams, showing the various Kessler Plan parts in their entirety in the study of this chapter.

George Kessler, who did a fine job laying out Kansas City, was called by the City Council of Dallas in 1910 to submit a plan for Dallas. As a lad George Kessler worked as a cash boy at Sanger Brothers Store. Now, he was returning to Dallas as a professional city planner, and he was planning to render immeasurable service in remaking the city. The 1927 *Forest Avenue Annual* was dedicated to the Kessler Plan.

George Kessler first demanded that a railway station, a union terminal, be built. He claimed that it would become the front door of the city and that a plaza should be built in front of it. He insisted that the railway tracks on Pacific Avenue be removed to eliminate a dangerous grade crossing in town and that those tracks be put on the south side of the street. He suggested that more roadways be built into Oak Cliff. He had great plans for the Trinity River. He spoke of the traffic congestion on St. Paul, Ervay, Main, Commerce, Ross, Greenville, and Lemmon. He showed how that traffic could be alleviated. He mentioned ways of beautifying the parks. He demanded that there be a Central Boulevard, a large thoroughfare for traffic, that would go north.

The school children of Dallas studied all of these plans — never knowing that years later a union terminal would still be a front door to the city with Dealy Plaza in sight, that railroad tracks would be used on the south side of Pacific, that there would be many viaducts going into Oak Cliff, that there would *still* be great plans for the Trinity River, that traffic would seemingly *always* be backed up on St. Paul, Ervay, Main, Commerce, Ross, Greenville, and Lemmon, that the parks would be beautiful and well kept, and that Central Expressway would be a vital thoroughfare filled with cars bumper-to-bumper day and night.

Dr. Kimball included chapters on city government. He explained how the officials were elected and how they functioned in their jobs. There were pictures of the mayor and the council at that time. There was a chapter on citizenship. Judge Atwell's court was shown. The judge was accepting the oath of allegiance from foreign-born who were becoming citizens of the country, of the state, and of Dallas. There were several chapters concerning municipal functions — the fire department, the police department, the water department. Problems in building codes, street pavings, and city wastes were defined and possible solutions were listed.

On the concluding pages in the book, Dr. Kimball asked for a "great art gallery." He mentioned the movement under discussion to build one by general subscription or by municipal bonds — and he lived to see the gallery built at the Fair Park in 1936 for the Centennial celebration. He would be most pleased with the new one that fills a large spot in the proposed arts district that also includes the Dallas Arts Magnet School where students come to study art, music, theatre, and dance.

On the last page of his book, Dr. Kimball left a challenge to the students in the public schools of Dallas.

> Some of you boys and girls must serve Dallas as mayors, as commissioners, as policemen, as businessmen, as bankers, as merchants, and in thousands of other ways. Some of you must teach in her schools, preach in her pulpits, and lead men to the highest and finest and best that is in the lives of the city. Others will do other types of service in the busy working world or in making homes. All are needed in the service of the city. If you shall seek your own selfish ends and your own selfish desires and riches in serving the city as a public servant, as a mayor, as a commissioner, as a preacher, or as a teacher, it will be a day of great disaster for you and for the city. What America needs most and has needed most at all times — and the same is true of Texas, and of Dallas — are men and women who shall serve devotedly, unselfishly and without thought of gain. A few of you boys and girls must serve as leaders, thousands must serve in the ranks, to each alike shall come happiness and success as Dallas grows to be a finer and a better place in which to live. It may be that your life will be spent somewhere else as men and women; in this case we hope that it will still be that you show the Dallas spirit of service for others, of loyalty and of friendliness throughout all your lives.

Chapter Four

Shortage Of Teachers And Of Money

How you gonna keep 'em down on the farm,
After they've seen Paree?

were not only the first lines of a World War I song, but was also a sociological question dealing with the times. In 1918 the doughboys returned not to the farms, but to the cities. The population in Dallas rose, and thus, the city schools' enrollments increased. Also, the war caused a rise in the birthrate. There were more new Dallasites to be educated in Dallas.

In 1914 there were 17,415 children enrolled in the Dallas schools with 506 teachers. In 1923 there were 36,796 children enrolled with only 885 teachers. Obviously, there was a critical teacher shortage, the first one experienced by the Dallas schools. It was at this time that Dr. Kimball initiated the platoon system.The system squeezed added teaching time out of the teachers, but still, more educators were needed.

Miss Mary C. Spears was brought to Dallas to establish a teacher recruiting program. Her first steps took her to the education department at SMU where she worked with the head of the teacher training program there in planning teacher recruitment for the Dallas schools. SMU and Miss Spears worked out a plan whereby the junior and senior girls could continue in their studies on the campus for a half day, and then the selected young ladies could teach in the Dallas schools for the other half of the day. They would be paid for their teaching services, and they would also get college credit. They were assured that they would graduate with their class, but they would have added advantages — some money and some grand experience.

Mary Louis Henry (nee Speer) and Gertrude Cave (nee Ballard) were two of these SMU girls who joined this program. Mrs. Henry remembered that her father was very opposed to her agreeing to study and to teach. He was only concerned about his daughter graduating.

"But putting me in a classroom with kids to teach was like putting Brer Rabbit in the briar patch. I couldn't wait to get started."

Besides the fact that the girls really all wanted to teach, they were also caught up in the charm of Miss Spears. No one could resist her. When Miss Spears walked into the classroom to tell the girls about this opportunity, they were immediately spellbound by her fascinating personality. She instantly became their idol.

"We all wanted to be just like her. She could speak. She was dressed so beautifully. She was witty and enchanting. She was intelligent, and she was offering us a chance to be just like her. Naturally, we all jumped at the chance," recalls Mrs. Henry.

The girls who were selected to be a part of this training were called Cadet Teachers. They attended their classes at SMU, they attended teacher training classes led by Miss Spears, and they taught classes in the Dallas schools. Their teaching was monitored by a critic teacher in the Dallas schools.

"We were so young and inexperienced, but we learned from our critic teachers, and, of course, from Miss Spears. And too, Miss Spears became a good friend to each of us."

Mrs. Cave recalled a party that she and Mary Louis were planning. They were thinking more of their party than of the teacher training work, since they were young, typical college girls. Miss Spears sensed that their interest was elsewhere, so she inquired about their absentmindedness. The girls told her about the party that evening. She told them to go home, get the party over, and come back to the class the next week ready to concentrate on education.

"One day we were late getting to class," Mrs. Cave related. "My father had provided a car for us in order to get to all the classes, and on the way to teacher training we had two flat tires. We told Miss Spears that we were so sorry, but we had had two flat tires. She hastily replied, 'Really, Miss Ballard, one flat tire would have been enough for your excuse.'"

When Mary Louis and Gertrude graduated from SMU, they started teaching that next fall for the Dallas schools as planned. They were joined by their good friend Katheryn Branan (nee Cole) who had just graduated from Baylor. All three girls were products of the Dallas school system, and now they were returning as teachers in the system they loved. Miss Ballard had graduated from Forest High when E.B. Cauthorn was a teacher there. Now, he was assistant superintendent in charge of employing teachers.He was most pleased to engage this former student. Miss Alice Muldrow, who was then principal of Rosemont School, had taught Miss Ballard in the third grade at Reagan School. She had also been Miss Ballard's Sunday School teacher. So when Gertrude was going to teach in the Dallas schools, Miss Muldrow arranged for her to come to Rosemont. Miss Ballard taught for a number of years until she resigned from her career to marry Joe Bob Cave, the first man to graduate from the Dallas schools.

Mary Louis Speer and Katheryn Cole went to teach at Obadiah Knight School until they committed the unpardonable sin. They both married. Katheryn Cole married Judge Walter Branan, and Mary Louis married Pat Henry, who served as vice-president of Republic National Bank for many years.

However, even before Mrs. Henry was married, she was condemned as a sinner by Superintendent Justin Kimball, because she had committed the *other* unpardonable sin — she bobbed her hair. The Marcel bob became fashionable, but anyone who got a marcel was immediately called a flapper. Mary Louis, young and impressionable, one day decided to shear off that distinction of Victorian dignity, long hair, and get a marcel, the sign of a loose woman of the twenties. When Mary Louis realized the awful truth, that she had probably lost her job, she rushed back to the beauty shop, gathered up the fallen tresses from the floor, and arranged them into a bun. She hoped that she could pin her hair back on. She feared that her father, like Dr. Kimball, would be horribly distressed.

Eventually, the Marcel hairdo won out over any protests, and short hair was accepted. However, it was several years before a woman with short hair was not viewed only from the corners of the eyes of the straitlaced godly types.

The cadet teacher recruitment plan continued through the thirties. It was then that Mozelle Welch, a student at SMU, decided that she would enter the program. Mrs. Welch is today one of the administrators of the media and library service program for the Dallas schools. She was inspired to teach by her teacher at Obadiah Knight, Nell McCorkle. This teacher was most encouraging and loving when the kids really needed some extra attention. Mozelle and her friends were all settled into Maple Lawn School when the boundary was changed, and they had to transfer to Knight School. Miss McCorkel made the change less painful. Knight School was out in a cotton field, and the school didn't look inviting to the children who were in the well established Maple Lawn. Miss McCorkle made them all happy that they were in Knight School. Mozelle was so impressed with the whole situation, that after she graduated from the Dallas schools, finished her college work, obtained a teacher's certificate, she requested that she be given a teaching position at Knight School.

Another fine Cadet Teacher was Wanda Barnett, who taught for a number of years and then became a principal. She was called into the cadet program for love and money. "I was lured into the Cadet program by the $40 a month we received. Those were depression years."

The Cadet teacher training program continued until the start of World War II. At that time another critical teacher shortage evolved. Young men who were teaching were called into the service. In order to get more teachers, an old rule was abandoned. It was decided that married ladies could teach in the Dallas system. The repealing of this law drew some qualified teachers into the district.

Dr. White loves to tell the story of Elizabeth Dice, the beloved math teacher at North Dallas High School. Miss Dice started teaching at North Dallas in 1922 when the school opened. She continued teaching there until she retired. When the rule about married women not being able to teach was stricken from the books during World War II, Dr. White teased his charming, capable teacher.

"Elizabeth, you can get married because of World War II." She shrugged her shoulders and replied, "Dr. White, you're one war too late."

Everyone who ever had Elizabeth Dice for math at North Dallas was well prepared for any college course in mathematics. Miss Dice really didn't have time for marriage. She gave her energy and time to the students at North Dallas.

In 1950 there was another teacher shortage. The depression babies, comparatively few in number, were coming out of college, and the war babies, comparatively large in number, were entering school. There were not enough depression babies to care for the war babies. Besides that, the depression babies, having enough economic stress, were not readily drawn into the low paying teaching jobs. Instead, they were looking toward the riches that could be made in that postwar era.

So, there were all sorts of programs, plans, and promotions in the colleges to lure good students into the teaching profession. At North Texas State, the Future Teachers organization each year elected a Miss and Mister Future Teacher. I served as Miss Future Teacher one year and had a great time visiting other college campuses and going to banquets, parties, and dances. It was at one of these grand functions that I met the most beautiful teacher in America, Mrs. Nell Owen, a teacher at James B. Bonham School, Dallas, Texas. *Our Miss Brooks*, a TV series about a school teacher, sponsored a contest to find the most beautiful teacher in America; the kids at Bonham School entered their teacher, Mrs. Owen, and she won.

The sponsors of the *Our Miss Brooks* series decided to prove that all teachers did not pose for Halloween masks in their spare time. There were beautiful teachers, and the sponsors set out to find the most beautiful of all. The children at Bonham, the school on Henderson Street, entered a picture of their speech arts teacher, Mrs. Owen, and out of 5,000 entries, she was chosen as the most beautiful. Nell had been a Rotunda Beauty at SMU, and she had taken her beauty and her teaching skills to Bonham Elementary School. As the winner, she received a free trip to Hollywood, a part on the TV series, and her picture plastered on the cover of *Life* magazine, February

23, 1953. *Life* called her "durable and fetching," two qualities that made for good teaching. She was also termed patient as well as loving. The *Our Miss Brooks* series was such good PR for the teaching profession — even though the show's teacher Connie Brooks was in poverty, she still had a great time with her bashful beau, the biology teacher, who taught of life but couldn't live it up, and her paranoid principal, who needed to be worshipped and obeyed in order to function. The contest was terrific PR for the teaching profession as well as for the series.

In the spring of 1950, North Texas State University created a new type of student teaching program that was so successful that it was immediately put into operation all over the country. It lured good students into the program, and it provided better training for those who had decided to become teachers. Usually a student in education during his senior year spent one hour a day at a high school teaching one class in the subject that was his major teaching field. The teacher of that class at the school would observe the student teacher and give a grade. This one hour a day for one semester was really all the teaching experience the prospective teacher received. Dr. Wayne Adams, who was head of the student teaching at North Texas felt that the student teachers needed more classroom experience, and they needed to get the real "feel" of teaching. Therefore, two students from the education department at North Texas were selected to experiment in a pilot program that would place these two student teachers in Dallas schools to teach all day for six weeks. They would be guided and observed in their teaching by selected teachers from the Dallas system. These student teachers would stay for all after school activities, they would get to know all the other teachers in the school in which they were student teaching, and they would attend faculty meetings at the school. Dr. Adams along with Dr. R.V. Holland, who was head of the speech and drama department at North Texas, asked me if I would be one of the experimental student teachers. I would leave the NTSU Denton campus and live in Dallas for six weeks and teach at Hillcrest High School. The classes in which I was enrolled, of course, would continue for the six weeks during which I was gone, but I would be given special assignments to make up the work. Would I go? It was a great opportunity, so I left North Texas the middle six weeks of my senior year, moved to Dallas, and taught at Hillcrest for six weeks.

Mrs. Clair Cunningham was the speech and drama teacher at Hillcrest. A recent graduate of SMU, she was a national debating champion while at SMU, and she was now proving to be an outstanding and effective teacher at Hillcrest High. I was inspired and impressed with her immediately, and she promptly called me "her little shadow," because that was exactly what I became. Since her love was debate, she gave me the drama work. She was able to give more of her attention to the 1952 debate topic: Resolved, that all American citizens would be subject to conscription for essential service in time of war. (The truce talks in Korea had failed, so this was an apt topic.)

I was in charge of the senior play. She had chosen the play, but she hadn't cast it or selected the backstage crew. This was up to me. I called for tryouts one afternoon, discovered all the great talent at Hillcrest (a small school at the time existing only in the original Vickery Place building plus a few portables), chose the most appropriate cast and crew, and posted a rehearsal schedule. I became a part of the school just as the plan had proposed, and through this close contact with teachers and students, I was "hooked" on teaching.

I went on all the debate tournaments too with Mrs. Cunningham, met the other coaches, and saw the inside of tournaments as a teacher. I myself had debated in high school, but the role of coach was so different from that of contestant. I had debating experience but no coaching experience. At one of the tournaments during the coffee break, I had an opportunity to talk with Mr. CC. Nutley, debate coach at Adamson. He gave me some coaching tips. He wrote them on a napkin, the only paper handy at the time. I have that napkin carefully glued in a scrapbook that I kept of this whole experience. The tips are still timely.

The same feeling that I had about coaching debate, I had about directing a play. I had been a member of many play casts, but the role of director of high school students was a new experience.

Paul Salzberger, who is today a prominent Dallas attorney, played the lead in the play. A secondary role was taken by Arnold Margolin, a fine actor, in whose family runs quite a bit of dramatic talent. Younger brother, Stuart Margolin, also a Hillcrest graduate, created the character of Angel on the *Rockford Files*, the James Garner television series. Today Arnold and Stuart Margolin are doing quite a bit of directing.

Those six weeks at Hillcrest were outstanding days in my college career. The whole experience was memorable and beneficial to my teaching career. The educators who came to observe the program decided that it was an excellent student teaching procedure, and this extended student teaching experience was adopted throughout the country. Today, sometimes a whole semester is devoted to actual classroom experience for the student planning to make teaching a career.

During the sixties there was not a critical teacher shortage, because there was a drop in the birthrate. Also, the hippie generation claimed to have a strictly humanitarian attitude, devoted to helping others and not to making money. The colleges were turning out teachers and social workers who claimed that service to others and not money was the answer to human happiness.

Today, there is a rise in the birthrate, and because monetary gain is more popular than humanitarian services, there is a teacher shortage. If one does become a teacher, one is often looking for a way to get out of the profession as soon as possible. There is not only a shortage of teachers, but there is a shortage of role models. There are not too many Miss Spearses or Mrs. Cunninghams.

The teachers are moonlighting more than ever, and many times these second jobs become the first jobs. Teachers also claim burnout. Some are charred by their hectic schedules. Discipline problems are overwhelming, and the morale is low. Where's all the fun?

The colleges must start wooing good students into teacher education. North Texas State University with the Meadows Foundation has started a program for undergraduate elementary and secondary education majors called Excellence in Teaching. It is a five-year program that is offered to only those students who have B averages during their freshman and sophomore years. Then in the junior years special courses of study are begun. During the three years that the students are in the college of education under this program, they will have plenty of field work at the NTSU Pupil Appraisal Center and juvenile agencies throughout the metroplex area. Financial assistance during the fifth year will be given and the students will be assigned to schools for one semester as paid teachers' aides. Student teaching will be extended to a full semester. When the students graduate from the Excellence in Teaching program they will have bachelors' and masters' degrees. Hopefully, they can bring Excellence in Teaching to the Dallas schools.

SHORTAGES — OF MONEY

> One of the outstanding events which took place during the past year, was the election which increased the salaries of the teachers in the public schools of our city. The election came on April 6, 1920, and the school bonds and taxes carried by a large majority.
> Before that time, the salaries of the school teachers were shamefully low. It was a thing which was a discredit to the City of Dallas — that the teachers in the public schools should receive such low salaries, when they are one of the most important groups of people in the whole nation today.

This was written by Russell Birdwell, the editor of the 1920 *Dal-Hi Annual.* This student used the annual as a platform, and he voiced his opinion which obviously was shared by the people of Dallas, because the bond issue did pass. Still, the teachers were not being paid enough for their work.

If I came home from elementary school and complained about a teacher, insisting that, "She's so mean — mean old teacher," my father would always answer, "Honey, teachers are not mean. They're hungry." My father admired school teachers, and he was always concerned about their low, starvation wages.

When I was in college at North Texas State University, one of my favorite education teachers, Dr. Robert Marquis, came into class on a brisk fall day late in November and sighed, "Well, I just got last Christmas paid for." All of us prospective teachers who at that time were well supported by our parents, laughed heartily, thinking that Dr. Marquis was joking. When we entered the teaching field, we realized that Dr. Marquis spoke the truth, and that teachers do not make nearly enough money for the amount of education that they must have in order to enter the teaching profession.

The old TV series *Our Miss Brooks*, showed the financial desperation of the school teacher. Miss Brooks roomed with Miss Davis who had a cat that was living much better than Connie Brooks was. Minerva the cat enjoyed gourmet food, while Connie dined in the school lunchroom.

Nevertheless, even with low salaries, teachers have always managed to survive, and some of the teachers have survived very well. Miss Pappenhagen who taught at Dallas High for over forty years, died in January, 1930, and the *Dallas News* ran an editorial about her entitled, "Miss Pap's Estate." She left an estate that was larger than that of an ordinary businessman, $40,000, an enormous sum of money for those dark depression days. The editorial went on to say that Miss Pappenhagen had *not* lived as a miser. She was just a good manager. She managed her life well, along with another teacher, Miss Ruth DeCapree. These two lived together and enjoyed almost everything together. They even owned a car together. When they drove up to Central High in their car, one could not help notice that on the door at the driver's side there was a name printed, Miss Pappenhagen, and on the door at the passenger's side, there was a name printed, Miss DeCapree. They traveled together, they taught together, they owned a car together, and they evidently managed their money together.

My mother's class from Columbian Elementary School had a reunion on Valentine's Day, 1974. This was a reunion of a class that started together in 1900, so needless to say, there wasn't a big mob at the reunion. In fact, there were three students and one teacher. The students were Mrs. Dorsey Gregory (Lucille Cloud), who taught in the Highland Park Schools for a number of years, Mrs. Alfred Horton (nee Weiland), whose family owned the funeral home, and my mother, Mrs. Phil Brau (nee Hass). Their teacher, who entertained the former students at her home, was Mrs. Lannes Hicks Smith, who also taught in the Highland Park Schools after leaving the Dallas Schools. At this reunion, Mrs. Smith was in her nineties, not too much older than her former students, because in 1900 a young lady started teaching at sixteen, right out of high school and just after taking the teacher preparatory class. The petite Mrs. Smith had been the little darling of Columbian Elementary School, and she remained a darling to these students who enjoyed seeing her that day. My mother told of having a picture of the class, and she asked Mrs. Smith if she had a picture.

"Of course not, my dear. I didn't have the twenty-five cents to buy one. Remember, I was a teacher." Still, in spite of a low teacher's salary, Mrs. Smith had enjoyed a full and fruitful life. She was a good manager.

There was a teacher at Columbian Elementary School, Miss Norma Wormser, who used my grandfather to keep financially afloat. She bought bread from my grandfather's bakery, one loaf every other day, which was delivered right to her home. When my grandfather arrived with the loaf, Miss Wormser would always comment on how she loved rolls, so my grandfather was trapped into giving her a couple of rolls, actually three — one for Miss Wormser, one for her mother with whom she lived, and one for their maid. Miss Wormser was not wealthy, but she had a maid — pure class and good management! Those two traits always seem present in a teacher's personality.

Now, Miss Wormser had another method of gaining something extra from my grandfather and from the other parents. Teachers were only paid for the nine months of teaching time, so if the school year was lean, one can imagine what the summers were like. Miss Wormser had an ingenious method for raising summer money. She sent notes home with the students who she thought could afford what she called "summer conditioning." In other words, she'd handpick herself a summer school class of those students who could afford to come. She always insisted that my mother, her brother, and her sister needed "conditioning." They really didn't need this special attention, but Miss Wormser said that they did. She knew that my grandfather could afford it. Besides, it didn't hurt the kids any, and Miss Wormser was then able financially to get through the summer. She had it made with the extra teaching and the extra rolls. (She never had to dismiss her maid.)

Teachers throughout the years have managed, and a lot of them survived, because of their summer jobs or of their moonlighting during the semester. Teachers with their moonlighting have always brought problems to the administration, who ask, *Do they have the energy to teach if they have another job in the evening or on Saturday?* The *Times Herald*, September 9, 1932, carried this observation of L. V. Stockard, Superintendent in charge of High Schools. "Teachers must conserve their energies for their real duties which are undoubtedly the imparting of knowledge to pupils. They must minimize their attention to outside activities." This has always been the cry of the administration, but moonlighting and teaching will always go together, for many teachers moonlight in the first place so that they can stay in the teaching profession.

One of the early successful moonlighters was Miss Emma Pettey. Her second job was so much a part of the first, teaching at W.B. Travis School, that really the moonlighting enhanced her teaching more than anything else really could. She had a marionette company, and with the help of three puppeteers who were all graduates of the Woodrow School of Expression, Dallas, she offered as many as nine different shows in repertory. The Emma Pettey Marionettes could be engaged for a single performance, one hour for $30. One could engage the group to bring *Goldlilocks, Red Riding Hood, Punch and the Dragon, Puppet Vaudeville, Jack and the Beanstalk, Rumpelstiltskin, Three Wishes, Hansel and Gretel, and Cinderella* to any school or civic organization. One had only to call Miss Emma Pettey, 1416 S. Pearl Street, Dallas. Miss Pettey lived her whole long and creative life in the house on Pearl.

She was a member of the First Baptist Church, and Dr. George W. Truett called her whenever he wanted a service enhanced by drama. She was called upon to direct the presentations.

During the day, as a teacher at W.B. Travis School, she could entertain her classes with the marionettes herself. However, she had the classes work up shows using her priceless puppets and marionettes. There was a fine acting troup coming right out of the third grade at Travis School.

During World War II many teachers moonlighted, because the extra jobs were plentiful with most of the men overseas. Miss Faye Catledge worked in the men's shoe department at E.M. Kahn on Saturday. There wasn't a man available to sell men's shoes, so the efficient teacher took on the job. Dr. W.T. White, the new Superintendent of Schools, came in to buy some shoes, and Miss Catledge happened to wait on him. Later someone asked Miss Catledge, "Have you seen the new superintendent? He's so handsome." She replied, "You ought to see him without his shoes on."

Coach Earl Adkins, one of our favorite teachers at North Dallas, worked at Sears on Saturdays, and we girls would go down to Sears just to see him. We didn't realize that he was moonlighting. We just thought he liked Sears. Every Monday morning he'd come into our history class and announce, "Shop at Sears and save. Work at Sears and slave." No amount of moonlighting could have hampered his teaching ability.

Dr. Otto M. Fridia, presently deputy superintendent of the DISD, had this to say about moonlighting.

> I think it's a serious problem that impacts our ability to deliver education to the kids. I see it as having a serious impact on the effectiveness of teachers. But moonlighting has become a necessity because of the inadequacy of teacher salaries. Inflation too is taking its toll. It just costs more to live.

This was from an article that went on to point out that some teachers moonlight so that they can continue teaching. One stated,

"I don't want to quit teaching, but let's be blunt about it. You can't live on loving kids alone."

Some teachers say that if their salaries were raised they would immediately quit moonlighting, but others call the extra job their salvation. They feel that it's a good time to get away from kids and associate with adults. "It's refreshing to do something creative out of the classroom," one teacher remarked.

Dr. Fridia is working toward salary increase and less moonlighting. "If we're talking about a sound investment in the lives of young people who are going to be our future leaders, then reward teachers and reward them well."

In the meantime, teachers go on with various ways to make extra money. In the summertime, the coaches and physical education instructors are seen working for the park department. Mr. William Morris, our physics teacher and coach at North Dallas, always worked at Tietze Park swimming pool in the summertime, so we enjoyed him during our vacation. Coach Billy Kidd from Greiner ran the paddle boat concession at Bachman Lake. Some coaches invent things. Coach Wallace Davis considered the marker at the goal line on the field. It was there to mark the line, but also it was a hazard to players who were crossing the line. They could fall on it or stumble on it, so Coach Davis invented a marker that would flip over and give way to the player rather than hurt him.

Mr. C. Ford, teacher at Forest Avenue High, conducted a summer camp for girls, Camp Kickapoo. He never had trouble getting guys to be life guards. They eagerly asked for jobs so that they could see the girls all summer. He bribed the boys. The ones with the best grades got the jobs.

Most of the Dallas band directors are first quality musicians, so aside from their duties as band directors, they're also jobbing musicians. The list of the Dallas band directors and the membership roll of the Dallas Musicians Union are almost one and the same. They're good teachers,and with the professional experience they get from moonlighting, they're even better teachers. Two great band directors moonlighted themselves right out of teaching. While a band director, Mr. Bill Everett worked part time for Brook Mays Music Store on weekends. Now, he owns Brook Mays. Virgil Watkins sold band instruments on the side, and eventually opened his own store, Watkins Music Store.

Two other very talented musicians moonlighted themselves out of teaching. Mal and Betty Fitch were adored by the students at W.W. Samuell. The talented duo always performed in the evenings. Mal played piano and conducted the band and Betty sang. Today Mal Fitch conducts the house band at the Fairmont Hotel. Betty is singing.

The science teachers often used their knowledge of science and math outside of the classroom. Mr. Louis Murray, who taught science at Bryan Adams for a number of years is also an inventor. He has over sixteen patents in audiovisual aid equipment. Aside from teaching he also helped out at the local funeral home, because he was a mortician. He taught chemistry by day and embalmed by night. Where else could you get a chemistry teacher with firsthand experience like that?

The shop teachers took their talents home with them and used them outside of school. Mr. Alfred Malone built fine houses in the Forest Hills area. He was the shop teacher at Alex Spence and Bryan Adams.

The home economics teachers may slave over a hot stove all day at school and then demonstrate their talents at department stores in the evening. Nancy Beseler and the girls at Sunset High cook, clean, sew, and study nutrition all semester, but during the summer Mrs. Beseler can be seen standing by a microwave oven telling the customers of its fine qualities. She takes her professional experience back into the classroom along with some new recipes.

Whenever a textbook is needed, who is better qualified to write one than the teacher of the subject for which the text is needed? Miss Wilhelmina Hedde, speech teacher for many years at Adamson, wrote *The New American Speech Book,* a text for public speaking classes. The book was adopted by the State of Texas, and Miss Hedde did profit greatly from her writing talent. The book was adopted by several other states,so she brought fame to her school and some good fortune to herself.

Another writer plus teacher, Miss Leland Watkins, used to edit the *Texas Almanac* for Ted Dealey. She made quite a sum of money doing this, but she also absorbed enough Texas history to qualify as a master historian.

"I'd give my class enough work to choke a horse, and then I'd run across the street to the church and play the organ for a funeral," stated Mrs. Erma Beard, teacher at Urban Park Elementary School, who played the organ at the church on Sunday. A problem came only when there was a funeral during the week, and organ music was needed for the service. Because the congregation was healthy, and there were not too many funerals, it all worked out for this fine teacher. Principal Garland Reed never complained when Mrs. Beard left to play for the funeral. The class didn't either. The students were too busy completing the work that she left for them to do while she was across the street doing some quick work for the Lord. No one suffered from her extra job, and the church was most grateful for her services.

A recent article in the *Dallas Times Herald* stated that about twenty-nine percent of Texas teachers moonlight. They are readily hired for these second jobs because they are efficient and intelligent, well-organized and well-versed.

When another article came out stating that administrators are paid so much more than teachers, Jerry Brown, governor of California, stated, "Why in the world are salaries higher for administrators when the basic mission is teaching? "

He made this statement as a governmental administrator, but he wasn't ready to give up his salary in order for a truly dedicated teacher to get an increase. People keep talking about teacher pay raises, because the words are cheap. However, the cost of living keeps getting higher, and the teachers are so far behind on the pay scale, it would be difficult to catch them up. Actually, the question of teacher's pay will never be settled, because there will always be the called, chosen few who must teach and who will manage somehow, regardless of the fact that they are making substandard wages. The dedicated teacher will teach well and probably will also sell things, write books, and invent things just to be able to teach.

Once when she was teaching, Miss Wanda Barnett failed to pick up her pay check in the office, so the principal brought it down to her room. As she was slipping the envelope into her purse, a little first grader asked her what it was that the principal had brought to her.

"That's my pay check," she replied. The little boy looked surprised. "Oh, where do you work?"

No teacher would want that child along when she went to plead for a pay raise. Someone might get the idea that teaching school was all fun and games. Of course, it was fun for Miss Barnett, because she was one of those teachers who loved every minute spent in the classroom, and she certainly never taught for the money. There are a lot of happy, underpaid teachers who are such artists in the classrooms that the students don't even realize that their teacher is working.

THE GILMER–AIKIN BILL, 1947

The Texas State Legislature in 1947 had big plans to improve the state's public educational system. The war was over, and hopefully peace would be forever, so interest leaned toward the improvement of education. The Gilmer-Aikin Committee made up of legislators, educators, and other selected citizens was created to study the situation and to make recommendations as to how education could be improved in Texas. State Representative Claud H. Gilmer, attorney and rancher, from Rocksprings and Senator James E. Taylor, county newspaper editor recently returned from World War II, were behind the creation of the committee. The fight of the regular session of the fiftieth legislature over the method of financing the state salary schedule for teachers in the public schools of Texas also led to the creation of the committee.

The Texas State Teachers Association really wasn't too happy with the committee, because they wanted action and not study. The teachers wanted more money — not more talk. Senator A.M. Aikin, Jr. of Paris was named cosponsor, because he had always been a friend of Texas educators. The men really did not like all the politics that were involved with the dispensing of state funds for education. The laws that finally came from this committee made sweeping changes in the financing of Texas schools. There was such intense interest and study that all three Senate Bills (115, 116, and 117) passed in the regular session.

The program was successful, because it moved Texas to the forefront in the realm of educational policy and administration. Senate Bill 115 created new offices. There was to be a twenty-one member State Board of Education elected November 8, 1949. High caliber men were chosen to put the bills into effect. The first chairman of the new State Board of Education was Robert B. Anders, former state legislator. The first Commissioner of Education, an office also established by the bill, was Dr. J.W. Edgar, who had been Superintendent of Schools in Austin and Orange.

Senate Bill 116 was the longest and most complicated, because it contained the formulas for establishing more equal educational opportunity for all Texas children. Many small expensive schools were consolidated. Then there was a total reorganization of the funding for Texas schools with special attention given to maintenance, textbook selection, and school curriculum. State funds were distributed according to the average daily attendance. This was a strong inducement to administrators to get and keep the kids in school. Equal treatment then was given to all races financially. The new laws stopped some school boards from spending monies intended for black education on white schools. Hispanics were to be segregated only in the first grade while these children were learning English. After that, there was to be equal funds for each child regardless of race. The Bill also provided special service teachers such as counselors, nurses, librarians, and supervisors.

Bill number 117 provided a plan of automatic financing whereby the necessary money to pay the state's part of the guaranteed program was there.

The bills did give some credibility and stability to the educational system in Texas. The basic salary scale was a blessing. There was another statement often noted that also was a blessing and music to the ears of any teacher applying for a position.

"We would love to have you join our faculty, and yes, *we pay above Gilmer-Aikin*."

A TEACHERS CREDIT UNION

"Credit Union for Teachers: Dallas Instructors Oraganize to Thwart Loan Sharks," was the headline in the *Dallas Morning News*, March 22, 1931. The article went on to read, "Teachers borrow more money than any other of the professionals." The piece heralded the financial needs of the teachers, but at least the debtors were called professionals. A group of educators in Dallas studied the national situation and found that in 1930 teachers in the United States threw away $5,000,000 in high interest rates. This was a shocking statement, since it's hard to imagine that the teachers in the United States in 1930 even had $5,000,000 — to pay out on anything.

During those financially bleak days my father was credit manager for Mr. Ira McColister at McColister Chevrolet, and if ever a school teacher came in to purchase a car, that teacher came in with only promisory notes from the school district. There just wasn't money enough to pay the teachers, so they were given "promises" of money that was eventually to come into their hands. Mr. McColister took promisory notes, since in 1930 a car sold with a promise of payment was better than no car sold at all.

Nevertheless, the Dallas teachers decided that a credit union would serve them in systematic savings and assist them in taking care of their own credit problems at a legitimate rate of interest. In this they followed the trend in the nation at that time. By 1931, two thousand credit unions of all kinds had been organized in the United States, and the Credit Union National Extension Bureau in Boston was eager to offer advise to any group interested in their own union. The teachers in Dallas were interested. At least, thirteen of them were. These thirteen teachers, under the leadership of H.B. Yates, a Forest Avenue High teacher, resolved to stop paying high interests on money borrowed. They vowed to put some buying power into the hands of the Dallas instructors. These thirteen, H.B.

Yates, F.M. Delaney, Miss James Ellen Stiff, J.S. Henry, C.L. Ford, H.B. Hester, E.D. Walker, Arthur W. Harris, W.J. Edmonston, Bulah Baker, Grace Simpson, S. Stanley Knapp, and W.P. Fulton contributed five dollars each, and with the original sixty-five dollars the Dallas Teachers Credit Union was formed, January 17, 1931. This was the first *teachers* credit union in the state of Texas.

The union charged only seven percent interest on loans and paid from six to eight percent dividends on the funds that were deposited in the union. An early ledger showed that the teachers continued contributing five dollars regularly each month. The only teacher who was able to put in much more was H.B. Yates, who one month came up with the whopping amount of ninety-five dollars. Yates was a bachelor who lived at the YMCA, and according to the early ledgers had more money to invest than the other teachers. But every organization needs a leader and Yates took on the leadership in action and in heavier financing. He got the whole thing off the ground.

"This union will put money in the pockets of Dallas teachers and insure their financial rating," he assured his eager followers.

The credit union operated out of H.B. Yates's desk drawer at Forest High, until eventually the union could afford an office. The first office was in the Kirby Building. It was open for business every school day at 4 P.M. Betty McCree, the finest secretarial student at Forest High, was selected by Yates to assist him in running the office. Betty left Forest High at 3:30 P.M. and arrived at the Kirby Building every day by 4 P.M. to handle all the credit union business. She received twenty-five dollars a month, but she eventually realized much more from the job. She was given a lifetime career, because Miss McCree today serves as membership secretary. She handles credit union business from her fine office on Ross Avenue and not from a desk drawer where she began.

When the credit union was only a month old, the membership tripled. During the lean years of the depression, those teachers in one month had a capitol of $200. The growth continued and in the early forties the credit union had more than 2,300 members with $900,000 in assets. During the war, the growth was erratic, but the members' savings steadily increased. However, after the war, like most businesses, the union experienced phenominal growth. Buy on credit became a way of life, because there was so much to buy. New cars were available. Vacation plans that had been shelved during the war were brought out. People wanted to see the United States and the world that everyone had put forth so much effort to save. New furniture appeared in the stores. Those signs that had been placed in store windows during the war reading, *Sorry we're out*, were replaced with signs that enticed one to buy immediately. The price was right, and everyone was getting everything.

Early in the fifties assets reached one million, and by the end of that decade the union was in excess of nine million. In 1959, the offices moved from the Kirby Building into a new building at 4600 Ross. The Dallas Teachers Credit Union was one of the first unions in the country to own its own building.

By the end of the sixties financial service was given to all school employees who lived or worked in Dallas, Collin, or Rockwall Counties. The union had 27,149 members. It became a $28 million financial institution.

At the end of 1979, assets stood at $120,207,882 with a membership of 66,058. With all this growth in business, the union had to build a new wing to the building on Ross Avenue. Two branch offices were opened—one in Richardson and one in Southwest Dallas. An in-house computer system was purchased, and payroll deduction and bank draft services were introduced.

The inflation and economic pressures were at an all time high in 1981, the fiftieth anniversary of the union. Still, the members continued to save, and 29,000 loans totaling $64,270,638 were made. The Board of Directors is both optimistic and creative in its thinking. The property adjacent to the Ross Avenue headquarters has been purchased for more building expansion. At the last credit union convention, Alvin Toffler, author of *Future Shock* and *The Third Wave* was the speaker. His shock waves continued as he explained a future with more and more electronic technology.

The executives of the credit union are definitely considering the use of every possible new technology that is offered in the business and financial world. The credit union will see that the members get the finest and most modern conveniences. Thirteen teachers with $65 dreamed of "putting money in the pockets" of the Dallas teachers. It's obvious that their dreams were realized.

Chapter Five

School Traditions

The twenty-eighth president of the United States, Thomas Woodrow Wilson, was a self-proclaimed "mama's boy." He loved his noble, strong, saintly mother, Jessie Woodrow, so much that he dropped his first name, Thomas, and demanded that he be called Woodrow, his mother's maiden name. It was no surprise to anyone when in 1914, President Wilson signed the proclamation to set aside the second Sunday of every May to honor mothers all over the country.

In 1928 Woodrow Wilson High School opened, and from opening day on, the school was never called Wilson High, but always Woodrow. No one knows why this was, but certainly, unknowingly, the students and faculty paid greater tribute to the president than they realized. A tribute was paid when the school was named for him, but a greater tribute was paid when they began to call the school by his mother's maiden name.

The school sits in the heart of East Dallas, the land of traditions. The Lakewood Country Club is one of the oldest in the city, White Rock Lake was used as the camping ground for the Beemans, Dallas's second family, and Father R.C. Buckner looked eastward when he dreamed of establishing a home for children. Therefore, East Dallas has always had a special inbred heritage that has lasted through the years.

Just recently the Lakewood Library published a book entitled *Reminiscences: A Glimpse Of Old East Dallas*. The library had been working for some time on an oral history of East Dallas, and it was brought to the public in this book. The old timers in East Dallas told the fascinating stories of the area, and they told them with love. No other area in Dallas has published such a book, because there is just something special about East Dallas and its heritage.

One of the first and largest clubs that was organized at Woodrow High was the Early Dallas History Club sponsored by Mr. B.B. Cobb, a teacher in the business department. The club met each week to hear the various members bring reports on the early history of their city. The members felt that a student needed to know where he came from in order to know where he was going, so it's no wonder that a school creed evolved from these early Dallas historians. Every student at Woodrow accepted this creed along with the responsibilities of good scholarship. It was published in every annual for years opposite the picture of the principal who guided the students for almost thirty years.

THE CREED

We believe in honest work, in friendly comradeship and in the high courage that leads to right conduct.

We believe that from contact with the truest and best in people, in books, and in life, will come our inspiration for success.

We believe in loyalty to our Woodrow Wilson High School, which was named for a great man and is dedicated to his ideals; we believe in loyalty to our community, the City of Dallas, which has fostered our education and our pleasures; we believe in loyalty to our country, the United States of America, which was founded by great men, has been protected by great men and will always be the producer of great men.

We pledge our allegiance to these three agencies and hope, by our own lives, to make them all stronger and more potent factors in the advancement of humanity.

We publish this, Our Creed, opposite the picture of our principal, G.L. Ashburn, because by his example and precept, he has helped us to formulate these beliefs.

MORE STUDY OF EAST DALLAS

For years the Early Dallas History Club went on supporting the school, delving more into Dallas history, and favoring Principal Pop Ashburn. Today it doesn't exist, but fortunately the study of early Dallas history has not been abandoned by the students of East Dallas. Since the city is growing so fast, it might appear that a changing population really wouldn't care too much for an intensive study of Dallas. This is not true, for down the street from Woodrow High is William Lipscomb Elementary School where there are students still probing into the past of our city and where children are still investigating their Dallas ancestry. These are the third grade TAG students. These Talented and Gifted students have been tested, and their test scores have placed them in this special class where they have projects which challenge their exceptional abilities and creativeness. At Lipscomb School one of these projects centered around Dallas history. The TAG students were studying about old Dallas; they were looking into the old families of East Dallas, and some were looking into their own East Dallas backgrounds.

One of the third graders, Dawn Hulsopple, decided that she would investigate the Dallas school system as it was in the early 1900s. Dawn wanted to know what it was like to go to school then. What was it like to teach then? She chose this subject because education figured in the roots of her family. Her great grandmother, Mrs. Mary Cornelia "Minnie" (Bradfield) Scott, was a teacher in the Dallas schools at that time. Mrs. Scott taught at Fannin from 1911 to 1912. She then moved to teach at Travis from 1912 to 1941. Then she retired. Dawn learned that while teaching the third grade at Travis, her great grandmother had fallen and had broken her leg. She had to be away from school for three months. Her students visited her every day, because they missed her so much, and one of the larger boys begged,

"If you'll come back, Mrs. Scott, I'll carry you."

Mrs. Scott was the sister of John Sherman Bradfield who was president of the Park Cities School Board for thirty-three years. An elementary school in Highland Park bears his name. Dawn had to dig for all this information. She learned how to investigate, how to bring all her materials together under a central theme, and how to present this theme to the class in an interesting manner.

The whole class project was to climax in a slide show with script. So actually, the whole class had to learn to sift through information brought in by the various members and to assimilate this information so that the final product was an interesting and entertaining slide show. The children were responsible for making their own slides. Vivian Wilkinson, the teacher, worked closely with these children, and she had the blessings of her principal, a veteran with the DISD, Mrs. Brenda Gilliland. Mrs. Wilkinson's husband got into the final act of the project. He came to school with tape recorder and taped each child as that child narrated his part of the script. The city of Dallas never looked better. Its history was never presented so well.

These third grade TAG students also published a newspaper during the semester. Again each student was assigned a special project in order to get the paper together — selling ads to merchants in the neighborhood, writing news stories about the school and East Dallas, drawing comic strips, creating a crossword puzzle, taking pictures. Finally each project was put together and the newspaper was published.

The bankers down at InterFirst Bank were attracted to the activities at Lipscomb, so the bank adopted the school. The students enjoy restored and carpeted rooms and the secretaries enjoy electric typewriters, because of the interest and generosity of InterFirst Bank.

Children may inherit a large sum of money from their parents. The money can be spent and is gone forever. A child may acquire a grandmother's desk, a rocking chair, a sugar bowl, and that child might cherish these possessions, but these gifts can be destroyed. But when a child inherits some good solid roots, he's holding to a priceless commodity. A story from parents, grandparents, aunts or uncles will live forever in the mind and can be recalled when a connection with the past is needed for security. When families lose their traditions, when they forget their ancestry, then they have lost their very being. Unfortunately today in this mobile society, families travel very light, and in the many moves a family can lose some of the customs and memories.

I looked over my 1949 North Dallas High annual and discovered that most of us in that graduating class had been born in Dallas. What homogeneous groups we were. When I was growing up in North East Dallas, I wasn't aware of the fact that my playmates and I were so much alike.

My mother use to say, "Don't play with those kids. They're renters." Now, it wasn't that my mother hated people who didn't own their houses. She just thought it best that I not associate with transient people. Actually, she didn't have much of a problem, because everyone was deeply entrenched into the neighborhood. My mother was not a snob. She was just abiding by the old Southern way of life. She was a typical Southern lady who constantly warned me that I must always be aware of my associates. I had to behave beautifully at all times.

"You can't do that. What would the neighbors think! " she warned. Today, most people don't know their neighbors. This is sad, and to make things even sadder, they don't know what their neighbors are thinking. And the saddest story of all is that they could care less.

The study of history is most important. Knowing that children are still studying the history of their city and are still learning about the struggles and victories that have gone before them, can assure us of a crop of youngsters who will know where they're going. Students must know where they've been. Then they can move toward a good education which can bring earned prosperity and merited happiness.

Allegiance to the school will make the student more aware of his good performance. Being aware of a city's past accomplishments will make a citizen want to do better. The creed at Woodrow was recited by students, some of whom are the most prominent and well-educated citizens of Dallas today.

Now, in our modern truncated society the creed is a bit long, so the students of Woodrow now abide by a motto that if followed will lift their spirits as well as their grade averages. "Keep thy heart with all diligence, for out of it comes the issues of life."

TUESDAY — BANKING DAY

For years, every school child in Dallas "banked" on Tuesday. It was a tradition. Oliver Wendell Holmes, Sr., said, "Put not your trust in money, but put your money in trust."

In 1922 Dr. Kimball decided that this was what the school

children of Dallas should do. The average child wasn't wealthy enough for a trust fund, but he was certainly ready for a bank account, so the teaching of thrift became a part of the curriculum. The schools worked first in thrift education with the Southwest National Bank. This bank became North Texas National Bank which merged with Republic National Bank. In the early days of the savings program the children would buy ten cent bank stamps at the school. They would stick the stamps into books until each book was worth five dollars. This gave a child enough capital to start a real account with Republic National Bank. J.M. Cumbie, a vice-president at Republic, with the blessings of Fred Florence, president of the bank, set up a program that enabled every child in the Dallas schools not only to have an account, but also to have a cherished passbook from which they could watch their savings grow.

The bank appointed J. Frank Fields to oversee the whole school thrift program. Mr. Fields worked with the appointed banking teacher at each school. Tuesday morning was banking day. Students would deposit a little money each week, and the students and the teachers would watch the amount on the bottom line increase. It was really exciting to see how rich a student could become with just a little savings.

Every Tuesday afternoon Mr. Fields would go to the schools and collect the money. Warren Clements was the banking teacher at Adamson High School. His student assistant was Jim Young. Jim took a real interest in Mr. Fields's banking duties. He would watch Mr. Fields collect money, count money, come in with an adding machine for a regular audit. This was all so very impressive to the Adamson High student, that he decided then that the banking business was for him. Today Mr. Jim Young is a vice-president at Republic National Bank assigned to property management. His career really started back at Adamson when he helped Mr. Clements and Mr. Fields with the school accounts.

Trophies were given to the schools which had the most accounts and deposits. In other words, the awards were based on the amount of banking activity not on the amount of money involved. It didn't matter how much a student banked, for the goal of the program was to encourage a student to save something.

Fred Florence thoroughly enjoyed going to the schools to

award the trophies, and Mr. Fields thoroughly enjoyed overseeing the whole operation. Working with the students, the teachers, and the school administrators was a delight to this banker. When Mr. Fields retired from Republic Bank, seventeen years ago, the thrift program came to an end. This end wasn't brought on entirely by his retirement, but rather by the vast change in the saving and spending habits of people who had been given credit cards. VISA and Master Card never figured in the thrift program engendered by Dr. Kimball, Fred Florence, Mr. Cumbie and Mr. Fields. The old "save for and get later" theory was replaced by the "Charge it! " philosophy.

My account with Republic Bank that I started in 1939 as an elementary school student and closed as a graduate in 1949, paid for my room and board the first two years of college. My own children who graduated from high school in the seventies enrolled in college with VISA. In 1987 my husband and I will make the last payment on our son's senior year. Who's to say which was the better plan? I'll leave it to the sociologists and my creditors.

THE LUNCHROOM

Culinary artists claim that there are two sources of cuisine. There is the family cuisine prepared by the adoring mother, slaving over the kitchen stove for her hungry and precious brood. There is the cuisine of the professionals — the chefs who devote their lives to cooking and consider it an art. But actually there is another form of cuisine — traditional with schools. That is the food served in the school lunchroom. This is food that mothers will stand behind since they don't have to cook it. Their only hope is that their children will eat it. The artistic professional chef doesn't understand it. Nevertheless, all through the years, American kids have become healthy, hearty grownups from eating (at least sometimes) the school lunch.

The school lunch is not a bad lunch. It's a miracle. When one compares the number fed with the money spent, one can only conclude that the whole operation is a marvel. Parents will not balk one instant at paying three or four dollars for a glorified hamburger at a fast-food stand, but the school lunch should never exceed twenty-five cents. Surprisingly enough, it is still very inexpensive in spite of inflation.

The scene is the school lunchroom. It's the first day of school. A patroling teacher walks silently up and down between the tables watching hawk-eyed as the little children stuff their faces. They are not to throw food, only eat it. The background sound in the cafeteria is an identifiable noise that everyone who has ever gone to a school can remember. There is a muffled monotonous vocal sound mixed with a full roar of chewing. There is a frequent *Ding!* of the cash register.

Suddenly there is the sound of shattering glass and crashing garbage can. A child stands by the garbage can blinking back the tears. The lunchroom lady in charge of dirty dishes rushes out.

"Why did you throw the whole tray with the dishes on it into the garbage can?"

In a sobbing voice, the little first grader answers, "Because you told me to."

"I did not." The lunchroom lady is hysterical. She takes her job of keeping the steady flow of dirty dishes and trays going very seriously.

"You asked me what to do with the food left on your plate. I told you to *rake* it in the garbage can."

"Ooooooooooooh, I thought you said to *break* it into the garbage can."

The child had misunderstood the order and had thrown the tray with the dishes as hard as she could into the trash can. What else could a first grader do?

"No, no, no. You rake it into the garbage and put the dishes here and the tray there."

"I'll know next time." And off goes the little girl, not crying, and ready for play outside.

Thousands of children each day buy their lunches in the cafeterias and thousands clean their plates by eating the food or by *raking* the leftover food into the garbage cans. What do they rake in? A masters thesis was written on plate waste, preference and acceptance in the cafeterias of the Dallas schools. It was discovered conclusively that if a kid doesn't like the food, he won't eat it. No amount of nutritonal education will get him to change his mind. It doesn't take a master's thesis to figure that out.

Sam Levenson, comic and lecturer, told of his Jewish mother who said, "There is no bad food; only spoiled children."

The thesis pointed out that two foods were raked into the garbage regularly — cottage cheese and liver. Most vegetables were discarded. Hamburgers were a favorite. Most fruit was eaten, especially grapes. But as far as prunes were concerned, the dietician shouldn't even bother to serve them, unless she has something against prunes herself and just likes to see them in the garbage can. Taco salad was a favorite, but as far as spinach was concerned, it went from serving table, to plate, to garbage can. Chili pie, chicken fried steak, barbecued chicken, chili mac, and corney dogs all went down for nourishment. Pizza was popular with the taste buds, but buttered carrots only added color to the garbage can.

Today, the Dallas Independent School District serves food to all one hundred and eighty-one schools and one hundred and seventy-one preparation sites (kitchens). For the other ten the food is catered. The cafeteria managers order food for their particular cafeteria, and their orders are governed by the standard school menu. The menus are prepared and cycled for a five-week period, so the manager knows exactly what is to be served on a particular day. Special days are now observed. On May 5, Cinco De Mayo, enchiladas and seasoned pintos, shredded lettuce, and the ever popular congealed fruit cup are served.

In the sixties two radio disc jockeys, Charlie Brown and Irving Harrigan who is now known as Ron Chapman (real name), would always give the school menus on their early morning wake-up program. Congealed fruit cup always took a beating from them, since that name sounded much better than calling it the plain old Jello and fruit cocktail that it really was. These two gentlemen played havoc with the whole menu each morning, but the children of Dallas continued to buy their lunches in spite of what they said. In fact, because these two men were so popular and because they spent so much time announcing the school menu, they probably sold more plate lunches than anyone realized.

One snowy morning when the schools were closed because of the bad weather, Irving Harrigan stated that he was going to give the school menu in spite of the fact that the schools were closed.

"Here it is, kids. Here's the school menu *were* the schools open today: Rib eyes, baked potato with sour cream, tossed salad, and strawberry cheesecake. And of course, the ever popular congealed fruit cup."

Actually that day, the menu probably consisted of Salisbury steak, parsley buttered potatoes, sliced peaches, and an oatmeal cookie.

Dieticians would never call a potato a potato. A more descriptive name was necessary. This was to assure the public that the cooks were not just opening an institutional size can of something and pouring it into the pot. They must do something to the contents of the can, and by all means they must give it an exotic name. If it's only adding the word "seasoned" to the name, the dietician added it. It's not green beans; it's "seasoned" green beans. Anna Lee Blount, who was one of the supervisors for the school lunch program, insisted that a delectable name was necessary.

"Who would want to eat a potato patty, when one could eat a 'golden' potato patty? " Obviously it read better in the paper and sounded better on TV. Today the menus are announced each day on Channel 2, DISD cable TV station.

In the beginning of the public school system there were no lunchrooms. The children at the Akard Street School left the school grounds for one-half hour to skip down to Mrs. Rubenstein's boardinghouse for lunch. Mrs. Rubenstein had a boardinghouse at 271 South Akard, and she fed not only the Dallas school kids, but the Dallas businessmen as well. She had the best chili in the world, and it only cost a nickel a bowl. The crackers were free. The kids thrived on the Rubenstein chili. On occasion they would have time to stop at the meat market next door to get one of those gigantic pickles for two cents.

So much time, money, effort and expertise goes into the planning of the school menus today. In the early days the gang survived on Rubenstein chili and big pickles. Regardless, it must have been a healthy diet, because a lot of people grew up to tell about it.

For those students in schools who didn't have a boardinghouse close by, there was the janitor's house just across the street. The janitor's wife would also fix chili for the group at lunchtime. She would either have the kids over at the house for lunch where they would eat out in the front yard, or she would bring the food over to the school and serve it in the classrooms.

The first lunchroom was built in 1907 at the new high

school on Bryan Street. Rosa Spearman was director of school lunchrooms at that time, and she took much pride in her work. "We aim to serve warm wholesome lunches of high nutritive value, carefully prepared under sanitary conditions, sold at the lowest possible cost per serving, and to implant in the mind of the child an intelligent understanding of wise food selection."

She set down the ground rules that still remain. "The servers cannot idly just stand and stir vegetables when not busy." This stirring is such a natural act. I wonder how Mrs. Spearman controlled it.

"The server will not chew gum or taste the food at the counter." Seeing a server lick the spoon could still the appetite of any hungry patron.

"The server will not shout an order from the counter to the cook." There was certainly no class in a shouting server, and Rosa Spearman ran a high-class lunchroom. Dallas businessmen regularly ate at the Bryan Street High Cafeteria when it first opened.

Frances Welch was head of the school cafeterias for a number of years, and she was responsible for standardizing the recipes. When a child got used to the taste of a certain food, then that food must always taste as the child expected it to taste. The cooks seasoned according to the recipes — not according to their tastes. All the food was prepared in the same manner. This rule holds true today.

The cafeterias order hamburger patties that are already pressed and ready for cooking. One particular year, the patty was square instead of round. A child returned the hamburger because of the shape of it. The lunchroom manager assured the child that it was the same meat and that it had the same taste as the round hamburger — it just happened to be square. The child was still determined not to eat the odd-shaped hamburger. Finally in desperation the child approached the lunchroom manager.

"I'm allergic to square hamburgers."

The depression days brought the song, *Brother Can You Spare A Dime?* and a dime (actually eleven cents) was all one needed to buy a plate lunch in the high school. The elementary kids got their lunches for eight cents.

There were never any fried foods served from the cafeterias then. The only drinks offered were milk and hot chocolate.

The vegetable soup contained six vegetables, and it was only a nickel a bowl. The desserts were not fancy, but wholesome. While the children ate, they were told of the "need of complete mastication." Hence the food was properly digested. A child never left the table until all the food was gone.

Each year more cafeterias were added to the school system. Sometimes there would be a dedication ceremony. Such a ceremony took place on October 1, 1932, when the Maple Lawn lunchroom was dedicated. The festivities started at 6 P.M. with a dinner of wieners and chili and noodles. There was coffee and root beer for the parents. The children had milk. E.B. Cauthorn was the MC for the program. The ROTC band from North Dallas High played, and Alex W. Spence, attorney, spoke. The evening was completed when the Maple Lawn students sang the loyalty song.

At Cedar Lawn there was no cafeteria. It was long in coming, so Katie Clark, teacher, fixed the food for her class. She would put the pot of stew on the wood-burning stove to simmer each morning. By lunch time, the stew was ready to eat. She raised the vegetables on the school grounds, sowing the seeds right under the classroom window. Sometimes a child whose family could afford it would bring a few vegetables. The PTA furnished the soup bone which cost ten cents. The mothers also brought the crackers. Miss Clark kept a teakettle on the fire, so that the children would have hot water to wash the dishes after lunch. Times were tough in the thirties, but Katie Clark and her class were not aware of those hard times. They were eating too well.

Those of us who went to school during the war still have trouble throwing away food. We were continually told of the starving children in China. The sight of their hungry faces on the cover of *Life* magazine haunted us so much that we stuffed ourselves thinking that it would help the Chinese.

The free lunch at school did not exist in the beginning. If a child could not pay for the lunch, he would work in the cafeteria for his meal. Later as the system grew, the PTAs took care of the needy children. Then the Community Chest and the United Fund took over the job of supplying lunches for poor children. Now, there is federal funding. The process is so involved that a whole office on Ross Avenue is devoted just to the handling of this money.

Today in the lunchrooms there are salad bars and short lines for pizza and tacos. Of course, there are the standard school plate lunches always available. This never seems to change. There is another factor that never changes — the kids are still hungry. Hungry kids must be fed before they can be taught. Frances Welch summed it up well.

"In the broad program of the school, we feel that we have as much to do with the children's education progress card report as the teacher has and that credit for the successful health program should be partly ours."

CHERISHED MESSAGES

Sociologists and behavioral scientists should never overlook the scribblings in autograph books, annuals, and scrapbooks, for these scribblings bring to vivid light the human actions and reactions of the times. And too, a linguist with his fascination for the language can latch on to some of the word usages and word changes that are shown in these particular types of writings.

School children go to school with autograph books. They gather the thoughts of friends and these thoughts are preserved forever. Ofttimes these friends make helpful suggestions. Someone suggested to my mother in her autograph book, 1906,

> Be on time. Be kind, Be gentle. Be obedient. Be truthful.
> Signed,
> Your schoolmate

One friend requested,

> *Remember me early,*
> *Remember me late,*
> *Remember me as your old schoolmate.*

These sweet and moralistic notes were signed by schoolmates, a descriptive title seldom used today. *Schoolmate* was replaced by the word *Chum*. This contemplative thought was discovered in an autograph book dated, 1927.

> *We have been chumming together for two years.*
> *I hope that I will always be chumming with you.*
> Your chum

There were lots of popular verses written in autograph books during the twenties, and most of them were signed by "chums."

If scribbling in classbooks remembrance insures,
With the greatest of pleasure I'll scribble in yours.
                                        Your Chum

A friend is one who takes your hand
And talks a speech you understand.
A friend is constant, honest, true,
In short — she's just like you.
                                        Your chum

As sure as comes your wedding day
A broom to you I'll send.
In sunshine use the brushy part
In storm, the other end.
                                        Your chum

When you catch a fellow handsome and gay,
Swing to his coattail night and day.
When you're in the kitchen cooking meat,
Think of me and my big feet.
                                        Your chum

Some autograph books had special pages designated for the listing of school colors, the school flower, the school song, schoolmates, and schoolteachers. Popular colors for schools were purple and gold, and the flower was usually a pansy. Many a pansy was found crushed between the pages of the school memory book. Sometimes there was a special section set aside just for the report on a school function.

Mrs. H.R. Beachum, Jr. (nee Dorothy Keahey) wrote the whole story of the May Fete at James Hogg Elementary School. She also mentioned her favorite club and favorite teacher.

Friday, May 6, 1927, 6:30 P.M., the May Fete was held. It was a Grecian Court. We worked hard for it so it would be a success. The election was held and the following were elected: Duke, John Harris; Duchess, Darrie Ann Lynn; King, Earl Bauer; Queen, Dorothy Keahey. Miss Wilson conducted the May Fete. Miss Wilson also organized the Good Citizenship Club. Every Friday the club met. John Harris was president, Elizabeth Peeler was secretary and Mary Gamble was treasurer. At the end of school three girls were given gold medals for being good citizens. They were Mary Gamble, Elizabeth

> Peeler, and Carrie Ann Lynn. Every Friday we wore pink
> and also wore a sweet pea.

Surely pink and sweet peas were only worn by the girls. John
Harris being a Duke and also a president wouldn't have been
caught dead in pink with a sweet pea attached.

At one meeting someone that was definitely not bent toward good citizenship must have sneaked the book from its
owner and hastily scrawled in the margin next to the lovely account of Miss Wilson's marvelous work, "Old lady Wilson is
off! " Mary had tried to erase the disparaging remark, but the
culprit had borne down too hard with his pencil. A readable
image remained.

A special page was set aside for special chums, and Mary
wrote, *Ouida Hughes is my favorite chum. She will always be
first.* This was written on the day Mary was leaving James
Hogg Elementary School and going on to Oak Cliff High. But
allegiance to Oak Cliff proved to be greater than the love of a
chum, for later on the next page of the book, Mary wrote, *Much
to my sorrow, Ouida Hughes changed schools and is now going
to Sunset. I must get another chum.* The rivalry had always run
deep between the two schools. An Oak Cliff High student
would not *chum* with someone from Sunset!

World War I influenced the writings in the autograph
books. Written on the first page of a high school memory book
owned by Miss Mattie French Shannon is a poem that captured
the feelings of Americans about the world situation at that
time. Actually, this little ditty revealed the attitudes of students toward the other countries of the world better, perhaps,
than a prolonged essay written by a renowned sociologist.

A   stands for America, allies and all,
B   stands for Britain, a nation that must not fall.
C   stands for Canada, England's big son,
      And in this great war great fighting was done.
D   stands for destruction, demolish, — destroy,
      The ruin of Belgium was the Kaiser's joy.
E   stands for Europe, where the war was begun.
F   stands for France, where the fighting is done.
G   stands for Germany the cause of it all,
H   stands for hell where the Kaiser will fall.
I   stands for Italy, another ally
      That took the oath 'autocracy must die!'

J   stands for Japan, a brother of the east,
     Who looks upon the Kaiser as a great wild beast.
K   stands for Kaiser, the devil on earth.
     For him the ruler of hell has a reserved berth.
L   stands for little, like the heart of a Hun,
     Whose only desire is to master a gun.
M   stands for Mexico, Villa's domain,
     Where he and his army hundreds have slain.
N   stands for Napoleon, a warrior of the past,
     Who won many victories but was conquered at last.
O   stands for order, like the German gave,
     That put women and children in a watery grave.
P   stands for Peace, the prayer of the world
     For which in the war *Old Glory* is unfurled.
Q   stands for Quitter, Uncle Sam has none,
     Though the battles are bitter, he fears not the Hun.
R   stands for Russia, who ran off to hide
     Until her women the Germans defied.
S   stands for Submarine, the monster of the deep.
     For fear of their presence sailors cannot sleep.
T   stands for Time that rolls swiftly by
     While our boys are in France, to fight and to die.
U   stands for Union in which we are strong
     If not for it we could not stand long.
V   stands for Vinny Ridge, where the Canadians fought well,
     And to the tune Yankee Doodle gave the Kaiser hell.
W   stands for Washington, Wilson and World,
     From whence came the command that *Old Glory* be unfurled.
X   stands for Xmas, the brightest day of them all,
     And before it comes again autocracy must fall.
Y   stands for You, who Uncle Sam is calling
     For somewhere in France our boys are falling.
Z   stands for Zest of which our army is full,
     And along with the Tommies, our Sammies will pull.

Mattie had tucked away in her memory book a letter she had received from a doughboy overseas in France. A thought expressed in the letter showed that Mattie was quite a girl and that her doughboy was a soldier first in time of war, but who never lost sight of what he was fighting for — to be home with his girl!

My dear . . . How is school? Received your letter and pictures. You certainly look fine. The girls over here do not know what a low neck dress is.

The boys did not have autograph books, but they never

hesitated to write in one. And they never aired many deep emotions in the poetry that they wrote.

> *Kisses have germs*
> *I've heard stated.*
> *Kiss me kid,*
> *I'm vaccinated.*

> *Although we may fuss and fight all night*
> *I still think that you're all right.*

> *Down by a river*
> *Hanging on a tree*
> *Four little words,*
> *Do you love me?*

> *Cows like pumpkins*
> *Pigs like squash,*
> *I like you,*
> *I do, by gosh!*

> *Our eyes have met,*
> *Our lips not yet,*
> *But, Oh! You Kid,*
> *I'll get you yet.*

> *Sure as the grass grows around the stump,*
> *You're my darling sugar lump.*

The invention of the automobile was a real boon to romance. Couples went out riding, and if the young man was smart, he would run out of gas on Lovers Lane. This poem, "A Motor Romance," was found in a 1932 annual.

> Alice and her beau, Frank, one day,
> Went riding in his Chevrolet.
> They climbed a hill and then 'twas seen,
> The tank contained no gasoline.
> They coasted downward toward the lake
> But Frank, he couldn't work the brake.
> They struck a tree a moment later,
> That almost wrecked the carburetor.

> They journeyed home with Frank's pushin',
> While Alice sobbed upon a cushion.
> She'd not forgive, she vowed with scorn,
> Till Angel Gabriel blew his horn.
> So poor Frank's hopes were doomed to blight
> For Alice married Willys Knight.

Before its demise, the Willys Knight automobile was just as popular as the Chevrolet. At least this message said so.

There was still a lot of advice, good wishes, and pensive thoughts given during the thirties as can be seen from this collection of verse found in various autograph books of the period.

> *May your life be bright and sunny,*
> *And your husband fat and funny.*

> *When you get married and have twins,*
> *Don't come to me for safety pins.*

> *Remember the girl from the country,*
> *Remember the girl from the town,*
> *Remember the girl who spoiled your book*
> *By writing in it upside down.*

> *When you get married and the old man gets cross,*
> *Pick up the broom and tell him you're boss.*

> *Little Oscar Shay,*
> *Decided to his sorrow,*
> *To speed across the right-of-way.*
> *His funeral is tomorrow.*

> *I thought,*
> *I thought,*
> *I thought in vain,*
> *Until I finally signed my name.*

> *Roses are red*
> *Violets are blue,*
> *I am hungry.*
> *What about you?*

Don't it make you mad?
Don't it get your goat?
When you get in the bathtub
Without a cake of soap?

Some write for love,
Some write for fame,
I write simply
To sign my name.

They laughed when I sat down to play,
Some fool had pulled the stool away.

When the golden sun is setting,
And your heart from care is free,
When of others you are thinking,
Won't you sometimes think of me?

When World War II was raging, the kids back home had Adolph Hitler to belittle in their autograph books.

Yours until Hitler gets Hungary and eats Turkey in Greece.

Your pal.

In the forties *Pal* was used in place of *Chum*. Also, because the war news brought reports from all over the world, the names of distant countries often crept into the doggerel.

When you're in Africa up in a tree,
Send me a coconut C.O.D.

When you get married and live in France,
Send me a piece of your old man's pants.

The ladies in the forties wore hairdos that were governed by the powerful bobby pin. This practice was mentioned in the memory books:

Can't think, brain dumb,
Inspiration, won't come.
Can't write, bum pen,
Best wishes, Amen.

Yours 'til the bobby pins get seasick riding the permanent waves.

Because of the sobriety of the world situation in the forties
some of the messages were ofttimes a bit grim. They were also
a bit philosophical.

> *I went to the river,*
> *I went to drown,*
> *I thought of you*
> *And couldn't go down.*

> *There is a book in heaven,*
> *It's leaves are white as snow.*
> *And may your name be written there,*
> *When you are called to go.*

> *In your golden chain of friendship*
> *Regard me as a link.*

> *When you climb the bannister of life,*
> *Remember me as a splinter in your career.*

Annual signers in the forties always told their friends that
they were "swell" and "all round." In the fifties their *Buddy*,
the name that was then used for *Pal*, was told to,

> *Stay as sweet as you are,*
> *And you will go far.*

There were others that were used to bringing kind thoughts
and wishes.

> *Oranges grow in California,*
> *Lemons grow there too.*
> *But it takes a State like Texas*
> *To grow a Peach like you.*

> *When you are old and cannot see,*
> *Put on your glasses and think of me.*

The "tell it like it is" spirit moved into the annuals. I noticed in my son's 1974 annual, two people in particular didn't pull any punches.

> To a nice boy whom I've *learned* to like . . . good luck!

> To a neat guy who has some weak spots . . . best wishes!

The whole point of the autograph book and of the customary annual signing was to wish the *Classmate*, the *Chum*, the *Pal*, or the *Buddy* the very best and to make sure that the friendship would always be remembered.

> *To a cool chick . . .*
> *I was here but now I'm not,*
> *So I left a note so I won't be forgot.*

SCHOOL CORRESPONDENCE

Three factors separate the business world from the educational world. Whenever a businessman looks at the schools, frowns in disgust, and sighs in dismay over the way the schools are being run (thinking he could run them so much better if given the chance) he'd better think twice and consider these three points:

First, schools are nonprofit. There is no money being made in the schools. Humanitarianism reigns supreme, not the dollar bill. This factor alters the thought processes for all concerned in education.

Secondly, when a crisis arises in the business world, it is handled with a called meeting. Files are checked, agreements are recalled, contracts are reread. In a school crisis, there is no time for a meeting. Schools are almost combustible at times. A kid throws up or breaks an arm, a kid sasses a teacher, a kid clobbers another kid — there are no files to check or contracts to reevaluate. In school a teacher must handle the situation as he or she had learned to do so in an education class back in college or by reacting effectively using all the years of experience in the classroom as a guide. After the smoke clears, a note is usually written to someone explaining the situation.

Thirdly, the stationery and the correspondence of the educational world are so very different from that of the business world. In an office, everything is fairly orderly. Office memos are sent on paper stating, "FROM THE DESK OF . . ." these interoffice

memos are typed or written neatly. However, in a school there
is no memo. There is a note scratched out on Big Chief tablet
paper, or notebook paper with three holes in it, the back of a
hall pass, or anything else that might be handy.

Now, these notes are not only written by teachers. Crises
arise at the home, and the parents write notes. Then the principals write notes to the parents and to the teachers. Teachers,
in turn, respond to the principals. Then, of course, in the middle of all this the kids write to each other about all sorts of
things.

In a million years a businessman would never be exposed
to any of the following gathered correspondence. These scribblings could only come out of the traditional school situation.

[Note to band director when child missed halftime show:]
Mr. Band Director,
    Please excuse Orson for not being in the halftime show.
He was stopped and detained for a long period of time by the
police, therefore, he was late getting to the high school to
meet with the band. This was no fault of his own and he was
innocent and very disappointed. Please understand.

His mother

[Note to band director at the end of the school year:]
Mr. Rumbley,
    Mary Jones left her trumpet in the band room. Please
leave it there over the summer.

Mrs. Jones

[Note to principal from the dean of students:]
    Mrs. Firestone brought this little girl in to see me be-
cause she (the little girl) is afraid the world is coming to an
end on Monday. She is terribly worried. She told me that she
goes to the Holiness Church and her mother and father read
it to her from a paper. I don't know exactly what to do about
it. At the moment she is content to watch me use the type-
writer. Please don't tell my minister that I am attempting to
keep the world from coming to an end. What shall I do with
her? Shall I try to convince her that she will need to know
how to read and do her numbers in heaven next week?

[Note to principal from mother:]
    Dear Principal,
    Will you please give Charles back his belt to keep his
clothes up? If you don't give him his belt, then pay him for it.

His mother

Some notes are obviously forged. A little first grader asked teacher Aleen Hurlbut if she could be excused from music class. Ms. Hurlbut told the little girl that she would have to have a note from *her mother* in order to leave music. This note came the next day printed as only a first grader could print it.

Dear teacher,
Mary will not be in music anymore.

Her mother

And then there are hall passes:

Hall Pass:
     Name: Henry
        To: Office
  Reason: For bringing four bullets to school.
     P.S.:   They are in the envelope with Henry.

Hall Pass:
     Name: Gilbert
        To: Office
  Reason: Gilbert hit Pete on head with a Yo-yo. (I now have yo-yo — he's unarmed.)

Dear Teacher,
    Rebecca didn't went to school Friday because we took her to Waco, Texas to see her grandfather's father of her father. The one with who she is staying is her grandmother's mother of her mother.

Thank you,
A parent

Glendon Shirley told her class that she didn't want them to forget the true meaning of Easter.

"I'm Jewish," piped up a little boy.

Glendon, not wanting to offend in any way, replied, "Well, Jesus was a Jew."

The little boy seemed surprised. "I knew that God was a Baptist, but I didn't know that Jesus was a Jew." Some Rabbi was falling down on his job.

Mary Frances Walsh announced, "It's Education Week. What do we do when our parents come in?"

With wide eyes, the little boy came up with what some parents might consider a pretty good answer. "We say, 'Welcome,' and give them a cold beer."

Another child asked with a hopeful look on his face, "Teacher, are you taking that aspirin so you'll be nice to us?"

[Note to principal from mother:]

Please let Janice come home at lunch. She has an appointment at the beauty shop and I have to get her some shoes for tonight's piano recital.

Thank you,
Her mother.

[Note sent back to parent from principal:]

The policy of the school board does not permit us to excuse students for the above reason. It will be necessary for Janice to check with her teachers to make up the missed work.

The child said that he had a stomachache. The teacher sent him to the nurse. He came back with his shirt rolled up and his stomach totally exposed. The teacher asked,

"Why is your shirt rolled up?"

"I told the nurse about my stomachache and she told me to stick it out to the end of the period and then I could go home."

The little girl brought the library book back very late. "I over dooed it," she explained.

[Note to principal from parent:]

Please excuse Nora from square dancing. She has started a different religion.

Thank you,
Her mother

[Note to principal from mother:]
Dear Principal,

Joe told me that you had punched him. And he also told me what he had done in school. After he told me what he had done I didn't like it, so I punched him again.

Thank you,
His mother

[Note to principal from teacher:]

Glen told me that his cousin died and he was going to the funeral. Called his cousin and found him very much alive and disturbed that he had had a funeral.

Signed,
Teacher.

FROM THE LIPS OF BABES

Teachers get together, and will, as tradition demands, tell school stories. Here are some choice examples.

Principal Pauline James asked a little boy why he was sitting out in the hall.

"That teacher put me out here."

"Which teacher?"

"That teacher." He pointed to a teacher who was substituting for another teacher who was ill. "That *prostitute* teacher."

A child threw up in the door way. When the bell rang, the class could not get out. This message was sent.

"Trapped in room by vomit."

True integration can only come when there is total respect and admiration between the races. Elizabeth Adams welcomed the first little black boy into Fannin Elementary School. This school had many Mexican American children in classes. When the class celebrated with a fiesta in the true Mexican style, the little black boy put on a sombrero and entered into all the fun. He stood there grinning, eyes shining, wearing this oversized sombrero and exclaimed,

"Oh, Miss Adams, I wish I were a Mexican."

A group of Rotarians including principal Harold Lichtenwald were laughing and carrying on at one of their meetings. One little first grader, who was there for a program, observed,

"I hope I can grow up and have fun like those old men."

The little black boy opened the door for his new white teacher.

"You're such a fine little gentleman. Thank you for opening the door."

"Oh, teacher, you're going to make me blush."

That teacher knew that she was going to learn more from her little black students than she ever dreamed that she would.

With real interest the little boys asked teacher Adele Haynes, "If God had a son, then he was married. Who was his wife?"

The bell rang and Adele thought she was off the hook. She

was saved by the bell and by the little boy sitting next to the one with the question, for that child answered the question.

"Silly, God wasn't married. There's not a woman good enough for Him."

Martha McCall told the children in her auditorium activities class that they could all be angels in the Christmas pageant if they came with their own wings. She reported that children came in wings that had been made with everything from chicken wire to shingles. There were wings of foil, feathers, and tin cans and wrapping paper. She held to her promise and they all went on stage in their assorted wings for the annual Christmas pageant.

A similar Christmas pageant was given across town. A parent asked the child what part he was playing.

"I'm Lo."

"Lo?" asked the parent.

"Yeah, you know. Lo, the angel of the Lord."

That same child told his mother that he would not join the Red Cross at school, because Christ had been hung on it.

REUNIONS

The beauty shop appointment is made months in advance, hours are spent finding just the right dress or suit, an immediate effort is made to lose weight, and there's a mad rush on for Clairol and Grecian Formula. All this is done in preparation for the high school reunion. Everyone goes and tries to look young, rich, and thin, the three important assets that make one appear successful.

These reunions take place for three reasons. First, and foremost, they bring back memories. Stagg Rentz, insurance man, president of the Forest Avenue Alumni Association, called the meeting to order. The minutes from the previous reunion were read. The secretary concluded with an appropriate statement.

"God gave us memory so we can enjoy the June roses in December."

The Forest Avenue High graduates are well organized. They are a unique bunch in that the school opened in 1917 and closed as Forest High in 1957. Only forty years of graduates must be contacted. The Dal-Tech alumni have much more work in getting their grads together. The school — like the system — is one hundred years old, since it was the first public high school in Dallas. Nevertheless, the Dallas High School-Crozier Technical High alumni worked toward a big, big reunion spring (1984). Mr. Steve Allen, Class of 1947, got it all together.

The Forest Avenue Alumni collect dues in order to pay for the news letter that is sent to each member. The treasurer noted:

"Teachers, don't pay dues. You've *paid your* dues."

Which brings us to the second reason for reunions. Graduates enjoy seeing friends and teachers. One is amazed when one sees a teacher years later, after graduation. A teacher who seemed all of ninety years old when one was in school turns out to have been really sort of young. I remember one of our history teachers who we thought was *very* old. She was a terrific teacher of the Civil War, and we decided that she knew all about the war because she probably "kissed the boys goodby." When I saw this teacher about twenty years after graduation, I discovered that she was only about fifty years old which would have made her about thirty when we all thought she was part of the nineteenth century.

It's great to see old classmates. When North Dallas High was fifty years old, we had a reunion at the school. A program was planned for the alumni that included some of the well-known graduates. Congressman Earl Cabell spoke; and also Dr. Ralph Phelps, who now is president of Howard Payne University. And of course, Judge Barefoot Sanders was present.

When Sunset High School was fifty years old in 1975, a history was published for the occasion. Principal Harold Filgo scrounged for the funds and Mrs. Vivian Silvan, journalism teacher, got the book all together. During the 1975 school term every student at Sunset had to bring a story or historical fact, or anecdote about the school. The best were collected for the history book.

Usually only high schools hold reunions. However, the Mount Auburn Elementary bunch sometimes gets together. The Minyard boys, now food store proprietors, were expected at that gathering.

Lastly, reunions bring evaluations. They sometimes give people feelings of regret. When Woodrow Wilson High celebrated its fiftieth anniversary, all the grads gathered. One lady graduate looked across the table at a well-known and extremely wealthy gentleman, also a Woodrow graduate. She sighed as she murmured to the friend next to her.

"Well, there he is. I knew I should have paid more attention to Trammell Crow."

Chapter Six

Changes After World War I

Until Dr. Norman Crozier became Superintendent of Schools in 1924 there was not a hard and fast rule set for the age at which a child would start to school. Children started to school when their parents wanted to put them there. There were kindergartens, and some of the children came, or rather were sent, even though they were not old enough to be part of a semiformal educational group.

There was a lot of child dumping. Miss Leland Watkins, who served as a Dallas educator for fifty-one years, recalled a case of this early in her teaching career. Pinky Lou came to school at the age of four, and it soon became obvious that Pinky Lou did not belong in school. By 10:30 in the morning she was asleep at her little desk, and in her sleep she would wet her little pants. Leland had to dry the pants either on the tree outside or on the radiator inside, depending on which was warmer — dryer.

"I finally faced Pinky Lou's father. 'You have a choice. Stop bringing Pinky Lou, or bring her with two pairs of pants.'"

Pinky's father was so impressed with the young sassy teacher, Leland Watkins, that he abided by her first suggestion and did not bring Pinky Lou until the next year when she was physically able to control herself. The father did spread the word that the school had a very impressive, spunky teacher who was doing a great job.

When Dr. Crozier came on the scene, he cut out the kindergartens, and he set the age for entrance into the first grade at six years. First graders had to be six years old, and they had to be six by the first of September, or they could not enroll.

Unfortunately, I was born on the fourteenth of September, and because nature ran two weeks behind on my birth, I could not enroll in school the year that I was six. I was going to be a whole year behind! At least, that's what my parents thought, so by the time I was four years old, I began to hear talk at home about my having to go to *private* school.

"Should we send her to private school or hold her back?"

I could tell from the grim attitudes during these discussions that both could be bad. In the thirties, private schools were for the very wealthy kids or for those children who couldn't adapt to the normal situation, which was the public school. It was fine, fashionable, popular, and sensible to send a child to public school. That was where most of the kids were.

Finally, my parents decided on the better of the two disfavored choices. I would go to private school for the first grade. So, in September, 1938, I enrolled in Ludie Rae Gardner's private first grade class, corner of Vickery and McMillan, and it really turned out to be a fairly good situation. I remember that during that first month, we didn't learn too much, because we were having so many birthday parties for the kids who were enrolled. However, by the middle of October, with most of the birthdays out of the way, we settled down into serious reading, writing, and arithmetic lessons. The teachers in these private first grade schools (that sprang up all over town) worked closely with the public schools so that the children coming from these one-year schools would be ready for second grade work offered at the public schools.

To send a child to private school during the late twenties and during the thirties cost a lot of money. Not wanting to hold their child back and not being able to spend the money on a private school, some parents lied about their child's birthdate. These parents would declare an August birthdate for their child and attempt to enroll him in public school. Dr. Crozier had to get tough and demand that the birth certificate be brought to school with the child. Still parents continued to lie about the age of the child. Mrs. Martha Foster was the secretary in charge of checking birthdays, especially the suspicious ones that were on the thirty-first of August. She would check on birthdays and Dr. Crozier would check with her.

"Any more Ananiases today?" he'd ask at the close of a busy afternoon.

Dr. Crozier was not referring to the good Ananias in the *Bible* who baptized Paul after he had healed him of his temporary blindness. He was speaking of the Ananias in Acts 5 who, with his wife Sapphira, *lied* about the amount of money that they were giving to the church. Dr. Crozier called all of these birthdate liars, "Ananiases." In the Bible, Ananias and his wife both dropped dead at the feet of Peter. Dr. Crozier didn't wish death upon these prevaricators — he just didn't want them to bring their kids to school unless their children were six by the first of September.

JUNIOR HIGHS

The California School System, which began to set the pace for education in the country in 1920, had a number of schools operating quite successfully which they called Junior High Schools. These schools held grades seven, eight, and sometimes nine. They were for those students who were twelve and thirteen years old, difficult years of growth and of mental adjustment. These students were not children, but they were not really ready to take on any adult responsibilities. They were at an age where they needed some extra care and attention as they grew physically into adulthood.

In 1930 there were twenty-five junior high schools in the United States. The idea was catching on. The Dallas School Board in January of 1932, decided to adopt the junior high plan, and as soon as the money was acquired, a new building was built to house the kids of the "in between" age. At this junior high level, more attention would be paid to physical growth than to mental growth, because the major function of the body at eleven years was to grow. Special teachers would be acquired just to deal with these students. The shock of going from a childlike elementary school situation into an adult atmosphere of the high school was going to be alleviated. The whole program was carefully studied.

Finally, the School Board got the money, and plans to build Boude Storey Junior High were put into action. However, even before the plans were on the drawing board, Dr. Crozier had selected the principal. James T. Whittlesey was the chosen man, and he went to California for further study of the program. Whittlesey returned with grand plans, and these plans included a California look to the building. The structure acquired a Spanish flare. The principal returned saturated with junior high school information.

The Dallas School Board was so sold on this movement that in 1933 they opened not one junior high, but two. The other school was J.L. Long and Mr. C.W. Morris was chosen to be the principal. Together the two men, Whittlesey and Morris, shared knowledge of the junior high students and of programs for these students.

In 1939, another junior high was built to serve the north part of Dallas. It was named for the school board member who had been so intensely interested in junior highs, Alex W. Spence, young attorney whose untimely death saddened the citizens of Dallas. M.M. Myers was appointed principal and remained the principal of Spence Junior High for over thirty years. "Pop" Myers, with his big heart and broad grin welcomed hundreds of students into their preteen and early teen years.

"Students, you're in junior high now. It's a challenge. Make new friends. Start a new life. Learn new things. Be loyal to your teachers, to me, and to your new school, Alex W. Spence."

REPORT CARDS

Dr. Crozier changed the report cards in 1929. They were to reflect character training. Children received grades in obedience, cooperation, courtesy, and independence. Until 1929, the students were graded as Excellent, Good, Average, Poor, and Unsatisfactory. Dr. Crozier changed the grading system to rate the students alphabetically. In the elementary schools the students were graded on only three levels — Satisfactory, Needing help, and Failure, (S,N, or F.)

In February, 1931, 10,000 educators gathered in Washington at the National Educators Convention, and Dr. Crozier presided as the president of this prestigious group. The educators gathered to discuss the well-being of the 27,000,000 school children who were in school at that time in the United States. The teachers and the administrators all had one thing in common. There was no money to speak of to use for the advancement of education. But there was a determined spirit to try to do the most with what funds were available. The speaker at the convention was Admiral Richard Byrd — whose topic was Character in Action. Dr. Crozier made a marginal note in his report on the convention to the effect that Admiral Byrd loved kids so much that he didn't make his "usual charge for the lecture." The admiral gave a cut-rate for the teachers. This was good, since in those days money—or rather the lack of it—was a primary issue. There was no money to build any schools in Dallas, so all the buildings were crowded and crammed and overflowing with kids.

The *Dallas Times Herald* reported that Dr. Crozier warned the school board that there was danger in slipping back into the old ways of education. The three R's were not everything.

"We must have other programs for the students—especially athletics." A stadium was finally built with WPA funds.

Dr. Crozier guided the schools through the depression years, and it was difficult because the city grew larger and the funds grew smaller. This gentleman was able to do it somehow. He was born in Mississippi, September 14, 1877. (He and I have the same birthdate. I wonder if *he* had to go to private school!) His family moved to Texas where he attended school. His degrees came from The University of Texas, Austin College and SMU. In Dallas he served as the principal of Dallas High in 1914. He was assistant superintendent in 1919 under Dr. Kimball, and then in 1924 he was appointed superintendent and served until his death in 1940.

The *Dallas Morning News* reported in 1932, on Dr. Crozier's birthday, that a dinner had been prepared in honor of the occasion. He was fifty-five. He insisted that there be "no fuss."

"Give me quince preserves, hot biscuits, butter, and a glass of good rich sweet milk and you'll be giving me food fit for a king."

This statement came from the man who guided the schools through a time when there were very little kingly things about. Those were depression days, but Dr. Crozier never seemed depressed.

Chapter Seven

Support Systems

A teacher cannot stand alone. Teachers must have help from the parents of the students, and must have help from the members of their own families. Teachers must have help from all sorts of people.

THE PTA

When a woman gives birth, the new little life is brought to her all wrapped up in a small cuddley blanket, attached to the precious bundle somewhere should be the mother's membership card to the PTA, because in a couple of years she's going to have to join anyway. PTA membership goes along with motherhood. For super parenting, the father too must join.

I had been at Robert E. Lee School only a couple of days when I brought home the slip that said, "Do you want your child to be in a class that has 100% membership in the PTA? Sure you do! Fill out this slip and send it with $2 and you will be thought of as a loyal, American citizen and a fine parent. If you do not do this, you will be considered a despicable reprobate." Of course, my mother and father, both, immediately joined, and my class was 100% the very next day. Some classes lagged behind a day or two, but my bunch was top drawer!

When my daughter went to Umphrey Lee Elementary School in the fall of 1961, she was in school only a couple of days when *she* brought home the slip that read, "Do you want your child to be in a class that has 100% etc., etc." The only thing on the slip that had changed through all the years was the amount of dues. That had gone up fifty cents. I immediately joined. My husband reluctantly sent his two fifty even though he claimed it wasn't fair. He was teaching at W.E. Greiner Junior High, was a member of that PTA, and felt that one membership was all he could handle. I convinced him that this was for his daughter, and he needed to show his unfailing support.

Our PTA — like all the PTAs through the years — was constantly sponsoring something to make money. Umphrey Lee was a new school, so it needed everything — curtains in the auditorium, fans in the auditorium, and a piano for the auditorium. Our PTA was going to tackle all those needs.

In the fall the first thing under the PTA sponsorship was usually the gigantic Halloween carnival. A lot of work went into those carnivals, but a lot of money came out. I myself made quite a bundle in the fortune teller's tent. Of course, I suffered a lot for it. The black wig I had rented gave me a headache, the hoop earrings almost destroyed my lobes, and all the other jewelry and all the makeup that I was wearing caused me to perspire violently. I was snapped into that fortune-teller's tent promptly at 6 P.M. with all those kids and that crystal ball, and four hours later when I was released I gazed into that ball and saw no future for myself whatsoever. I was so hot in that tent with all those kids breathing on me and extending grimy little hands for a reading into the future that I thought I had died and missed heaven.

On top of enduring the heat, I had to think more creatively than I ever had in my whole life. Every one had to have a different future, and what kind of future does a fourth grader have anyway?

"Oh, yes, I see eight more years of school ahead for you." They looked so disappointed at that, it seemed imperative that I think of something else.

"Ah, yes, I see that you will meet a tall handsome stranger on the playground."

One kid answered, "My mother told me not to talk to tall

handsome strangers." For myself I saw one thing clearly. The next year I would *not* be the Umphrey Lee School fortune-teller. I was going to sell snow cones and that was all there was to it.

At Christmastime, the PTA sponsored a cake baking contest and Julie Benell, Dallas actress and food editor of the *Dallas News* at that time, was the judge. I decided that I would win by baking a Julie Benell cake. I bought one of her cookbooks with the recipe for her famous carrot cake in it. I decided that she'd taste my entry, recognize her own recipe, and declare me the winner. The evening arrived and so did Miss Benell, to begin her tasting. She'd taste, meditate, drink water, and then taste another cake, meditate, drink water, and so on. A coconut cake won, and the famous carrot cake didn't even place. It was obvious that Miss Benell did not recognize her own cake, because the coconut cake was made with a recipe of Miss Benell's gourmet cooking rival from the Neiman Marcus Zodiac Room, Helen Corbitt. Nevertheless, the PTA made some money off the prize winning and us non-winning cooks.

With the carnival money and the cake baking money the PTA had enough to buy the curtains, fans, and piano for the auditorium. In fact, we made the auditorium look so great, we decided we would use it ourselves to give a show — the next big money-making project. Like most PTAs the Umphrey Lee crowd was really a bunch of ham actors and actresses. Charles Parr, a devoted parent, and I wrote the script, entitled, "Gunsmoke At Umphrey Lee." Farrar Whitten played Matt Dillon, Bill Lewis was Doc, Jim Bruce was the bartender, Charles Parr was Chester, and I was Miss Kitty. (Since Charles and I wrote the script, we gave ourselves choice parts.) Of course, we shared the limelight with other devoted parents, and anyone who wanted to participate filled in the barroom scene. C.L. Duke, the principal, played the one tune that he knew on his harmonica during one of the quiet times in the barroom. It was a great show, and we made enough money to buy some equipment for the physical educational department.

I continued working for the PTA all the years my children were in school. I never was a fortune-teller again, but I did write a marvelous program for the David W. Carter PTA that honored the principal, Harold Lichtenwald. We did the whole program around refrigerator packing boxes. To really honor

Mr. Lichtenwald it was necessary to tell of all the schools with which he had been associated. He had attended schools, he had taught in schools, and he had been principal at several schools. We decided that someone from each of these schools would come out and tell about their association with Mr. Lichtenwald at that school. But instead of just coming out from the wings of the stage to do this, it would be best to build little school houses, put them all over the stage, and let the speakers step out of them and speak their parts. We collected refrigerator packing boxes, and my stage design class at Dallas Baptist College turned the boxes into schools just big enough to hold a speaker. One of my students, Mike Owens, headed the project. Today, Mr. Owens is programmer for Channel 2, (cable) for the Dallas Independent School District. He's doing a lot of scene design for the school district, but his career really started with refrigerator boxes that so ably honored Mr. Lichtenwald.

THE FIRST PTA

The story of the PTA in Dallas really started with a mothers' club. This first mothers' club in Dallas was organized in 1895 at the McKinney Avenue School, now known as William B. Travis, and Mrs. George B. Dealey was the founder. Her son, Ted, came home from school one day very muddy, so Mrs. Dealey went up to the school to see just why little Ted was so dirty. She discovered that after a rain the playground remained a muddy bog for days, and there were no walks whatsoever around the school. Something had to be done. Some gravel for that playground was badly needed. Mrs. Dealey rallied together twelve mothers: Mrs. T.W. Griffith, Mrs. J.B. Adoue, Mrs. A.V. Lane, Mrs. Oliver Thomas, Mrs. Wendel Spence, Mrs. J.W. Spake, Mrs. Walter D. Want, Mrs. J.B. Shelmire, Mrs. Richard R. Nelms, Mrs. Arthur Simpson, and Mrs. Robert Trumbull. They each donated five dollars to pay for the gravel. Colonel R.E.L. Knight, an Oak Lawn property owner, was contacted for the gravel. Colonel Knight was able to supply the gravel from the bed of Turtle Creek, but he refused to accept any money for it. His daughter, Mary Watts Knight, was in the school, and he felt that she too should play on gravel rather than in mud. Ted Dealey told in his book, *Diaper Days of Dallas,* that his first real date was with Mary Knight. A romance blossomed on the gravel.

Mrs. Dealey had some money now, since the gravel was donated, so her newly founded mother's club decided to spend the funds on something else for the school. A woman from Chicago was invited to bring a program for one of their meetings. She spoke on art in the school, and the mothers were awakened to the fact that the rooms in which their children studied were downright *drab*. So the ladies decided to get some good reproductions of famous paintings for the children to enjoy in class. Because the first money that they spent was for art, they named their club, The Public School Art League. It was good that Colonel Knight donated the gravel, because The Public School Gravel League was a name that wouldn't have fit those highly-refined ladies.

Nevertheless, the paintings were purchased and hung on the walls. When the mothers viewed the treasures, they decided that the walls were too dingy to hold the art, so they immediately took the pictures down and had the walls painted. When the walls looked worthy of the art, the pictures were again hung in the classrooms. This happened a day before a Texas blue norther blew in. The janitor started the faulty furnace the next day at school, and clouds of soot blackened the walls. The ladies were horrified and immediately petitioned the Board of Education for a new furnace. After that was installed, the ladies had the walls painted once again, and the treasured art was hung for the third time.

For their next project, the ladies planned to replace the outdoor toilets with a more modern convenience, the water closet or a flushing commode. The mayor refused to listen to such a demand. He wasn't about to bring in one of those new fangled flushing toilets. Besides, water closets really weren't too popular. When President Millard Fillmore installed the first water closet in the White House, he was criticized for doing something that was both unsanitary and undemocratic. For, a by-product of the installation of a water closet which required gallons of water for each flush, was the enormous increase in the public demand for water. And furthermore, it was undemocratic to give only a select group the power to flush. However, Mrs. Dealey was not to be defeated in her cause, so with the group she visited the mayor at frequent and regular intervals, and finally, to get the ladies off his back, the mayor replaced the outhouses. After all, Mrs. Dealey had the *Dallas*

Morning News behind her. Her husband was running the paper.

The group of mothers was well organized, and more and more mothers were joining. Since the group was dealing in services way beyond the art field, the club was renamed, The Mother's Club.

The second mother's club to be organized in Dallas was at San Jacinto School. The third club was at Colonial Hill School. Mrs. William M. Reilley was elected president of the Colonial Hill Mother's Club in 1905. That was the year that Miss Birdie Alexander was relieved of her duties as music supervisor. School money was running short, something had to be cut, so the school board decided that music was to go. Mrs. Reilley got the support of the presidents of the other two mother's clubs, and the ladies rose in protest over the removal of Miss Alexander. The ladies won out. Music instruction remained in the schools of Dallas. After this victory, Mrs. Reilley realized that the mothers did have some influence, so on March 24, 1906, she organized the Dallas Mother's Club Congress with the members coming from six schools — San Jacinto, Colonial Hill, William B. Travis, Stephen F. Austin, James W. Fannin, Davy Crockett, and The Fair Park School.

Two days before the Mother's Congress came into being, the new Woman's Forum of Dallas was organized with its various departments. The Congress was invited to be one of the departments with Mrs. A.V. Lane chairman of the school section and Mrs. J.N. Porter (Ella Caruthers Porter) chairman of the home section.

Mother's Clubs in the high schools started organizing. Mrs. George Sprague was the charter member of the Oak Cliff High Club. One of her responsibilities was to provide Professor Adamson with a birthday cake each year on his birthday.

All the ladies diligently moved on in their work of improving the schools. They demanded and got a probation officer and a sanitary inspector for the schools. And in 1908, they campaigned and got two women elected to the School Board, Mrs. E.P. Turner and Mrs. P.P. Tucker. The Dal-Hi Annual of 1911 proudly boasted:

"Mothers of the land know best what is good for their children. If all school boards were made up of mothers, the schools of the nation in general would be far better off."

The Congress of Mothers had been organized in Washington, 1897, and it was the dream of Mrs. Reilley that the Dallas Congress be affiliated with the national group. Her dream was realized on March 31, 1909. Even when she became seriously ill with typhoid fever that spring, this illness did not deter Mrs. Reilley. She had never been stopped before, so at her request she was taken in a horse-drawn surrey and literally carried into the meeting so that she could see her dream fulfilled.

The Congress of Mothers strengthened its ranks by creating an advisory board made up of such Dallas leaders as Judge F.B. Muse, Dr. William Deatherage, Dr. C.I. Schofield, Arthur LeFevre, superintendent of schools, 1910–11, Dr. George W. Truett, Alex Sanger, and George B. Dealey. The Congress formed the following working committees: the extension committee, the school improvement committee, the anti-cigarette committee, the entertainment committee, and the committee to find a meeting place.

Eight schools were represented at that first session, the six original schools with added representation from John H. Reagan and Alamo Schools. During the first month, the council initiated plans for the observance of the first Mother's Day in Texas. Mrs. Albert Gantt was chairman, and she, with Professor Arthur LeFevre, were to see that special Mother's Day programs were given at all the Dallas schools. The council received a letter of appreciation from Miss Anna Jarvis, the founder of Mother's Day, for its work in the observance of this memorial. In her letter Miss Jarvis stated that she was most pleased that the schools would stop to observe a day to honor mother.

The committee for finding a meeting place completed its assignment, because the Congress of Mothers began to meet at the Chamber of Commerce building, 1308 Commerce Street. The biggest problem that faced the mothers at that time, 1910, dealt with the censorship of movies, which were becoming very popular with the kids. The mothers were really not as concerned about the movies themselves as they were about the darkened theatres in which they were shown. Those darkened theatres just might encourage unbecoming behavior on the part of the young people sitting in them. There was a committee to investigate the possibility of showing movies in a lighted area.

The mother's clubs were starting libraries in the schools. They were also looking into the possibility of a nurse who could visit the schools. Mrs. John S. Turner who became president in 1911 was able to get the school board to employ a nurse. The mothers furnished the medicine chests and any other needed supplies for a nurse at each school. Lunchrooms as well were being equipped by the mother's clubs. Things were moving right along.

In the fall of 1914, a dress code for the girls was put into effect by the congress. The girls were to adopt a simpler and more hygienic dress. There were to be no high heels, silk stockings, elaborate hairdos, or dresses of "party dress material" worn to school. Extremely low necks and short sleeves with excessive jewelry and stage makeup were out! Physical culture was to be taught to the girls. The course would include lessons in correct posture, sitting, walking, and breathing. The mothers condemned girls in skirts that were slit, girls with painted faces, and girls wearing evening dresses in high school classes. The mothers went on to imply that tight fitting skirts were causing delinquency in boys. Those slits in the skirts were just as harmful to the young men as cigarette smoking, staying out late at night, or playing hookey. For the girls, the acceptable dress became the innocent middy blouse and the pleated skirt.

To bar the sale of alcohol from the fairgrounds was the next goal of the mothers. The moms got word to R.E.L. Knight, president of the State Fair, that they wished the sale of alcohol to be stopped on the fairgrounds. Colonel Knight, who had been so generous with the gravel, sent a word to the mother's congress stating that it would be best if the mothers were to let their efforts and attentions go only to the schools and to let the directors of the state fair put their minds to the annual celebration. In other words, the mothers were not to meddle into the concerns and functions of the state fair. The sale of alcohol at the fair was none of their business.

Well, the mothers considered that it *was* their business, so a mass rally as held at City Hall, June 28, 1916. This poem, written by a *Dallas News* poet was read,

THE FAIR WILL DIE

The Fair will die! The fathers have said
The Fair will die without liquor red!
Such kind advice do the fathers give,

> Telling the mothers that the Fair must live;
> That the fathers run the great State Fair —
> Mothers' duty ends with household care!

The matter of alcohol was taken to the voters of Dallas, and the sales of liquor were barred from the fairgrounds in 1916. The vote supported the ninth amendment against the saloon. In spite of the barring of alcohol, the fair lived on!

Mr. Jake Golman of Cliff Baking Company saw the power of the mother's group and went directly to the mothers club to convince them that his bread was the best for the school lunchrooms. The ladies did decide that Mr. Golman's bread was the best for the kids. He in turn, for this vote of confidence, gave $900 a year toward the purchase of lunches for those children who couldn't afford to buy a lunch. Actually, Dallas mothers were often used to endorse products. A full page ad ran in the Dallas News stating that Mrs. Clarence Echols, PTA member, served Welch's Grape Juice to her family. The PTA got the money from the endorsement.

Every time a school was built and filled with children, the mothers of the students at the school got busy and organized a group, so that by 1920 there was a mother's club at every school. Dallas had so many active groups that in October, 1920, the State Congress of Mothers met in Dallas at the First Methodist Church. The first constitution and bylaws were drawn up, and Mrs. Ella Caruthers Porter from Dallas was elected the first president of the Texas Congress. This poem was read at that meeting.

TRIBUTE TO OUR PIONEERS

> We cannot list the things they did,
>   the weary hours they spent,
> Their toil observe, their trials sore,
>   as to their test they bent.
> Let us who reap the blessings now,
>   the fruits of their labors unceasing,
> Remember them with fondest love;
>   and, as the work, increasing,
> Enriches all our Texas land
>   to bless our children dear,
> Let's lift our hearts in gratitude,
>   to the loyal pioneer.

The mothers went on to help in the start of Hope Cottage,

the adoption agency, and in the organization of better baby clinics. They saw to it that fire drills were held and that fire prevention was stressed. They played a large part in the renovation of the Royal Street School (Columbian School) which stood where the Convention Center stands today. This school was to become the administration building in 1922.

The mothers also worked to get preschool groups formed, and soon Dallas was known as a pioneer in preschool work. In May, 1925, the first parent institution and summer roundup was held at the First Baptist Church, Dallas, where over a thousand preschool-age children were examined for physical and mental defects. Leading physicians and psychiatrists gave their time to do the examining and also to hold classes relating to child care and education for parents and teachers. The mothers also never let down in the work to get student scholarships started. All of these plans and intentions took money, so the mothers continued with money-making projects — bingo, bridge tournaments, games, craft fairs, etc.

When the building of a new school was approved, the PTA was always on hand for the ground breaking ceremonies. On March 10, 1931, the *Times Herald* gave front page coverage to the ground breaking for Robert E. Lee School. A picture of Mrs. A.C. Fair, Mother's Club President, Dr. Norman Crozier, Superintent of Schools, and James Whittlesey, principal, was carried with the news coverage of the new school.

The Mother's Club was renamed, January 3, 1934. Those diligent mothers were now to be called the National Congress of Parent Teacher Association, the PTA. Fathers were now a part of the membership. The name changed, and the work continued. The PTA went on working against the sale of alcohol to minors and against horse racing in Texas. They worked for marble machine control, adequate truancy law and enforcement, clean motion pictures and stricter driver's license laws. They opposed gambling devices and objectionable dance halls.

World War II brought with it an influx of juvenile delinquency. The PTA moved to establish more youth centers to keep the kids off the street. There was a definite show of patriotism. The patriotic moms in Dallas, like patriotic moms all over the country, sold war bonds. Dallas was the first county in the United States to reach the quota in War Bond sales.

Mrs. Leon Price was elected president of the Dallas Council of PTAs in 1944. She was later elected president of the National Congress serving from 1953 to 1956. The year after Mrs. Price was elected president of the Dallas council, Dr. W.T. White was elected Superintendent of Schools. She and Dr. White closed the war bond booth that the PTA had run at Sanger Brothers Department Store from January 18, 1942 to December 22, 1945, after selling $1,678,941 in war bonds and stamps.

The postwar years were on their way with a whole new set of problems, and unfortunately people believed that the schools could solve them all. Dr. White emphasized close parent and school relationships which really was the only way a school could survive. Education was complete and effective (then just as it is now) only when the parents with the children were involved.

The Crime Commission of Dallas was organized, and the PTA was involved with its work. The PTA also moved with Mayor Erik Jonsson as he established the Dallas Motion Picture Review Board. The year that the board was established, 1948, Cecil B. De Mille was invited to speak at a luncheon sponsored by the movie review board and the PTA. Mr. De Mille told the audience that,

> . . . mass entertainment is the most democratic of the arts. The public gets what it wants. We have created and you have made possible an industry and art form that is the greatest medium of expression known to man. What it will say to the children of the atomic age depends on our vision.

Someone in the North Dallas High PTA must have had some extra power, because Mr. De Mille left the luncheon and came over to North Dallas to speak to the student body. As an aspiring actress, I was elated with this opportunity to hear the great man of films tell his inside stories of Hollywood. It was a rare priviledge for us to be able to hear and later to meet Mr. De Mille, and this occasion proved to be one of the highlights of my high school days.

A headline in the *Dallas News,* 1947, read, "All Out Campaign Shaping Up for School Severance." The public school system was going to break from the City of Dallas and become the Dallas *Independent* School District. Financial support would come directly from the people of Dallas without the intermediary approval from the City Council. The PTA endorsed this separation of the school system from the city council, because it would put the schools into professional hands and also increased revenues would come to the district. Today the DISD is one of the largest businesses in the city.

Things began to really hop in the fifties for the PTA. In 1954 the School Administration moved over on Ross Avenue into a new building that was built on the foundation of the old San Jacinto School. The PTA Council began to meet in the new auditorium. The fifties brought happy days and busy days. The parents and teachers rejoiced when Jonas Salk came up with a vaccine that would end the crippling disease of Polio. The council immediately went to work in getting the vaccine to every schoolchild.

There were other great things happening. The council endorsed driver education. The parents worked for getting floride in the water. They continued investigating and rating motion pictures. The magazine racks were carefully checked for obscene literature. This was especially done in the popular fifties' hangout — the drugstore. Of course, Doc Harrell, who catered to the Woodrow Wilson crowd, and OS. Castlen, who took care of the bunch from North Dallas, would never allow anything in their drugstores that would be detrimental to the good moral growth of their patrons. These drugstores were educational institutions. They were also the most popular after school social scenes for the kids in those two particular high schools. Doc and O.S. were adored and admired by parents and students.

One mishap in 1954 really saddened the hearts of the mothers. The old Travis School burned to the ground. This was the school in which Mrs. Dealey had started the mother's club, and for which she had acquired the needed gravel. This had been the birthplace of the PTA. A day of honor was given in honor of the old McKinney Avenue School after the destructive fire, and this story was told at the gathering.

> The school was built in 1890, a three room frame house. Miss Affie Johnson taught reading and writing and arithmetic. She also coached the football team and acted as surgeon for all the cuts. She was the disciplinarian and the sanitation expert. She remembered one small boy who attended the school. In the second grade he came to school with live animals in his pockets. Some thirty years later Miss Affie

telephoned this boy and asked him to give a lecture to her classes on his experiences. His name was Frank Buck.

The sixties and turmoil rolled in, but there were some great things recorded in the PTA minutes. The William B. Carrell School opened for the physically handicapped and also offered courses to the parents. The theme of the PTA was "Homes Create Community Strength Through Effective Learning."

In 1968, Dr. W.T. White retired and Dr. Nolen Estes came into the Dallas schools as superintendent. He came in at a time when the unpopular war in Vietnam was raging, when there was a hippie movement going strong within the colleges that was sifting down into the high schools, and when the federal courts were ready to pounce on the schools with more demands for integration. The PTA readied itself for turbulent times. Whereas Dr. White began his tenure as superintendent with women's fashions resembling those of the Victorian period, skirts falling to midcalf in length — thanks to Christian Dior and the "New Look" — Dr. Estes started serving the schools when girls were wearing skirts so short that a whole new line of lingerie had to be created just for the fashionable miniskirts. Clothing in the late forties and through the fifties reflected the social repression that characterized American attitudes. The movements of the late sixties voiced freedom from everything including clothes. A repressed spirit was encouraged to be a free spirit.

Dr. Estes did set up a dress code for the kids, and the PTA tried hard to help in the enforcement, but eventually the code went out with yesterday's news. The logic behind the code sometime appeared ridiculous. Girls were not allowed to wear pants. The long tunic over the pants was stylish. Pants and tunic covered the body well, but the pants were not allowed. So, the girls just took off the pants and wore the long tunic as a mini dress which was acceptable even though more body was exposed by these minis than at any time in fashion history.

Hair length for men was a scorching issue. There could be no long flowing locks on the boys. H.S. Griffin, deputy superintendent, after watching the 1973 New Year's Day Cotton Bowl game on television between Texas and Alabama, realized that a whole nation was cheering men whose hair was falling out of their football helmets. Mr. Griffin called Dr. Estes immediately and advised that the superintendent cancel the rule on hair length. With a whole nation cheering strong men with long hair, how could one expect high school boys to shear off the supposedly stylish and power-giving long curls.

Dr. White came into the service of the schools when Jack Armstrong was the All American Boy waving the flag for Hudson High. Dr. Estes arrived when there were flag burnings and so-called freedom riots. The guys of the forties adored Jack Armstrong on his radio show, because one minute he was at Hudson High and the next minute he was having a swell adventure in the Amazon River Basin. With gasoline ration stamps the Dallas students couldn't even drive out of the neighborhood during the war years, so they lived their lives through Jack.

The girls in the forties identified with Judy, with whom they had a date every Saturday morning on radio. Judy had great times with her friend, Fuffy Adams. Their only sin was letting the fudge boil over on the kitchen stove. Judy and Fuffy would have never understood the literature that was passed out to the girls in school during the sixties that dealt with the use of deadly drugs.

Dr. White came in 1945, the prelude to the "Best Years of Our Lives." Dr. Estes came in 1968, a year of the assassinations of Martin Luther King and Robert Kennedy, of the invasion of Czechoslovakia, and of the police war at the Chicago Democratic Convention. Dr. White came in when a man was a man and a woman was a woman. Dr. Estes entered when it was a little hard to tell the difference, especially from the back side.

The PTA took the theme "Family Involvement in Educational Change." That theme would stand as meaningful today as it did in the late sixties. The changes in education were so rapid that parents, teachers, and administrators remained in a constant turmoil. In 1972 the federal courts issued busing orders that caused a complete and instant change in the school population. White citizens flew into the surburbian school districts for their children to attend there, or they placed their children in private schools. People began to wonder if public education in the large cities would survive — and the PTA began work for its survival.

Positive Parents were organized with Mrs. Betty Vondracek in a leading role. She was the 1982–83 President of the City Council PTA. Her children had always attended public schools in Dallas. Son John is a senior at Hillcrest High, and he stated that he was well-prepared in math for his computer science major at A&M. Daughter Vickie is a sophomore who is in the honors group. Mrs. Vondracek praised the teachers at Hillcrest for her children's fine education.

Positive Parents was organized when the backbone of the business world went to Superintendent Linus Wright and demanded that something be done for positive publicity about the city schools. These men put a lot of tax money into public education and felt they were getting nothing in return but negative feedback. Mr. Wright went to the PTA first, since the PTA members were primarily the positive parents in the school system. Now, each school has its own positive parent group. There are no city-wide meetings, but rather, there are city-wide rallies to celebrate public education.

At Christmastime, 1982, there was a giant rally at the Union Station. Each high school presented the top five students from the previous five years, and the students came with their favorite teachers. Business executives were there to meet these students and teachers. Most of the graduates were attending colleges in Texas, but the Ivy League schools and the technical institutions were well represented by these recent DISD graduates.

On Labor Day from now on there will be a celebration featuring the vocational and magnet schools. The students who have graduated with a special trade and skill will be interviewed by businessmen who are looking for their particular skills and talents.

In the beginning, Mrs. Dealey had only to put gravel on the playground. The city grew and complications arose. The needs are no longer simple. However, the positive spirit of Mrs. Dealey and of all the mothers and fathers and teachers who have served in the Parent Teachers Association through all the years must and will live on. Public education will survive.

A CENTRAL DADS' CLUB

Bill Lewis, an executive with Dallas Power and Light, who was president of the Central Dads' Club, 1964–65, explained that the idea of a Dads' Club actually began when the fathers of the boys in the ROTC formed a club to promote interest in the ROTC and also to encourage the young men in their interest of the military.

Sunset High School took over the idea and established the first Dads' Club in 1925, the year that the school opened. Now, Dr. E.D. Walker claimed that North Dallas High had the first Dads' Club when the fathers of the athletes got together in 1923 to encourage the boys in their interest in sports. Regardless of which school was first, the point is that the dads were interested in the boys, and the boys developed into better men because of that interest. Dads' Clubs were organized in several schools as the idea caught on and the interest increased.

In 1931, Dr. George Sprague, President of the Adamson High Dads' Club, was concerned about some things that were happening at Adamson, and he wanted to take the problems up with the school board. He realized that he could get better results if there was a concerted action taken, so he arranged for a meeting to discuss the matter with the three Dads' Clubs that he knew existed, Sunset, North Dallas, and Adamson.

He learned that there were other Dads' Clubs springing up all over the city, so he suggested that probably a central organization of this kind could be founded. A month later a meeting was called at the downtown YMCA, and there the Central Dallas Dads' Club was organized with Dr. Sprague as the first president. These men then served as presidents after Dr. Sprague from 1932 to 1967, after which the organization ceased to function:

John C. Read, C.H. Shutte, R.T. Shiels, Dr. Sam L. Scothorn, Wimberly C. Goodman, E.E. Hendrix, M.A. Tracy, R.L. Brewer, Lewis C. Hugg, C.E. Cason, Romie Rasor, W.F. Pope, W.F. Welch, Harry Rubin, Lloyd Campbell, Alto B. Cervin, T.W. Ruthledge, Dr. J.H. Ray, Lonnie W. Wilson, Don L. Sterling, D. Lynn Crossley, C. Lawton Smith, Wilson Shelly, Alfred N. Sack, B.J. Ingram, J. Wesley Fry, Earl Holland, Port E. Stages, Jr., Coleman Cobb, George Johnson, Sam Money, William David Lewis, Keith Lukin, Charles E. Parr, and Charles Hodges.

In 1947 a constitution of the Central Dads' Club was drawn up with fourteen articles all in keeping with the object of the club,

. . . to support and maintain a charitable and educational undertaking, and its special field of activity shall be the providing of a centralized source through which the various Dads' Clubs of Texas now organized and to be organized may exchange ideas and combine their efforts for the advancement of education in Texas.

The constitution only verified what the clubs had been doing since the Central Dads' Club was first organized in 1931, supporting public education. All through the years there were awards created and given to the outstanding dads. In 1939 the T. Barney Thompson Award was first given. T. Barney Thompson was a country school teacher, an old-time Dads' Club worker, and a highly civic-minded gentleman for whom the award was named. In 1949 the T.A. Vines Award was established for outstanding work in the Dads' Club. Mr. Vines was a prominent member of the Boude Storey Dads' Club, and this club established the award in his honor. Myron Everts always gave the Everts award to an outstanding dad each year. These were ways of thanking energetic, intelligent, and resourceful fathers.

In 1936 the Central Dads' Club was called upon by the Tech High School Dads' Club to help clear away a nearby undersirable element. The final report on the action read:

> Through the concerted efforts of Central Dads' Club the Tech High School area was cleared of the 'red-light' district. The first result was a law prohibiting a female to accost a male, but this proved inadequate. Central Club was finally successful in getting police action which resulted in a thorough clean-up of the entire area.

The Dads' Club worked with the Park Board to get a park director and supervisor of playgrounds. The dads felt that having this officer would cut down on delinquency. The new supervisor was recommended, and his salary was agreed upon, $3,000 a year. This was a fine salary in 1940.

The February, 1940, issue of the *Dallas Dads' News* spoke of the increasing number of traffic deaths and injuries resulting from drunken driving. The Dads' Club worked to get stricter laws passed for this offence.

> Preliminary surveys by the traffic commission indicate that Dallas County had been far more lenient in dealing with this problem than most of the other counties in Texas. The

result has been scores of death and dying smeared over our streets and highways every year by alcohol crazed drunks at the wheels of ton and a half missiles of destruction. Let us hope that we have learned a lesson from the 1,158 traffic deaths and 15,000 traffic injuries that have occurred in Dallas County during the past ten years, the largest single factor of which has been drunken driving.

The dads put their hearts into this ever continuing problem.

An investigation of marble machines and amusement devices which might be used for gambling in the school district was conducted by the Dads' Club in 1948. The fathers felt that the machines were too near the schools. Also, there was a bingo game set up in the Lakewood Shopping Center. The dads leaped into action to rid that neighborhood of the gambling there.

Also, the clubs that year were working to correct the hazards of the railroad crossing by Dal-Hi Stadium. Their plea to the city was to act on the danger immediately rather than wait until some child was killed at that railroad crossing at Oak Lawn.

The Dads' Club made the front page of the *Times Herald*, November 12, 1952. Alongside a story of General Doolittle's warning the nation of a possible atomic attack, the Central Dads' announced that they were going to have a television show. Dallas High School students would quiz Dallas personalities on city events and problems. The program would be sponsored by the First National Bank in cooperation with the Central Dads' Club. The idea of this "Meet the Press" type show was well received.

It was a welcomed change from the wrestling matches, the cooking program, and *the Sid Ceasar Show*, all of which pretty well claimed the tubes in 1952.

The Central Dads' in 1961 looked into the possibility of setting up a student revolving fund to enable high school students to stay in school who were unable to finish high school because of financial reasons. This fund was made available for the 1963–64 school year, and it helped many a student finish high school without having to drop out and go to work.

An all-schools talent show was sponsored by the Central Dads' Club in the spring of 1953. This was the first of many that were given. All schools were extended an invitation to have their students audition for the show. This talent show became one of the most popular and outstanding events in the entire school year, especially with the elementary school crowd.

This first talent show in the spring of 1953 was such a success that the State Fair of Texas asked the Dads to sponsor another one in conjunction with the fair that next fall. This they did. The fall talent show was given on high school day through the years with the school system and the State Fair working together. The Dads' Club's venture into show biz proved successful and profitable — which is something that a lot of Broadway producers cannot say about their ventures. But these dads worked with youngsters who loved to get into the act, and they were supported by partners who wouldn't miss the act.

In 1965 the Rhythm Boys from Umphrey Lee Elementary School, a group of four darling little guys, Darwin Dulworth, Mickey Foster, (His mother Jill served on the School Board.) Kenneth Stewart, and my son, Phil, won a place in the Dads' Club talent show. The crowds poured into the State Fair Music Hall to see the winning acts, one of which was the Rhythm Boys doing the ever popular, *Hello Dolly.* It was exciting to know that all the money raised by the dads was going to make the Dallas schools better and to give some kids needed opportunities and encouragement in their work. Besides all this, the dads themselves had a great time. My father was active in the Dads' Club at North Dallas High. He loved the work, but the association with the other fathers offered him some close and lasting friendships.

The Central Dads' Club is no more, but dads will always be needed by the schools. There are different kinds of problems for the dads to solve today. The marble machines that fathers worked so hard to rid the neighborhoods of are now in game rooms displayed as a curiosity of the past. Today the kids spend hours hanging on to video games. Time with Pac Man could never replace time with father. Immorality is all around. It's not just down in an area around Tech High School. Besides, red-light districts are a thing of the past — one does not gasp over a house of ill repute. The subject today becomes a hit Broadway musical. Drunken drivers are so often fathers. There are so many more problems in our big city today, and unfortunately too many fathers are not around to help solve them. This fact is showing up in the personalities of the children. Teachers cannot be teachers and fathers too. Josh Billings, the American humorist, made this statement, and dads today need to take it seriously.

"To bring up a child in the way he should go, travel that way yourself once in a while."

THE CORNELIAN CLUB

On Saturday afternoons in the 1920s and 1930s at the movies between feature films, the kids enjoyed a short subject, *Our Gang Comedy*, starring Jackie Cooper and the Little Rascals. Later another gang starring Spanky McFarlin, Alfalfa, Buck Wheat, and Darla Hood appeared regularly in the local cinemas. In both series Miss Crabtree was the school teacher — beautiful, charming, patient. The remarkable thing was that she stayed that way even though some of the classroom antics of the gang would have caused any other teacher to lose all serenity. Miss Crabtree and the gang are still around today on television. The appeal of the Little Rascals never seems to fade.

Little Jackie Cooper (later it was Alfalfa) was always in love with the teacher. He could hardly hear himself recite because of the loud and rapid pounding of his heart as he gazed upon Miss Crabtree. The worst day of Jackie's life came when Miss Crabtree brought her fiancé to school. Jackie was crushed. However, at the end of the delightful one-reeler, Jackie accepted the fiancé, who turned out to be an all right guy, and soon Jackie was off to pursue the heart of the little girl who sat next to him in class. Still the audience knew that Jackie would never forget his first love, Miss Crabtree, the teacher.

Students all down the line have fallen in love with their teachers. At Alex W. Spence Junior High, I was so in love with Coach (and history) teacher Earl W. Adkins that I could hardly recite Roosevelt's cabinet for him, and to recite Roosevelt's cabinet was an easy task. We who went to school during the Roosevelt era had to memorize the president's cabinet only once. It never changed! My heart has always gone out to history and government students of today, since new cabinet appointments occur sometimes weekly.

Nevertheless, Mr. Adkins was my love and I had to really blink back the tears the day that he brought his wife and baby for all of us to see. I wasn't the only one in love with him. All the girls were. But, by the end of the day, we all decided that we'd accept his wife. There was really nothing else we could do. I decided to direct my attentions to the boy next to me even though he was seven inches shorter than I was.

Mrs. Billie Reece, whose husband is director of the DISD warehouse, remembered when Coach Ashburn got married. All the girls were crushed momentarily, but then they soon realized that they had to get over him. The class had a party for Coach Ashburn,and the students wore black arm bands. The girls mourned him, and the guys warned him. There would be no more days of the carefree bachelor life.

At Forest Avenue High School the girls' hearts went pitty-pat, pitter-patter over Coach Seldon Hutchinson. He was a big, handsome, virile man, whom guys admired and girls adored. He stayed single a little longer than gentlemen usually did in those days. He played the field and broke many a heart. Needless to say, the girls were interested in him, and they waited patiently to see the lucky lady who would capture Coach Hutchinson. At long last his engagement was announced. The young lady was met and approved. The wedding day came. Nine months and one hour after the wedding ceremony, Mrs. Hutchinson gave birth to a baby. The boys at Forest immediately responded with the locker room joke of the day.

"It would have come an hour sooner, except he had to go to the reception."

Students have always been interested in their teachers as people, and that interest obviously doesn't stop in the classroom. They want to know what that teacher's life is after school. The same feeling exists towards favored administrators. What does that principal do when he leaves his office? What about his family?

On Friday, May 13, 1983, the Cornelian Club met. The membership of this organization consists of the wives of the Dallas school administrators. This meeting in May was a very significant meeting, because the club was fifty years old that day. Mrs. Al Buschman, wife of the former Director of Athletics and also a charter member, gave the program. Mrs. Buschman was a professional actress before she married. When she came to Dallas with Al, she held private classes in expression and drama.

Mrs. Buschman announced her topic, "Let's Not Forget," and then she proceeded to tell the audience how to remember things. She was well qualified to speak on such a subject, since she was an actress and had always been able to memorize lines. She urged the ladies to memorize something new each day.

"Make a list and go the store without it. Read aloud as Lincoln did. Think of the brain as a muscle and use it."
All of this was an introduction to that which she truly wished the ladies of Cornelian to remember — their beginning. Mrs. Buschman recalled the first meeting fifty years ago:

Onnolee Schiebel, the wife of Walter Schiebel, the new principal of Dallas Technical High School, in 1933, called a group of the administrator's wives together. 'Walter and I have just come from Rochester, New York. He sees your husbands during the day and knows your husbands. I don't know any of the wives well and would so much like to get acquainted.' Our club was born.

The founder of the club was always a great support to her husband, Walter Schiebel, the principal who turned Dallas Technical High into one of the finest vocational schools in the nation. Mrs. Schiebel died in the fall of 1982, but she left fascinating diaries that told all about her activities with the schools of Dallas along with some news of the day.

Thursday, April 6, 1950: Gave a talk at the High School Teachers Wives Club. They seemed to enjoy it. Gave me a nice corsage. Square Dance Club hadn't met in three weeks, so we went. Afterward, ice cream at Ashburns — then television.

Friday, April 7, 1950: Son Dick is home! Flew over and wiggled his wings. Walter was in the yard. I cleaned a bit and then had the boys for lunch. Went to Jays for supper and then to the baseball game afterward. Tech won eleven to one over North Dallas.

Sunday, April 9, 1950: Big crowd in church and Sunday School. Took Dick. Japanese educator is in Dallas. Walter will have to entertain him until Wednesday.

Monday, April 10, 1950: Got groceries for Schubert Club. Walter went to court to fight the speeding ticket he got last week. Took the Japanese educator. Case dismissed. Russians have shot down a navy plane. Claimed it was violating Latvian territory. Was unarmed. Ten were aboard.

Tuesday, April 11, 1950: Schubert club met. I was a

hostess. Went to ballgame. Took the Japanese educator. No trace of the navy plane.

Friday, April 14, 1950: Cleaned and then went to PTA. Went to the social studies dinner at 6:30 p.m. at the school. We were the guests of Miss McEvay. Dr. and Mrs. Walker were there.

These few entries showed Mrs. Schiebel serving her family, the schools, and civic organizations. Dr. Schiebel retired in 1964, but he could not retire from the activities of Tech High. The students continued to be a part of his life.

Saturday, May 24, 1969: Went to a picnic that the class of 1936 sponsored. There were thirty-eight there. I brought potato salad. All well with Apollo 10.

Sunday, June 1, 1969: A group of Tech kids had a picnic at Tenison Park. We took the salad and potato chips. The Indianapolis 500 was won by Andretti.

A Christmas message from the Schiebels was sent in 1976. Dr. Schiebel, twelve years retired now, was not well. Mrs. Schiebel wrote:

Don't know if I'll be able to continue my volunteer work at Baylor. Walter taught his Lydian Bible Class until he was taken ill. He has been writing another volume of the *History Of Education In Dallas* covering the years since the first volume was published. He says it was easier to do the eighty-two years than these last twelve years. But it is nearly ready to go to the publishers. The Lord has been good to me. He gives me strength for each day as I need it.

The book that she spoke of *History of Education in Dallas*, Volume I, was published in 1966. It is an excellent reference book which contains a listing of the members of the school boards and of the principals of the schools as well as a comprehensive study of each school. Dr. W.T. White, who was superintendent of schools during the time of the writing of the book, requested that each school present a written history of that school to Dr. Schiebel, so that his book would be as complete as possible. Those histories are at the individual schools and hopefully are used at times to familiarize the students with the past activities of their school and with the great gentlemen and ladies for whom the schools were named. Dr. Schiebel's second volume on education has never been published. The material remains at the school board on Ross Avenue.

The 1976 Christmas message from the Schiebels went on to tell of their deciding to sell their big house on Munger, the one in which they had resided for thirty-two years. Selling the old homestead is a traumatic thing to which anyone approaching middle age can atest. It means giving up things. It means throwing away treasured junk. It means that one must change, and change is something with which only the extremely mature can cope. The Schiebels weathered the change.

> Bill (son) helped Walter clear the accumulation of years from the studio. Faculty notes, curriculum outlines, and other junk filled many boxes on the curb.

It must have been hard to accept the fact that there on the curb waiting for the trash man were notes from thirty-two years at Tech High. The outlines and the faculty notes were discarded, but the students who were taught by that faculty, led by those curriculum guides, encouraged and loved by Walter Schiebel live today as fine educated citizens, for those notes were in the hands of skilled teachers who gave their all to teaching. Those students have better lives because they had an education and they had an association with a great man and his wife, Walter and Onnolee Schiebel.

The remarkable Mrs. Schiebel was able to pass from one age to another without too much trauma.

> June, 1976: Walter and I sang our swan song in the choir — too many stairs to climb. I still spend a half a day at Baylor Hospital each week. It's been over twenty years since I started my volunteer work there.

The choir days were over, but the volunteer work went on. She just took whatever came in stride.

Mrs. Eva Dell Williams, whose husband Walter is an assistant principal at David W. Cater, is the new president of the Cornelians as they begin their next fifty years. Walter Williams, before going into administration work was band director at William Hawley Atwell Junior High, and his wife was a great supporter of the band. She sold just as much band candy and just as many magazine subscriptions and just as many light bulbs as the band kids sold. She — with band director husband — comforted my son through a traumatic experience. Son Phil was first trombone in the Atwell Band. That was the good news. The bad news was that the boundary was going to be changed because a new school was opening. Phil was going to spend his last year of Junior High at the new D.A. Hulcy Junior High School — he wouldn't be first chair trombone in the well-established Atwell Band. This meant that he would be who knows what chair in whatever band program would be established at the new school — all very frustrating to a junior high student.

In May the boundary was changed and Mr. Williams struck Phil's name off the Atwell Band list along with others who were no longer in the Atwell district. He offered all the comfort that he could to his now former band student. Phil and his buddy, Steve Crabtree, drummer in the band, plotted to blow up the new school, because they could not bear the thought of going to another school. I didn't worry too much about the planned blowup, since the most destructive acts the boys had ever committed were to fire water pistols at trash cans and to throw chinaberries at the neighbor's cat.

However, all my worry ceased to be, because Phil and Steve got phone calls from Mr. Don Daniel, who was going to be the new band director at Hulcy. He and his wife, Sue, were going to have all the prospective band members over to their house for a picnic. Here they would lay out the plans for the new Hulcy Band, and Phil with the other band members would have a big part in the making of the plans for the new band program. Mr. Daniel asked for their support, and he got it.

Don Daniel is now the band director at Bryan Adams High School, and Sue, his wife, is still mothering all the kids. Whenever the two of them meet one of Don's former students, Don won't always remember the name and everything about the student, but Sue will. The Bryan Adams Band is a traveling and performing band, and Sue is right there wherever they are. The band went to Washington for the inauguration of President Nixon. The band performs regularly at pro football games, and plays for special affairs. Sue is right there taking care of all the little ills, emotional traumas, and the thousand and one things that can happen to kids when they leave home.

Sue has taught school herself. She had as a student Robert Morgan whose father is Bill Morgan, an administrator with the DISD. In elementary school Sue taught Robert to write. While a member of the Bryan Adams Band, Robert forgot to get a permission slip from his parents allowing him to go on a band trip. He forged a note. Mr. Daniel found out about it and confronted Robert with the forged note.

"There's one thing good about this note. You write well. But after all, my wife taught you."

A student first respects a teacher. Then he admires a teacher, and then he loves a teacher. Then he'll get interested and nosey about the personal life of that teacher, and this is good.

"Are you married? Do you have children? Where are they?" A good teacher will open up and share his whole life with a student. His family will do the same. Teaching is a family affair.

JANITORS

A study was made a number of years ago to determine the power structure of the average public school system, and it was discovered, not really to the surprise of many, that the janitors in the school were really running the whole operation. It's fine to bring enlightenment to the kids, but it can't be done if there isn't any heat, and light, and water, and the other things that are necessary for physical comfort and thus, mental stimulation. The kids have always known that the custodian was one of the most important persons in their school life.

The Dallas School Board in the very beginning saw the importance of having reliable and dedicated janitors. In fact, when a school was built for students, a home adjacent to the new school was purchased for the janitor and his family. He got not only a salary, but also a house in which to live. This policy started in the beginning of the school system, and it was carried on for many years. Listings of the property owned by the Dallas schools included not only school buildings but also houses for janitors. The custodian lived nearby so that he could come in early and get the school warm in the winter, and so that he could open the windows on the hot sultry days. He would also be nearby to guard the building. All-night shifts are worked into the schedules of custodians today so that someone will always be at the school. This policy of having a live-in custodian is definitely cutting back on vandalism.

The duties of the janitors have changed down through the years. Here is a memo dated, March 15, 1906.

To the janitors of the Dallas Public Schools: You are hereby instructed to gather up at the close of school each day all cups and dippers in use by the children and for five minutes you are to thoroughly boil them. On Saturday of each week you will also scour with hand soap and hot water each and every cup and dipper so used thus keeping them bright and clean. At no time permit the use of old and rusty cups and dippers.

> Dr. Frank J. Hall and the Mother's Club.

This dipper cleaning only went on for five more years, because in 1910, a display at the State Fair featured something new — a sanitary drinking fountain. The dipper became a thing of the past. Janitors were elated over the fountain, so ideal for school. The Mother's Club was certainly sold on the idea, because the mothers manned the booth at the fair that featured the fountain. By the next year there were fountains bubbling forth in every school.

The janitors had to be uniformed and clean at all times, to set an example for the kids. A Dallas businessman who was appreciated and admired by the custodians (and really everyone who wore a uniform and served the schools) was Sam Dysterbach, who owned a dry goods store on Elm Street that specialized in uniforms. Mr. Sam saw to it that every janitor was outfitted in the best and most comfortable clothing, and if that janitor didn't have the ready cash for the goods, he could pay it off with no carrying charge. Every citizen (whether he wore a uniform or not) was Sam Dysterbach's friend. He was a man remembered for his generosity and civic spirit — a man especially loved by uniformed school personnel.

Elementary school custodians are so much more than just cleaning agents and guards. They are friends to the children, because elementary kids get lost a lot. Custodians are good guides for students who have not yet gained a sense of direction. The dearest friend I ever had in elementary school was the janitor. We all loved Mr. Langford at Robert E. Lee. I did feel sorry for him sometimes when one of us would throw up on the floor. I always thought he deserved so much more from us, but he never seemed to mind coming in with his sawdust, broom and air freshener when one of our overstuffed digestive tracts failed to function after lunch. Truly these men are loved for their work, and they are remembered.

At Pershing School there is a bust of General Pershing

standing prominently in the hall. The glass case that protects the cherished statue was given to the school in honor of the custodian, Mr. Agustus Tibbs, who faithfully served that school for many years. Mrs. Robbie Lee Mays who was the principal at Pershing, said that it was a joy to work in that school. Mr. Tibbs made it that way.

Custodians can teach. The *Dallas News*, September, 1963, ran a story about the extra activities of Mr. Spencer Chance, the custodian at Umphrey Lee Elementary School. He cleaned the school by day, and he watched the stars by night. Mr. Chance had a 200-power telescope and brought it to school in the evening, so that the children could engage in a little stargazing. My son was a part of that after school, late evening activity, and he, like many kids at Umphrey Lee, learned a lot about the heavens from Mr. Chance.

Some maintenance employees have special talents. This news came from a DISD dispatch dated January 12, 1983. The article explained that Mr. James Cole was the only carpet patcher in the district. When the carpet at Navarro School needed repairing, Mr. Cole was sent to do the work. He could not match the existing colors, so he cut colorful and contrasting designs for the patches. The carpet in the creative arts area had patches shaped like violins and musical notes. The patches in the library were book designs, and the office patches were typewriters. These were the most unique patches one could find anywhere.

"Our carpet was originally a solid color," said Navarro principal, Gwen Clark. "It's now multicolored, and it looks like it was designed to be that way. When Mr. Cole was doing the work, he took time to explain the process to the children and became a teacher."

Some custodians are called upon to plant trees, especially on Arbor Day. Barbara Farnell was the hostess for a TV show, "Inside DISD," which was broadcast on Channel 13. She planned a special program for Arbor Day using the Jim Hogg Elementary School seventh-grade classes to carry out the celebration, which would include a tree planting. It seemed that Jim Hogg, the first governor of Texas to be born in Texas, loved trees. In fact, he requested that on his gravesite there would be a pecan tree planted at his head and a walnut tree planted at his feet. Thinking of Jim Hogg's devotion to trees, Barbara

Farnell couldn't have chosen a better school for the the Arbor Day celebration than the one that bore Jim Hogg's name. Now, the school would plant a tree in his honor.

The seventh-grade teacher, Mrs. Mary Roberson was contacted about the program. She was to get the kids ready. Mr. Allen Dial, the principal, was to buy the tree that would be planted. Mr. Samuel Jackson, custodian, was to dig the hole for the tree.

Mrs. Roberson said that she had never seen a bigger hole than the one that Mr. Jackson dug. He filled it with water in order to have the soil perfectly moist for the promising roots. After school the kids came out in the yard and saw the gigantic hole full of water and thought that Hogg School was getting an outdoor pool. The children had to be forced to leave the school grounds that day — because what is more enticing to kids than a large hole full of muddy water?

The next day brought the video cameras and the tree to the school grounds. The tree didn't begin to fill the hole dug by Mr. Jackson, because it would have taken a redwood from Yosemite National Park to fill that hole. Still the kids were thrilled over their tree.

One student turned to Mrs. Roberson and exclaimed, "When I grow up and drive by the school and see this tree, I'll be so *inspired*. I can't wait for it to grow. *I'm just so inspired!*"

The cameras began to roll, the program began, the tree was dedicated, and it *was* all very inspiring. This happened on Wednesday. By Monday, the tree was gone. Not every kid at Jim Hogg was as impressed as the young man who couldn't wait to grow up with the tree — for that weekend a ball game was played much too close to the tree and it was victimized before it even had gotten a chance to grow and inspire anyone else.

Mrs. Roberson said that the students really enjoyed seeing the TV show about the tree even though it was shown a couple of days after the tree had been trampled to death. Its memory lived — on the video tape and in Mr. Jackson's enormous hole. And, a couple of days later Mr. Jackson proved to be just as good at filling in holes as he was at digging them out.

High school custodians live a totally different life than those in the elementary schools. They, of course, are always grand supporters of the athletic teams and once in a while they're asked to come in as cheer leaders and lead some yells at pep assemblies. This happened at David W. Carter High in 1972 when Coach Kedric Couch and his Carter Cowboys kept winning games and kept having pep assemblies. The custodians were called in to lead a couple of yells and they loved every minute of it. Two of these janitor cheer leaders were really unusual men. One was so large that he was appropriately and affectionately called "Tiny." The other was an ex-convict. One day, my husband, band director, accidentally locked his keys in the band hall. He was going to have to walk all the way back up and around to the office to get another key. This janitor, who had served time for burglary, came to my husband's rescue. Calling upon his past experience and talent at breaking and entering, this custodian picked the lock on the band hall in three seconds flat.

Janitors, like some of the teachers, moonlight. When my husband was the band director at W.E. Greiner Junior High, he shared the band hall with a charming lady, Mrs. Katheryn Riddle, who was the orchestra director and who taught violin the last period of the day. The custodian saved the band hall to clean last each day. The minute the final whisk of the broom was made, he left for his second job, delivery clerk at a nearby drugstore. The sooner he could leave Greiner, the more deliveries and money he could make. So, each day he quietly sneaked into the band hall before Mrs. Riddle was through teaching to begin his cleaning. Mrs. Riddle would only raise a dignified eyebrow when he entered with his broom, and then she would go on with her teaching. She didn't want him in the room until the lessons were over, but she never said anything. Each day, he came in a little earlier. One day when it had rained heavily, the floor was encrusted with a ton of mud. Each student brought in ten pounds of mud on a rainy day, so by the end of the day, there was almost a ton of the black glue on the floor. The janitor sneaked in even earlier and began to sweep — soon discovering that the broom was not working against the hardened silt. He left and came back with a hoe and started chopping the mud. This was too much for the sublime Mrs. Riddle.

"When I saw him with that hoe in the orchestra room, I knew I could endure his presence no longer. I screamed for him to take that hoe and get out."

From then on, that custodian started cleaning with the ringing of the final bell. Drugstore deliveries had to wait.

The winter of 1979 will long be remembered, because the ice storm that it brought literally paralyzed the city. The power lines were down, the water mains were frozen, the gas was scarce. The custodians stayed on duty around the clock until gas, electricity and water were restored to the schools. They made certain that all the machinery was cut off so that there would be no permanent damage to the equipment once all power was restored. There was a special television program about these men of the hour taped and presented in their honor on Channel 13.

A poet who wished to remain anonymous wrote this little ditty for the Forest Avenue 1919 Annual.

To The Janitors

There are none to whom we are indebted more
Than to the hard working janitors who mop up the floor.
We can tear up the school and do what we might,
But my morning the janitors have it looking all right.
The floors they dust, clean and oil,
And we kids go around and muss up and soil.
We praise those men who work all day,
They fix things up so the kids can play.
So come on gang, let's give three cheers,
Let's hope they'll be here years on years.

SCHOOL VOLUNTEERS

Sitting back and criticizing the school district is an easy thing to do, but if an individual is involved in the work of the district, then it's harder for that one to criticize. When one is involved with the workings of a system, then one has the insight into and the knowledge and understanding of the actions taken in the system, and one is less critical. There are many opportunities for a citizen to get involved with the DISD rather than to sit back and find fault with the schools.

The Dallas Independent School District Volunteer Program needs people who will go into the schools and help the kids in every way possible. There are many individual volunteers who devote their personal time to the volunteer tutoring program. They assist the teachers,and sometimes they just sit down and listen to the students. The people who do this are not publicly praised very often, and they are never paid in any way for their work, but the personal benefits are priceless. There are over fifty people who have been volunteering their time to tutor, teach, and listen for over thirteen years. These people are important to the district, because they give that little extra to the life of schoolchildren. Sometimes a student will succeed just because someone has told him that he *can* succeed.

Today some of the civic clubs and corporations are *adopting* a school. These organizations buy supplies, they offer jobs to the students, or they furnish needed equipment for the school. The great thing about this adoption plan is that a community spirit has begun to grow. This plan takes the school system back to the days when the Community Chest and the PTA furnished needed lunches and supplies. It goes back to the time when the neighbors were supporting the schools and there was a personal touch and a reaching out to help children. The federal government gives vast financial aid, but there's a definite need for a community spirit.

In the volunteer program there is also Co-op Education Partners. Local businesses provide jobs and supervision for the vocational students through this program. Going from school to the work world can be very difficult. This group offers assistance as students go out to work and plan for futures.

There are DOVES in Dallas. This is the Dallas Older Volunteers In Education. Who knows more about it and better how to do it than grandmother and grandfather? Some kids never see older people and never experience the wisdom an older person can share. These older adults who might, perhaps, have a little more time than anyone else, share some of their experiences. It's good for both parties.

There is my favorite program, SPARK. This is the Special Program for Additional Resources of Knowledge. This program features "sparkling" people who can bring all sorts of different kinds of presentations to the children. While I was head of the drama department at Dallas Baptist College in the seventies I had a children's theatre troup that traveled all over the city giving children's plays and puppet shows. We played libraries, nurseries, and hospitals. We also went to public schools whenever a teacher needed a play to further a teaching experience. Our troup was a member of the SPARK program.

One of our favorite places to go with a show was Navarro

School where Martha McCall was principal. This school had open classrooms with no walls, and the various groups were learning the basics in unconventional yet effective ways. The children learned math by going to the pretend grocery store and buying food. They added up the prices of the food they "purchased" to get the total grocery bill. Then they checked themselves on the cash register. The children were not only learning math, but also nutrition, because the teacher directed their selections of groceries. Each sack had to have some vegetables, milk, eggs, bread. No one could buy just candy.

Dr. McCall also conducted classes for the parents of these children who came from the projects in West Dallas. So often for these children, survival was primary in their lives, not gaining knowledge or learning appropriate behavior. In order for these children to alter their behavioral and learning-patterns, their home environment also had to change. Dr. McCall was trying to accomplish this.

Our theatre troup was requested to go to Pearl C. Anderson with an original play written for their library classes. Many of my students were musical, so often we would include an original song or two. For Pearl C. Anderson we wrote a jazzed-up version of *Sleeping Beauty*. The brothers Grimm would never have recognized their story, but the kids at Pearl C. Anderson loved it. A rock number was written and included in the show entitled "Man, We're Havin' A Party." When our troup finished giving the show and we were packing up the scenery and costumes, we could hear the kids singing that song as they were leaving the auditorium. My students agreed that they probably would never write a hit Broadway score, but it really didn't matter, because that day, their song was in the top ten at Pearl C. Anderson.

Jeanne Fagadau was instrumental in getting the volunteer program started in the DISD. Rosemary Morice and Sharlene Block are continuing with the service. The school system needs more volunteers and less criticism.

As Leila P. Cowart instructed in 1884, "Destructive criticism is something that one does not make at all."

Some of the fifth, sixth, and seventh grade classes in 1884 were held on the second floor of this building, corner of Elm and Akard. Besides the classes, the building housed a grocery store.

— From the collection of the Dallas Independent School District.

This building on Bryan Street was purchased from the Methodists. The first high school classes met here until the building was torn down in 1907 to make way for the new high school that still stands on Bryan Street. The business magnet is there.

— From the collection of the Dallas Independent School District.

This is the Chenoweth general store.
— Courtesy Dr. John Chenoweth

Leila P. Cowart arriving in her buggy pulled by the faithful horse, Patsy, and led by Miss Cowart's gardener, Mr. Creel.
— From Dallas Teachers Credit Union

This is my uncle, Carl Hass, with two of his buddies playing kick the can in the middle of Main Street, in front of my grandfather's West End Bakery, 1901.

—Author's collection.

My grandfather's first bakery, the West End Bakery, was on Main Street across from the old red courthouse. Later he opened another bakery *way out of town* at 439 South Lamar. This site today is just a few blocks away from the present convention center. My mother is on the right with her sister and old Shep.

—Author's collection.

Some first graders at Columbian Elementary School in 1906. My aunt, Katheryn Hass Sorells, is on the back row with a white bow in her hair.

—Author's collection.

The center picture is of Edna Rowe. Miss DeCapree is on the left. Miss Pappenhagen is on the right.

—From the collection of the Texas/Dallas History and Archives Division, Dallas Public Library.

Contestants in the Anti-Tobacco League Oratorical Contest

Miss Elizabeth W. Baker and the speakers at Oak Cliff High.

— From the collection of the Texas/Dallas History and Archives Division, Dallas Public Library.

The 1922 debate squad, Forest Avenue High, which included Stanley Marcus. He is second from right, center row. On the front row, second from the left is H.L. Peoples whose mother served on the school board and later organized the A&M Mothers Club.

— From the collection of the Texas/Dallas History and Archives Division, Dallas Public Library.

Mayor Frank Wozencraft, the "Boy Mayor." He graduated in 1916. Ten years later, he was mayor of Dallas.

— From the collection of the Texas/Dallas History and Archives Division, Dallas Public Library.

In 1917, Tom Clark, who became Attorney General of the United States, served as an officer in the literary society, Dallas High.

— From the collection of the Texas/Dallas History and Archives Division, Dallas Public Library.

Justin Ford Kimball, Superintendent, 1914–1924.

— From the collection of the Dallas Independent School District.

An early faculty at John Henry Brown School. Most of these lovely ladies did not have college degrees.

— Courtesy Miss Leland Watkins

A certificate from the Teacher Training School signed by Dr. Kimball, Superintendent, Mary Spears, Supervisor, W.E. Greiner, President of the School Board, and C.M. Moore, Secretary of the School Board.

— Courtesy Mrs. Joe Bob Cave

"We used to memorize a lot!"

— Courtesy Myrtle Hembree Jones

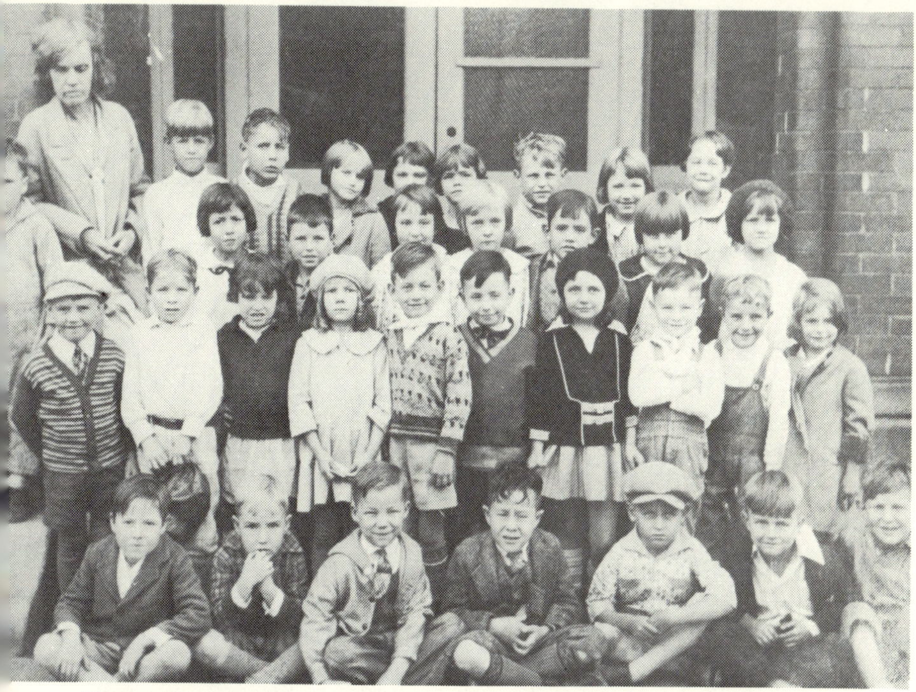

Emma Pettey with her brood at Travis School, McKinney Avenue, 1920.
Later in the 1930s she featured her students with their marionettes.

—From Mrs. W.P. Neblett, Royce City, Texas

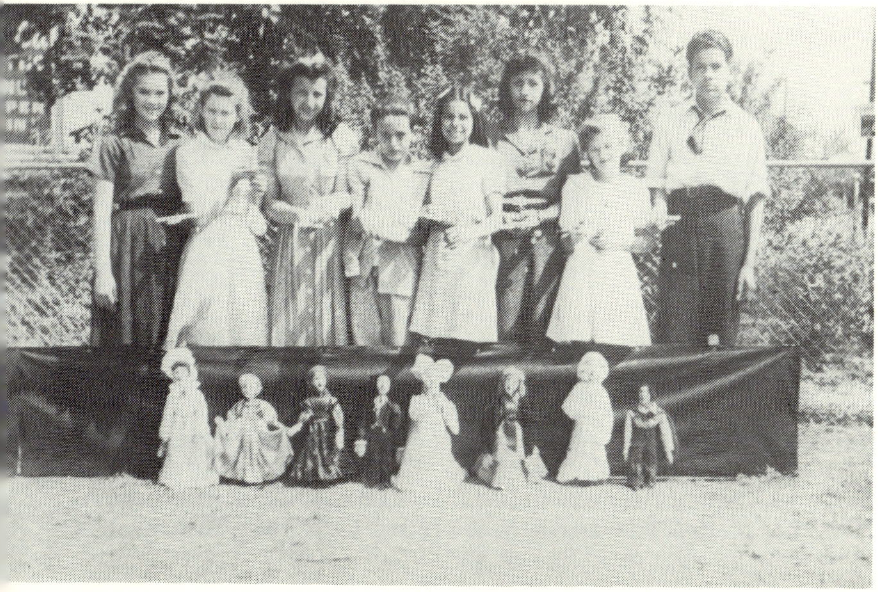

John Knott cartoon, *Times Herald*, December 19, 1932. Money was scarce then, and it still is!

—From the collection of the Dallas Independent School District.

The Dallas Teachers Credit Union Public Relations executive, Les McKee, left, discusses the future with Alvin Toffler, right, who brought us *Future Shock*.

—Author's collection.

Some of the gang at Woodrow rode in style. This was "Lena,"
1913 Model T, owned by Dorothy Dooley Headrick. As a senior
she wrote these lyrics, to tune: "Let Me Call You Sweetheart."

Let me call you Lena
I'm in debt for you.
Let me hear you rattle
As most Fords do.
Keep your headlights burning
And your gas tank full.
Let me call you Lena,
I'm in debt for you.

— Courtesy Dorothy Dooley Headrick

Co-operative Dinner Thrifty in This School

Teacher Kate Clark at Cedar Lawn Elementary School, corner of South Ervay and Browder, cooked for her students on the wood stove. This story was told in the *Dallas Times Herald*, March 10, 1932.

We girls at Alex W. Spence never sat with the boys at lunchtime.
— From the collection of the Dallas Independent School District.

Students study about China, and then they eat with chopsticks in the cafeteria.

— From the collection of the Dallas Independent School District.

The children celebrate Cinco de Mayo. Then tamales are served in the cafeteria.

— Author's collection.

The very first beauty pictured in an annual, Dallas High, 1917. Pollard Simons, developer of Prestonwood Shopping Center, was already a big businessman in high school.

— From the collection of the Texas/Dallas History and Archives Division, Dallas Public Library.

It was a tradition to join the Red Cross.

— From the collection of the Dallas Independent School Distric

Dr. Crozier, when he became superintendent, changed the grading system to rate alphabetically. Until 1924, numerical grades were given.
— *Courtesy Mattie French Shannon.*

Dr. Norman Crozier, center, in the white suit, and his staff in 1924.
— *From the collection of the Dallas Independent School District.*

Mrs. Leon Price was elected president of the National Congress of Parents and Teachers. This became an international honor when she was presented a painting by Madame Becourt-Foch, vice-president of the Paris council, pictured right. Mrs. Price appeared on the same program with Werner Von Braun, German rocket expert.

— *Courtesy Mrs. Leon Price*

Cecil B. De Mille chats with Gladys Barron and other PTA members about the art of movie making, 1948.

— Courtesy Gladys Barron

William B. Travis School, the birthplace of PTA, burned down in 1954.

— From the collection of the Dallas Independent School District.

Dr. Estes lost in the "long hair" issue. Here is the award winning David W. Carter High Stage Band with long hair. My husband smiles at the left. My son in the very center second row has bangs almost over his eyes.

—*Author's collection.*

Martha Taylor, a Woodrow Wilson High student who's mother, Esther Miller, was a graduate of North Dallas High, now owns Taylor's Book Store. Here she is with children's author Dr. Seuss and Dallas student, Danny Lovas, second grader at Pershing School.

—*Author's collection.*

The North Dallas Dad's Club executive board, 1949. My father, Phil Brau, stands in the center. A.W. Murray is at the left. Seated on the front row left to right, Fay Brown, E.E. Holland, Jr., Frank Elam. Standing on the back row on the right is teacher, Don Matthews. Mr. Matthews later became the public relations director for the school district appointed by Dr. White. The public relations today is handled by Larry Ascough, Bob Johnston, and Rodney Davis. Dr. White still enjoys pointing out that it took three people to replace the admired Don Matthews.

—Author's collection.

The Cornelian Club, 1934. Front row left to right Mesdames Phipps, Stockard, Comstock, White, Grafton, Oehler.
Standing left to right Mesdames Rorie, Budd, Turner, Lloyd, Muse, Myers, Whittlesey, Morris, Glasgow, Schiebel, Ashburn, Cobb, Reagan, Walker.

—Courtesy Mrs. Walter Williams

They check their math at the cash register.
— Author's collection, Pam Mitchell, photographer

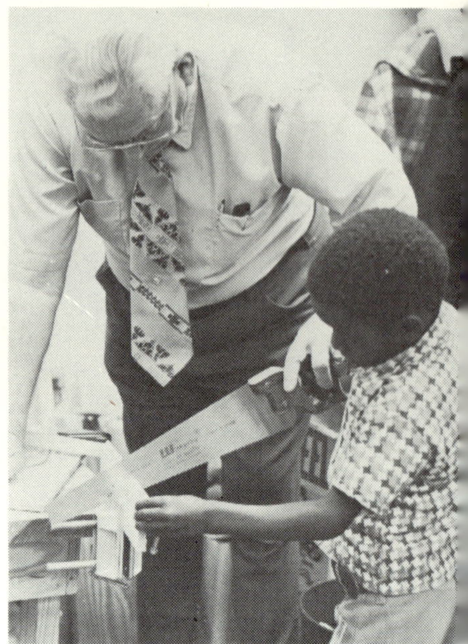

Older citizens are very helpful in the schools.
— Author's collection, Pam Mitchell, photographer

Acquiring manners is part of the curriculum. Principal, Mrs. Travis Sharp, always has tablecloths and flowers on the tables in the lunchroom at R. L. Thornton School.
— Author's collection, Pam Mitchell, photographer

Laura Alexander, one of the first real librarians.
*— From the collection of the Texas/Dallas History
and Archives Division, Dallas Public Library.*

Mattie Ruth Moore, one of the first elementary librarians, enjoys a moment with children's author, Tommie DePaulo.
— Author's collection.

Norvell Slater, quizmaster, tests the intelligence of the kids during a live broadcast of Quizdown.

— From the collection of the Dallas Independent School District.

Jerry Haynes, student of H. Bush Morgan, Woodrow Wilson High, conducted Quizdown on TV in the 1950s. This was before he became the beloved Mr. Peppermint.

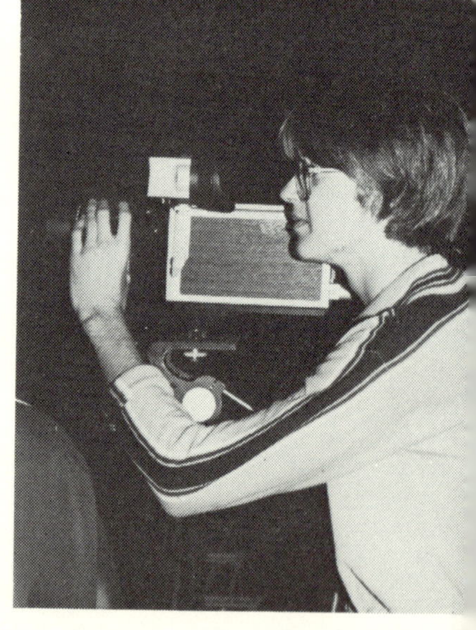

Now the school plays are video taped for future viewing.

The first ROTC unit, 1916. Clarence A. Maas, sixth from the left standing, Merwin Lee Bohan, second from the left sitting, and Pliny Del Valle, at the right, sitting — they were called the three musketeers.

— *Courtesy Mrs. Clarence A. Maas*

The 1951 ROTC at Camp Dallas. Professional photographer, Bob Mageors, is standing second from the right.

— *Courtesy Bob Mageors*

Professor Adamson in the center with his faculty in 1922.
— Courtesy Miss Roberta King

Fannie Basket with her students at Ben Milam School, 1912. That's Dallas businessman, John Lacy, seated on the front row second from the right with the apple for the teacher in his hand.
— Courtesy John Lacy

Wylie Parker was right! Dal-Hi Stadium was dedicated in 1939. In 1940 it was under water. River bottom did extend to Oak Lawn and Harry Hines. The pump station in the upper right hand corner needed to work a little harder.

— From the collection of the Dallas Independent School District.

Dr. E.D. Walker and famous son, Doak. Dr. Walker would bring Doak occasionally to North Dallas for us girls to "drool" and "swoon" over.

— Courtesy Dr. E.D. Walker

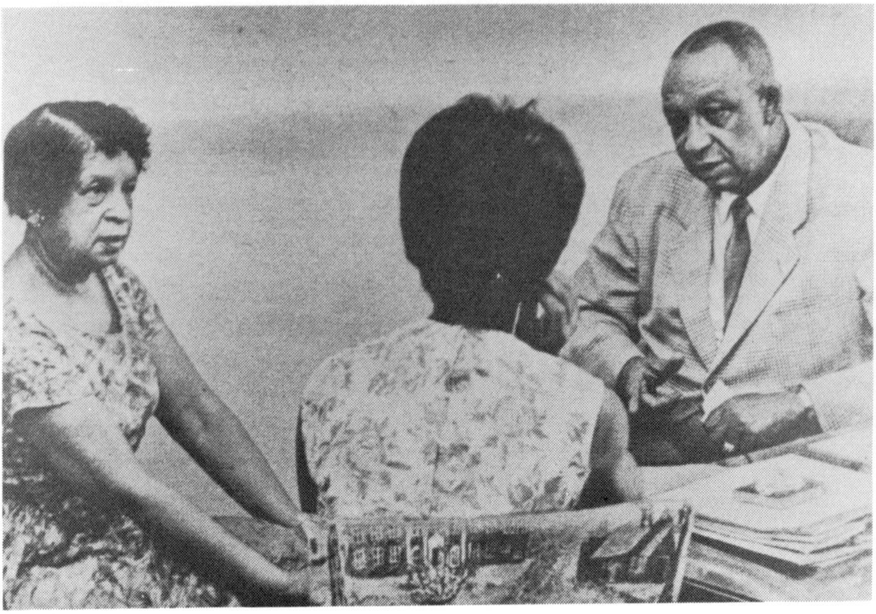

Dr. J.L. Patton, Jr. advising a student.

— From the collection of the Dallas Independent School District.

We knitted squares for the GIs at Robert E. Lee School.

— Author's collection.

We also collected scrap iron for the war effort.

— Author's collection.

These men drew the white beans. That's Big Foot Wallace standing on the back row third from the right. Richard Brown is seated in front of Wallace.

— Courtesy Leland Watkins

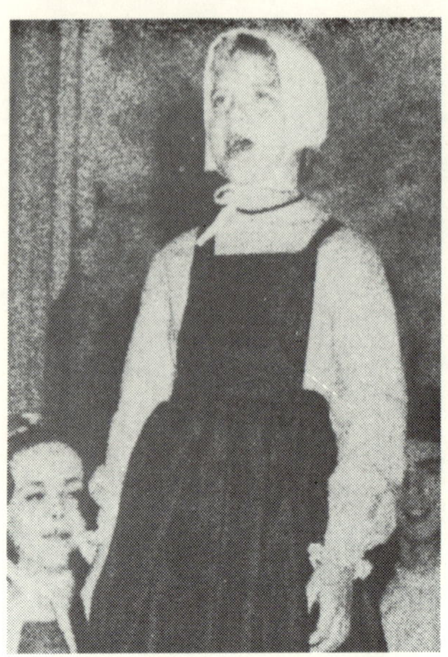

My daughter, Jill Rumbley Kerr, singing in the first musical given at Sunset, 1963. — *Courtesy Bill White*

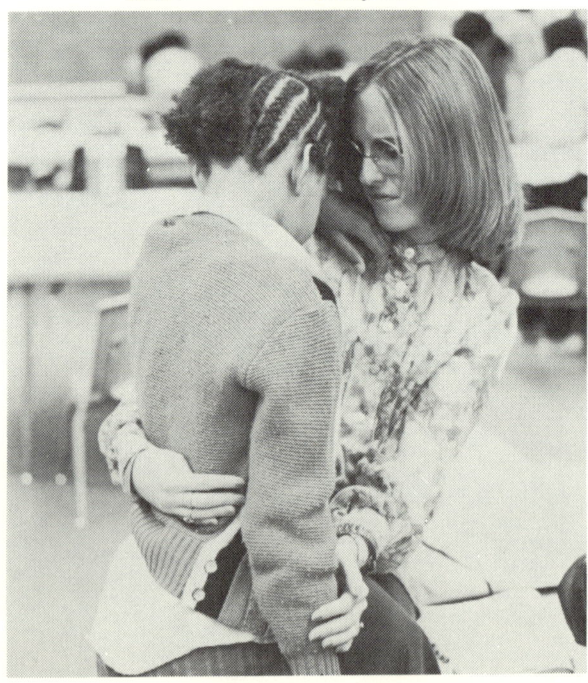

Teachers do so much more than just teach.

— *Author's collection, Pam Mitchell, photographer*

Students get a special welcome to Grady Spruce High from teachers Mary Baskett, Louise Thetford, and Ward English.

— Author's collection.

The presidents of the Dallas Classroom Teachers, 1953, from left to right, first row: Lela Lee Williams, Beulah Keeton Walker, Annie Kate Taylor, Lula Mock, Josephine Wilson. The second row: Quata Woods, Lillie Mae Spangler, Lola Hardy, Mayme Wheless, Myrtle Hembree, Jewel York, Sallye V. Graves, La-Verne Sweatmon, Sarah Tobolowsky.

— Courtesy Myrtle Hembree Jones

The prized trophy, an autographed picture of Linda Darnell.
—Author's collection.

Dr. W.T. White with General George Marshall bragging about Texas at the National Educators Convention, 1947.
—From the collection of the Dallas Independent School District.

Tom Hughes rules at the
Music Hall and the Majestic.
But he makes appearances
in several high schools to
judge contests and cast musicals.

In the 1950s, all teachers had
to sign a non-subversive
oath, declaring that they had
never been a communist.

Dr. White's "girl" principals, from left to right, Robbie Mays,
Wanda Barnett, Wilma Stewart, and Pauline James.

—Author's collection.

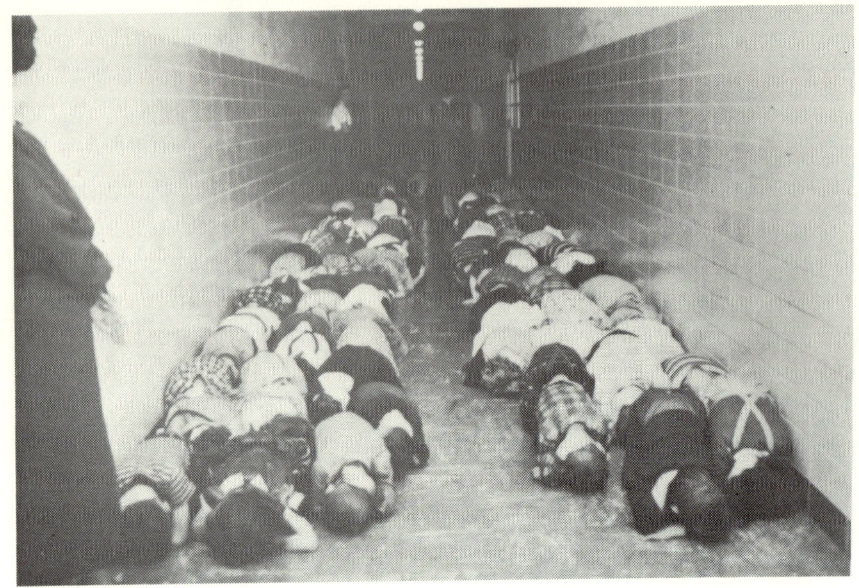

Students had to "duck and cover" during the sixties' drills "to learn how," in case of a possible atomic attack.

— From the collection of the Texas/Dallas History and Archives Division, Dallas Public Library.

"Adam and Eva"

The first senior play cast at North Dallas High, 1922.

— From the collection of the Dallas Independent School District.

The changing of the guard, 1968. Dr. Nolan Estes, second from the right, signs his contract as superintendent of schools in Dallas under the watchful eye of W.T. White, retiring superintendent. School board president, Lee McShan is seated at Estes's right. School board member Emmett Conrad is at the right of the picture, and J. Willard Gragg is at the far left.

— From the collection of the Dallas Independent School District.

Skyline principal, Frank Gusick, with one of his teachers, Dr. Martha Williams. The Kiwanians give much support to the schools. Pictured in the center is musician, composer, and positive parent Bob Piper, who also works with the schools through the Kiwanas Club.

— Author's collection.

Positive Parents President, Mrs. Betty Vondracek, with her children, John and Vickie. Mrs. Julia Jeffress, journalism teacher, is at the left.

— Author's collection.

My teachers at Robert E. Lee School, 1941. Helen Ardrey who inspired me to become an actress, is at the left.

— Author's collection.

Mrs. William Lipscomb at the top with her children at Lipscomb School. This group of children represent all the levels of the social echelon in 1926. Some are from the Juliet Fowler Home for Children. Some lived on Swiss Avenue. Mrs. Sheffield Kadane is standing center row far left with a barrette in her hair. Judge Lively's son, Hiram, is right below Mrs. Lipscomb in a dark suit and tie. Sammy Lobello is on the second row in the center behind the girl with the long curls. That's R. L. Thornton Jr. on the second row right with the handkerchief in his pocket. All of them hold their diplomas signifying that they had finished their work at Lipscomb school.

— Courtesy Mrs. Sheffield Kadane

Aaron Spelling, from the senior play at Forest High to the *Love Boat,* and *Fantasy Island.*

Suave actor, Neil Fletcher, in his leading man days of the forties. This was before he created the corny dog.

Beverly Renquist, teacher, but also professional actress, who appeared on stage with actors Preston Pearson and Too Tall Jones.

—Author's collection.

H.S. Griffin, second from the left, with some principals. That's Tom Coleman, far left, James Coalson, second from right and Carroll Bradford, right.

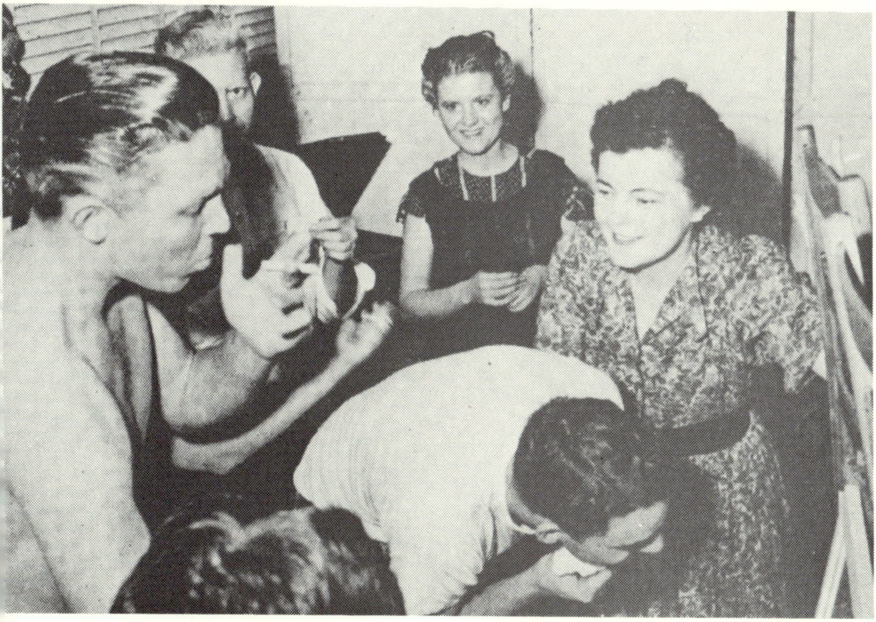

Margo Jones came backstage to greet the cast. I'm there behind her.

—Author's collection.

One-act play contest winners, District 10-AAAA, 1984. From left to right, Sonny Richardson, student, Bryan Adams High; John McCollum, drama teacher, Bryan Adams High; Jeff Morrow, drama teacher, W.W. Samuel High; and Nicole Erickson, student, Bryan Adams High.

— Author's collection.

Dorothy Huffstutler at Hillcrest High with a debater.
— Author's collection, Pam Mitchell, photographer

Quin Mathews, anchor newsman gives credit for his career in broadcasting to Tezzie Cox, Dorothy Huffstutler and Julia Jeffress at Hillcrest High.

As a butterfly, I'm ready to take off at the annual May fete, Robert E. Lee School, 1940.

— Author's collection.

Little flowers at Fannin School ready for performance, 1923.

— Courtesy Dorothy Dooley Headrick

At Bowie School Jan Lovvorn is a patient teacher. She moonlights for extra money for her classes at her grandmother's famous establishment, Highland Park Cafeteria. Jan with grandmother, Mrs. Carolyn Goodman.

Oak Cliff High graduate, Dallas lecturer, Mrs. Bard Paul, with author Anne Edwards who has written the biographies of Vivian Leigh and Margaret Mitchell.

Future authors at Bowie School with their self published books.
—Author's collection.

The cast of the first big Broadway musical *Oklahoma*, given in the Dallas schools, at Woodrow Wilson High.

Colonel William Herzog, band director, at the right being honored. A tree at Kiest Park was planted in his honor. There's a whole grove of trees at Kiest that were planted to honor prominent Dallas citizens.

— Courtesy Mrs. Sue Herzog Johnson

The first orchestra in Dallas High School, 1916. That's Hyman Charninsky seated on the second row fourth from the left behind the drum.

— From the collection of the Texas/Dallas History and Archives Division, Dallas Public Library.

Business giant, Ross Perot, left, is working diligently toward public education reform. He and Linus Wright, Superintendent of Schools, Dallas, are striving for quality education.

— Author's collection.

Congressman Earl Cabell as an actor in the senior play at North Dallas, 1922.

W.T. White is still teaching his Sunday School class after fifty-one years.

Director Don Daniel with the Bryan Adams stage band.

Violin teacher in the Dallas schools, Ruth Reed, gets a few musical suggestions from Maestro John Giordano of the Fort Worth Symphony.

— Author's collection.

Ruth plays with many professionals. Here she is with Roberta Peters, opera star.

— Author's collection.

When the girls went from bloomers to shorts, there were loud gasps from the puritanical forces.

— Courtesy Blanche Petzing

The first cheerleaders of Bryan High.
*— From the collection of the Texas/Dallas History
and Archives Division, Dallas Public Library.*

Cartoonist Jack Patton in 1922 for the *Dallas Journal* captured the proud feelings of Pop Ashburn for the winning Woodrow team coached by Hershel Forester.

— From the collection of the Dallas Independent School District.

Dallas businessmen supported the athletic program.

— From the collection of the Texas/Dallas History and Archives Division, Dallas Public Library.

The girls needed the exercise to become good strong mothers.
— From the collection of the Dallas Independent School District.

We're a nation that loves football. The dispute between the academia and the athletes has always been as shown in this 1939 cartoon that ran in the *Dallas Morning News*.
— From the collection of the Dallas Independent School District.

These fine football boys of 1917 finally got a gym.
— From the collection of the Dallas Independent School District.

Texas Sports Hall of Famer, Don January, fifth from the left, with the Sunset High golf team, 1947.
— From the collection of the Dallas Independent School District.

Teachers lead interesting lives. Here's counselor, Lynda Scurlock, socializing with Sue Herzog Johnson (Grandfather was the first band director) and movie star, Greer Garson. *— Author's collection.*

A lot of learning goes on in Seagoville with teacher Marcia Boone.
— Author's collection.

First Baptist Church, Dallas, honored their Dallas teachers with apples. Seated left to right: Nancy Tilley, Marcia Paschall. Standing left to right: Connie Christopher, Becky Vaughn, Jo Carol Mason, Edith Farmer, and Dr. Grace Wilson.

— Author's collection.

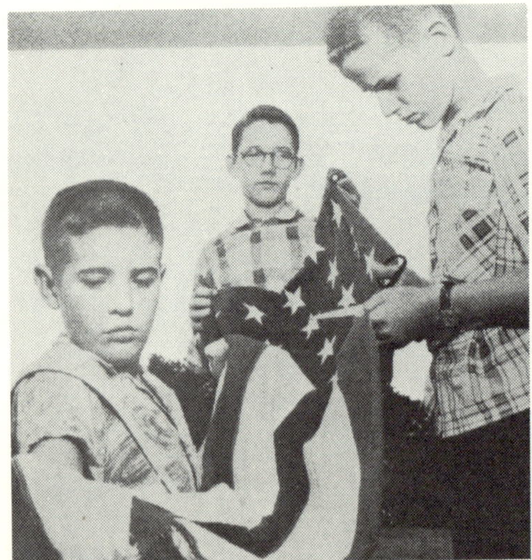

At the end of the school year, the flag is worn and consequently is destroyed. A new flag will fly the next year representing our democracy and our public schools where fine education must continue to be offered to all.

John Wade had great teachers at Thomas Jefferson High. Now, he's a great teacher.

— Author's collection.

Chapter Eight

Vive la Différence

There are some things that private funding, no matter how vast or how generous, cannot offer toward the education of a child. There are some things that public educators deem necessary in a child's educational career, that private education will *not* offer in the first place. There are some things that just go along with public funding that many think are necessary in the school system. *Vive la différence!*

THE LIBRARY

Superintendent J.L. Long placed all library duties upon the principals, who were named ex officio librarians. Every principal was responsible for the choice of the books, and each principal was responsible for the safety of the books. If a book was damaged by a child, that child paid for the damages. Principals were to see that books were fully and profitably used by the students. The teachers knew only that books were in the school.

The 1904 school board report went so far as to say that during vacation time the principal could be called, and that he would *gladly come down to the school* so that a student could get a book for summer reading.

One can imagine how excited the principal was, when on a hot summer afternoon he heard a faint tap at his door. He might open the door to a skinny little kid with a "craving for knowledge" look on his face.

"Yes?" The principal used only one word in order to keep the conversation short.

"I'd like to check out a book for my summer reading."

The principal then would "gladly come down to the school" and oversee the choice of the book for this young reader. Probably, this principal didn't mind that his listening and viewing pleasure was interrupted that afternoon, since there was no listening and viewing pleasure. In 1904 the media field consisted of the printed word and maybe a phonograph one wound up to hear a little of the "master's voice" — if one had the desire to crank the handle.

Needless to say, the "real" librarians were welcomed into three schools — Margaret Walraven at Bryan High, Laura Alexander at Oak Cliff High, and Cleo Irish at North Dallas to mention only a few of the pioneers. Elementary students enjoyed Mattie Ruth Moore, Myrtle Hembree Jones, Verbian Watkins Vaughn, Mate Hunt, and Jewel Bratton. All of these ladies added much to the school system.

Mattie Ruth Moore, who became head of library services for the district, was the first librarian at Sam Houston School. There wasn't enough money to buy books to even make a showing on the shelves, so the zealous librarian made a deal with the public library. If the public library would bring books to Sam Houston School, then the library at the school would open its doors to the children at the school as well as to the community around the school. The public library did send the books along with someone to keep the records. Miss Moore kept the books and the discipline in the library. This worked beautifully for awhile, and eventually there were enough books for both the school library and the public library. The school library continued to grow and the public library eventually put the books from Sam Houston School into the new Oak Lawn Branch Library.

There has always been a close relationship between school and public librarians. During her career (beginning in the 1930s) Miss Siddie Jo Johnson, author of children's books and children's public librarian, sponsored many book parades on

Saturday mornings at the downtown library. Our librarian at Robert E. Lee, Helen Morgan (like librarians all over the school district), helped us to find costumes resembling our favorite fictional characters. Then she'd take us downtown on a selected Saturday morning all dressed up in our character costumes, line us up behind Miss Johnson, and we'd be in the parade which began at the public library on Main Street. We'd march to Lamar, cross to Elm, and then trek back up to the library for our story hour. I was all dressed up as Alice in Wonderland one Saturday, marched in the parade, and returned to the library only to learn that the second floor of the old Carnegie library was condemned for the day. That old library was patched together for several years until finally after World War II, a new one was built. That Saturday, Miss Johnson read to us in the front hallway. She had a much bigger crowd than usual, because the adults joined in on the fun.

Miss Moore was my librarian at Alex W. Spence. She (like other librarians in the city) sponsored book review contests. In 1942, the contest at Spence was won by Zenia Michell, a little girl from England who was sent over during the war for safekeeping. She was part of England's Save the Children program. She came to Dallas, fitted right into our crowd, and won the book review contest. When VE day came, she cried. She was a totally confused little girl who wanted to go home but who, at the same time, knew she was going to miss us. She had come to stay during those formative years of a child's life, ten to thirteen, so she found it very difficult to return. She took home with her many wonderful memories and the prize trophy for the best book review.

Mrs. Myrtle Hembree Jones (like all the librarians in the district) used every way that she could think of to get children to read. At the Lakewood School library she arranged for a fireplace, overstuffed furniture, a braided rug — all adding to a cozy atmosphere for reading. At Thanksgiving time a picture of a featherless turkey was posted on the bulletin board. When a child read a book, a feather went on the turkey. At Christmastime a tree was lighted by the books that were read. A light went on every time a child read a book. There was a bank teller's window where a child could deposit memory work that was recited or a book that was read. His account increased with the knowledge that was gained.

Mrs. Verbian Watkins Vaughn (like all the elementary librarians in the district) gave programs that were based on the books that were required reading. She provided programs for teachers' groups when they met in Dallas. When Sarah Tabolowsky was elected national president of the prestigious teachers' sorority, Delta Kappa Gamma, she called upon her librarian friends to provide appropriate programs.

Today the library services are headed by Dr. Luouida Phillips, who assumed the duties and immediately saw to it that *every* school had a librarian at all times. There was to be no more sharing of librarians and schedules between the schools. Dr. Phillips has so much more to care for than just books. There are records, tapes, video tapes, tape cassettes, recorders, video recorders, and soon the whole operation will be on a computer serving every school in Dallas. There's a media explosion, and the DISD has been there in the middle of it all since the first fuse was lighted. Dallas education has come from the slate and has gone to the computer.

THE RECORD PLAYER

In the beginning there was one record player and one record. They were passed around from school to school so that the children could see and hear how the new talking- and singing-machine worked. Mrs. Dealey and her mothers bought the player and the record from funds raised with a lottery. The word lottery smacks of evil — the sin of gambling. However, the mothers and the school officials turned their heads from the evil suppositions, because they needed the equipment. If selling chances was the answer to their needs, then it was an acceptable answer. There was no budget for media equipment, because media equipment had not been invented. It was *being* invented. Each year brought a media surprise!

Later on, record players were acquired through various means. Dallas businessman, Joe Smallwood, remembers bringing thick Edison records to school. A record company was asking for those old records, because they needed the shellac from them. They promised the school a record player if the kids would bring the old records. They were brought and then smashed into bits for the shellac. Mr. Smallwood sighed and shook his head,

"There's no telling how many original Enrico Caruso recordings we smashed to get a record player for John Henry Brown School."

The kids also saved Masterpiece seals from composition books. It was un-American to have a composition book without a hole cut in the front cover where the seal had been. There was a time during the depression when I think the school system was financed by Masterpiece seals. The seals were traded for record players or anything else that was essential for learning. In those days it never occurred to anyone to do anything else but to save for things. Federal funding was as yet unheard of for education. Besides, if the schools had asked for help, President Franklin Roosevelt would probably have sent Masterpiece seals.

THE RADIO

In 1906 on Christmas Eve, Frederick Fesseden created a speaker that he thought just might be able to send out something besides dots and dashes. Marconi had arranged for the dits and the dots, and now it was time for some advancement. From Pennsylvania, Fesseden wished everyone a Merry Christmas vocally. Then he asked his wife to play *O, Holy Night* on the violin. He had no idea who would hear either, so he ended his broadcast with a statement that was going to become standard to a lot of broadcasts:
Keep those cards and letters coming.
Actually he was asking his hoped-for listening public to send letters if they heard him in the first place.

Meanwhile, shipboard off the coast of New Foundland, some sailors only use to hearing the code signals, suddenly heard a voice wishing them a Merry Christmas and a violin playing *O, Holy Night*, with a request for mail. They responded, and Fesseden knew he had something that would sell.

This was an humble beginning. However, it was not long before stations sprang up all over the place and people began to buy radios to pick up the broadcasts. When one did buy a radio, it was customary to put a lighted lamp in the window as a signal to the neighbors that they were welcome to come over and listen to the newfangled contraption.

The radio was used as a teaching tool. Whenever there was an important broadcast, school children heard it. That is —

some of them heard it — for the radios were scarce. They had to be shared until another great electronic miracle was invented — the public address system.

THE FIRST PA IN DALLAS

The news of the first public address system brought headlines. In the *Dallas Times Herald*, April 20, 1931, the headline read, "Park School Gets Novel Loudspeaker." The City Park School that is still called City Park School and is still located across from Old City Park was the first school in Dallas, actually the first school in the Southwest, to get an intercommunicating loudspeaker system. The school system was so proud of it, that a dedication ceremony was arranged. A demonstration was held at the school on a Sunday afternoon, 2 to 3:30 P.M., and all of Dallas was invited. The *Times Herald* reported that Dr. Crozier, Superintendent of Schools, spoke from his office at the administration building, blocks away. He was heard in every classroom at the City Park School. Then the principal of the school, W.A. Hamilton, spoke from his office to the classrooms and then to Dr. Crozier. Then Dr. Crozier made an address. After this speech a student who had been hauled over from the Cumberland Hill School sang *La Paloma*. It was all a miracle. To hear Dr. Crozier and *La Paloma* all in one afternoon and to hear it all in classrooms was overwhelming to the citizens and to the students at City Park School.

This was a primitive beginning, but the sad thing about school PA systems is that the programming has never advanced. In fact, Dr. Crozier and *La Paloma* were probably the best presentations ever given on a school PA.

I remember an assistant principal who spit into the speaker to see if it was on before he made his announcements. "Is it on?" *Spit, spit, spit!* Dr. Crozier did not do this.

In September of 1931 Sunset High School got a PA system, the first high school to have one. Principal W.T. White was heard to say, "Station SHS signing off. Your announcer has been W.T. White. I thank you." He said this after the daily announcements were given.

Most principals had announcements at the first of the school day or at the last, often at both times. However, Principal Perry Fite used the system at Grady Spruce High anytime he wished. When a problem arose he grabbed for the PA and spoke. He tapped for attention.

"*Tap-tap-tap.* This is Perry Fite, the principal, and I want to talk to you about some litter on the school grounds. There will be no litter. Here's what we're going to do . . ."

And action was taken immediately toward getting rid of the litter on the school grounds. Perry Fite was famous for his use of the PA — there was no waiting for announcements. They came when there was a problem, and the kids at Spruce listened. This was unusual, for usually the only children who really ever listened to the PA were the first-graders. That situation is pretty much the same today. The first-graders listen until they discover that the announcements remain the same. They always will. The only change that could occur is in the time of day at which the announcements are given, and this does vary with the principals.

At North Dallas High we didn't leave the school in the afternoons until Principal W.O. Pipes made his announcements. Mr. Pipes was a very dignified man, so his announcements and comments were very formal. There was always a lost and found report which Mr. Pipes turned over to a student to make. One afternoon the class was sitting in Miss Adele Epperson's room waiting for the announcements to end so that we could all rush over to O.S.'s Drugstore across the street when a student with the lost and found report came on the loudspeaker.

"Lost — a green girl's purse."

Miss Epperson, always the teacher, exclaimed, "Class, did you hear that misplaced modifier?"

Of course, we didn't, because we weren't listening. We were only waiting for the bell.

Miss Epperson never lost an opportunity to teach English. We had to stay a few minutes after school while she diagramed the sentence to show us that *green* needed to precede *purse*. *Green* modified *purse*, not *girl*. There were no green girls at North Dallas. We all readily agreed to that, and Miss Epperson dismissed us three minutes late which meant that I didn't get my usual stool at O.S.'s and that I missed the first chorus of *I'd Love to Get You, On a Slow Boat to China.*

Radio became a fine teaching tool, but it served and still serves the school children in another most important way — it wakes them up. Students cannot get to school on time unless their favorite wake-up program is blaring away on the home radio and later in the car.

The first wake-up program in Dallas was appropriately called "The Early Birds", a program which originated from the studios of WFAA. No one could get to work or to school in the thirties and forties without listening to that program, hosted by a little round man, Jimmie Jefferies, known to his listening public as Mr. Five by Five. His patter gave every mommy, daddy, and school kid just the spark they needed to get them off and running in the morning. Every Dallas family dressed, ate breakfast, and brushed teeth with the Early Birds. Jimmie told the stories and the jokes, the Early Bird band played the music.

One well-known member of the Early Bird band was Wilbur Ard, who played clarinet and saxaphone. He was known as Deacon Wilbur Ard, because he taught a Sunday School class for years and years at the White Rock Methodist Church. Later on Deacon Ard taught clarinet and saxaphone in the elementary schools of the DISD. He also had an elementary band.

It's hard to imagine, but there was always a studio audience down at WFAA which gathered at 5 A.M. to see a live broadcast of the Early Birds. On good days the audience would grow to about one hundred people.

When it rained the live audience dropped down to three or four. During the State Fair kids from all over Texas came into Dallas on buses and stopped off at WFAA to see the Early Bird broadcast before they descended on the fairgrounds for their day.

Well-known singers who appeared in one of the local supper clubs at the Adolphus or Baker Hotels would ring down the curtain at the club, go out for a late night snack, and then stop by and finish off their night singing a song or two with the Early Birds. This was an added thrill to the Dallas listening public, the majority of whom had to work too hard to make it to one of the fancy clubs.

Two major sponsors of the Early Birds were the Morning Glory Mattress Company with a singing Morning Glory Trio. Miss Inez, famous at the organ in cafeterias all over Dallas today, sang in that trio. Also Nutrina Chicken Feed picked up the tab for a lot of the broadcast time. Comedian Little Willie always managed to get in a few jokes about healthy chickens and roosters who were raised on Nutrina.

Fred Lowery the whistler was on hand to pucker up his talented lips and give out a few bird calls and some well-known melodies of the day. The Cass County Boys were on the Early Birds before they joined Gene Autry. There was Peg Moreland, the peg-legged ditty singer who could send the children off in a happy frame of mind with his "darn fool ditties." More comedy was added when the programmers gave Little Willie a side-kick, Hack Berry. Willie and Hack had some routines that would be much too corny and primitive for the worldly-wise, astute population of Dallas today, but in the thirties and for-ties, depression and wartimes, they were just fine.

Jimmie Jefferies decided to run for governor and had to give up his job as MC since the station had a policy that would not allow an employee to run for public office. Therefore, in 1941, Dallas welcomed a new voice on the Early Birds, that of Mr. Norvell Slater, a man who became a well-known announ-cer in Dallas. He was appreciated by Early Bird fans for his great voice, his wit, and his fine piano playing. Mr. Slater still has a radio program on KRQX, "Hymns We Love," and he's still in demand for programs.

A few years later Mr. Slater hosted a quiz show for the Dallas schools called "Quiz Down." Each week Norvell would don his cap and gown as the quizmaster and go to the various schools to test the knowledge of the students. Two schools were selected each week to compete against one another, and the kids from those schools would take turns answering questions. The answers to the questions were all found in the Dallas News, and the broadcast was made from the auditorium for one of the schools. Norvell always brought along a puppet, Webster Webfoot, the intelligent duck, to assist him in the competition.

And such competition there was! The nerves of the stu-dents, principals, and teachers were always on edge. The *Dal-las News* always covered the show, and in 1949, the *News* re-ported that Garland Reed, principal at Urban Park, was so excited that he was unable to remain in his seat. He had to be calmed down by one of the teachers.

As time went on, the competition grew. The *Dallas News* reported in the fall of 1952 that Woodrow Wilson High had a secret weapon, Mr. H. Bush Morgan. The infamous speech teacher at Woodrow was in charge of selecting the students who represented the school in "Quiz Down." He selected students who had "stickability, mental and stage presence." He demanded that the kids give their lives to preparation. Since the topics for testing were taken from the *Dallas Morning News*, Morgan set up a reading schedule for the students. They spent ten hours a week reading the *Sunday Dallas News*. They made notes. Then on Monday morning the chosen four would meet with Mr. Morgan to compare and share notes. On Monday evening the students and teacher gathered at one of the student's homes to go over the Monday paper. Then the group would again meet on Wednesday afternoon to discuss possible questions from the Tuesday and Wednesday papers. Then by one A.M. Thursday morning, they felt ready for the show that afternoon.

Woodrow Wilson held the championship for some time. The winners got books for the school library. One champion from Woodrow was heard to say after the competition, "It's a heck of a way to build a library, but we do it at Woodrow."

Mr. Slater had a Saturday morning radio program on WFAA for the schools, "Radio Frolics." The Dallas school kids got good exposure for their talents, and they enjoyed every minute of their performance time.

The "Early Birds" passed into Dallas history, but in the sixties a new early morning radio star began to shine on the horizon, Mr. Ron Chapman. He called himself Irving Harrigan, and as I've already related, he gave the school menus in the morning. However, he and his sidekick Charlie Brown also gave the weather report.

One of the most famous broadcasts of all times came in the winter of 1963. The schoolchildren and the teachers watched the snow and ice pile up around the windows while they listened to Irving Harrigan and Charlie Brown. They knew that any moment Irving would get the message from W.T. White, superintendent, that the schools would be closed for the day. But the announcement never came.

Irving Harrigan announced other closings.

"Well, Dallas, the Ford Motor Company is closed. So is Chevrolet. The Richardson School District is closed . . . but Dallas . . . well, there's no word. Dallas schools will be open. Here's a song that we're playing especially for Dr. W.T. White: *A Town Without Pity.*

The two men unmercifully tore Dr. White to shreds for not

closing the schools. However, the shreding was done in fun, because Ron Chapman is a funny man.

Where was Dr. White? Did he have no pity? Here's his
story.

"I woke up to clear skies early that morning, and by five
o'clock I was on my way to the school administration building
on Ross. It was still clear. But, before I got across the viaduct,
the horrible snowstorm had hit. In front of me an oil truck
skidded out of control, crashed and blocked the viaduct for four
hours. I sat there trapped in my car listening to those two radio
men rib me about my decision to leave the schools open. I didn't
make a decision. I couldn't get out of my car. I just sat there
and took the ribbing."

Dr. White vowed that he'd never be caught again. He
would never be in a situation where he couldn't contact the
outside world. That snowy morning when he finally reached
the administration building, he arranged for a phone to be put
into his car.

The *next* day, Dr. White closed the schools. The weather
had cleared, and Dallas school folk had a beautiful day off.
Nevertheless, for a long while the parents, students, teachers,
and administrators talked about the time when Dr. White
closed the schools on the wrong day.

Today Ron Chapman is still waking up Dallas on KVIL.
School kids still get the distinctive Chapman humor before
they meet their first classes each morning.

THE MOTION PICTURE

My mother loved to tell about the first movie that she ever
saw in Dallas. She was five years old when she saw this first
flick, so that would make the year, 1899. A gentleman went
from one store to another down Main Street and announced
that after the sun went down he would show a new thing called
a "Motion Picture." The showing was to be on a vacant lot that
was in the block that now holds Number One Main Place. That
evening after sundown, the townspeople gathered on the lot, a
sheet was hung up on a wire for the screen, and the movie was
shown. Mother didn't remember where the electrical juice originated, she just remembered the movie and the fact that the
plot was exceedingly thin. The pictures jerked a lot too.

In the first scene, a lady was shown in her kitchen. She

made a pie. She opened her oven and popped the pie into it, smiling all the while. She patted her foot once or twice to show patient waiting. The pie was done. She carefully took it out of the oven and placed it on the window sill to cool. This was when the plot (and hopefully the pie) thickened. A tramp passed by; his eyes fixed upon the pie. The lady turned to get the pie. It was gone! She saw the tramp holding and admiring his tasty loot. He started down the road. She came out of the house with a rolling pin in hand. He saw the angry glint in her eyes. He ran. She ran after him waving the rolling pin. They ran into the sunset until the reel ran out.

That was it. That was the whole one-reeler, but it was a terrific experience to see. The man showed it several times to the interested crowd. "It's a motion picture. Soon you'll be seeing it on a screen in a theatre." The man packed up the movie, the projector, the sheet, and departed.

But he had spoken the truth, because in a very short time a movie house opened in Dallas. My mother loved to tell about the first moving picture that she saw in a movie house. It was a tear-jerker. A little girl lived in a tenement. She leaned too far out of the upstairs window, lost her balance, and fell to the pavement below. Her whole funeral was shown on the screen. This really impressed my mother, because she had never been to a funeral. Now there was one projected on the screen for her to see.

She remembered her father turning to her and saying when the funeral was over, "See? See what happens when you lean out of windows!" My mother lived upstairs.

Those were humble beginnings for the motion pictures, but see how far they have advanced. Besides a funeral on the screen, we get all the blood and violence that precedes it.

The motion picture became a teaching tool. The new Dallas High School building, complete in 1908, had on the third floor a room called "the lantern room," in which movies and lantern slides were shown for educational purposes. Again as always, there was a money shortage, so later on when a school needed a movie projector, the money had to come from somewhere other than the budget. PTAs naturally raised money for movie machines. The *Dallas Times Herald*, March, 1931, carried a head-line, "Crockett School Gets Movie Machine with Money from PTA Bridge Tournament." The PTA had come through this time with a game of skill — not a questionable lottery.

TELEVISION

Just before World War II, I can remember going to the fair and seeing something new that was called television. The display at the fair was dominated by this huge cabinet holding a teeny-weeny nine-inch television screen. We viewed a show that we really couldn't see too well. It was still all in the experimental stage. All the experiments were stopped during the war, but by the late nineteen forties television was ready for the market. When Channel 8 opened in 1950, our acting troup from North Texas State was featured in a show. This was an humble beginning, and in two years the programming was still pretty humble. It was then that I was directing the senior play at Hillcrest, and I called Channel 8, offered them the play, and they took it. Network shows were scarce. Julie Benell cooked all day, and Gorgeous George wrestled all night, so the Hillcrest senior play was a welcomed artistic change.

Dallas eventually acquired a PBS station, Channel 13. This station in the sixties offered a program to the children that was hosted by teacher Eve Edmonds. She had been a fine teacher in the Dallas system, but she left the classroom to give full time to this popular children's TV program. She told stories. Because she stayed in touch with the classroom teachers she was able to help the children with their assignments. Paul Harris, an art teacher in the Dallas system, was also a part of the programming. He presented some art projects to the children that they could create at home. This was one of the first children's programs that was given on public television. It was the preview to what was coming.

The DISD today has its own cable, Channel 2. Cable television has been called the sleeping giant, and it will not be long before it wakes up. Talent will be needed for more and more program- and teaching-time on the cable. The teachers and students of the DISD are ready for the great awakening.

MEDIA MAGIC

Media magic is everywhere. At the Bryan Adams High School library Linda Garrett, the librarian showed off the cameras the library had for video taping. There were video tape players, audio tape recorders, audio tape players, and endless shelves of video and audio tapes for listening and viewing. The libraries are curriculum oriented — they are there to complement the course of study planned by the teacher. The students can find everything that they need in reference materials to complete their assignments, and extra audio or video equipment is available at the School Board on Ross Avenue.

Mrs. Garrett was formerly an elementary librarian. The elementary schools are also equipped with audio and video equipment, and a child can take an audio tape and cassette player home with him. In fact, there is a bag especially made to carry the tape and cassette player home for study. The bag reads, *Take ME-dia home!*

Bryan Adams High also has a video screen for sixteen millimeter cassettes that takes the students visually to college campuses all over the country. If a student wishes to know about a college, he slips the cassette into the player. He'll view the campus and while he's seeing the sights the tape will give him needed information about the school — strong points and weak points.

At Bryan Adams and at Skyline the libraries are equipped with a checking out devise similar to what the public libraries have. The student does not need to sign his name on a card — it's all automatic.

I was asked to serve as a critic for a drama festival held at David W. Carter High School. Every play that was given was video taped. When I gave my critique, I was video taped. The students left the festival with video tapes of their plays and video tapes of the critique. They could view these tapes at their schools for more study.

Mrs. Garrett mentioned that she enjoyed the high school students in the library, but she had warm memories of the little folks at the elementary school level.

One little second grader called her a "blueberrian."

"I'm a *li*brarian," Mrs. Garrett corrected him.

"Liberrian? I knew you were some sort of berry."

The library is a powerful place, and its power can be transferred to its patrons. I have always felt in control when I marched into a library, checked out any book I wished, and read it. Think of the power a student has today. He can check out a book, a record, a video tape and player, an audio tape and player, and who knows what is next in store in the media field. It's all so magical.

SPECIAL EDUCATION

The child with physical well-being and mental well-being was the center of early school efforts. It was around these normal intelligent students that the Dallas schools were built, for schools grow and thrive on the brilliant, healthy, quick-witted student. But this is America, and as citizens we must accept the responsibility of offering education to *all* children despite handicaps. Every person must be given the opportunity to achieve at his or her topmost ability. This is quite a challenge for the Dallas schools, especially since the system is so large. It is a great financial challenge, because any kind of special education is extremely expensive. Much of the program is federally funded, but there have been cutbacks, so more and more money is being taken from the local budget for the Special Education program.

The DISD is committed to educate this special child. There is the mentally retarded child who can be trained for a trade or educated to read and write. This child also must be offered an opportunity to gain communicative skills. There is the deaf child or the hard-of-hearing one who needs training in language and speech reading. With auditory training and phonetic practice, he can enter into the normal world. There is the orthopedically handicapped child who needs special transportation to school and who needs special facilities in that school when he gets there. This all must be provided. There is the partially-sighted child and the blind child who needs audio service and Braille textbooks. Speech therapy must be offered to the child whose verbal communication falls below normal. There is the child who is considered minimally neurologically impaired. Very special attention is necessary for this slightly brain damaged child. Then there is the emotionally disturbed child who is turning up more frequently in the classroom today, the child who is not able to cope with the normal routine of school life. The Dallas schools offer an education to everyone of these who suffer the mentioned disabilities. The opportunities are there for them, but these opportunities haven't always been there.

The first special education classes organized in the Dallas

schools were for the mentally retarded in 1914. Dr. Kimball started similar classes when he was superintendent in Temple, Texas, so when he arrived in Dallas he made these special educational classes available here. The children were called "unusual," not mentally retarded.

Whenever Dr. Kimball found a child in the regular classroom who was obviously not fitting into the routine or who was a hindrance to the learning activities of the other children, he would have that child placed in one of these special classes. In 1914, there were about four white elementary classes and one negro class with the average enrollment of about ten pupils per class. They were housed in elementary school buildings located in different sections of the city. One class was eventually established at the high school downtown. Shop work was offered to these students there whose learning ability, it was discovered, averaged at the fifth grade level. They were taught a skill.

In 1914 there was a tract of land (now Reverchon Park) called Woodchuck Hollow. This tract was used as a settlement for transient people. Some of these transients would stay a week; some would stay as long as a year. It all depended on their finding work. They lived in tents, wagons, shacks, and there were about twenty to thirty children living in this settlement. Dr. Kimball had a one-room structure built in the middle of the land, and he asked Miss Eleanor Winn, a beautiful lady with great sensitivity and intelligence, to go down to Woodchuck Hollow and teach. This she did.

The school system spent one dollar each day to feed these children. Additional food was given to the district for them by local grocers. The children cooked the food themselves. The mothers from these impoverished families also came to the schoolroom with the kids. They came to Miss Winn with their hopes and fears, their ambitions and their disappointments.

In his report Dr. Kimball stated that these people were not permanent residents — they moved on, but they needed to be mentioned because of the fine work of Miss Winn. Who knows what influence she may have had on those children and their parents — even though she only met with them a brief time. Eventually this tract of land was sold to the city for a park, and this special school closed.

Mrs. Carrie Firestone taught one special education class for the mentally retarded in 1925 at Trinity Heights Elementary School. Eventually she was teaching four classes. Then, as needed, special education classes were formed at Stephen Austin, San Jacinto, T.C. Hassell, Alamo, Asher Silberstein, Mirabeau Lamar, and James Bowie. The number of students enrolled in the classes never exceeded eighteen. The learning assignments were directed to all the ages, and there really was no fixed curriculum. All activities were supervised by the teacher or the principal of the school until the fall of 1950. Then a consultant for special education, Kathleen Varner, was engaged by the Dallas schools.

Even then with a consultant, these highly qualified teachers were left to use their own judgment as to what methods and techniques they used to instruct these children. The plan most favored called for each teacher to devote about one half of the class time to academic work and the other half to manual training or to some type of handiwork that was most suitable for the particular child. The consultant kept a record of what these children did when they were no longer in school. Some became delivery boys. Some were sack boys in the grocery store. Note was made of one boy who decided to become a bee-keeper. It was reported that in a few years he was shipping honey all over the country and was running a very profitable business.

Education for the deaf started in a limited way and also under the administration of Dr. Kimball. Miss Edna Washington taught deaf children in her home, a two-story residence on the corner of Washington and San Jacinto. She had twelve to sixteen students, and Dr. Kimball recognized her fine work and teaching abilities. However, the real start with deaf education came through the efforts of two Dallas couples who had deaf children. In 1915, Dr. Max Goldstein, a famous ear specialist and founder of Central Institute of St. Louis came and lectured in Dallas about deaf education. After hearing Dr. Goldstein, Dr. Guy Tittle, a pediatrician, and his wife took their little girl, Emmy Jane, who was deaf, up to the institute in St. Louis. They saw that the child really needed to stay in St. Louis for her education, but not wanting to leave their child there, they brought her back to Dallas and enrolled her with Miss Washington. Mrs. Tittle began to look for financial support for Miss Washington and found it from the Council of Jewish Women. This organization supported the school with money and volunteer help. The Jewish ladies even agreed to pay the rent on a house for another teacher who would come and teach at the school for the deaf.

Miss Forence Warner, who was on the staff at the Central Institute of the Deaf in St. Louis came down to see the work in Dallas. She had heard that some very special things were happening. She, in turn, went back to report on the very progressive school run by Miss Washington and caught the interest of a student at the institute, Miss Louise Hillyer.

Miss Hillyer held a music degree from Mary Hardin Baylor. She toured the area giving concerts until she went to Peabody for her master's degree. After graduation she went to Washington D.C. and worked for a time at the Capital just down the hall from the Undersecretary of the Navy, Franklin Roosevelt. The depression took its toll, she lost her job, and with a little money she decided to enroll in the institute at St. Louis. Here she met a little boy from Texas, Bruce Gabbard, who was deaf, and she took an interest in this little boy. His family had been torn apart by the fact that he was deaf, and she wanted to help him and the family. Miss Hillyer was the first graduate of the Central Institute for the Deaf. She was well-trained in lipreading and speech, and she was also very familiar with a new machine that had just been invented for testing hearing. With all this knowledge and with her little friend, Bruce, she came to Dallas, became a teacher of the deaf, and lived in the house that was furnished by the Council of Jewish Women.

Teaching hearing people to understand and accept deaf children and their problems was an added difficult task, but Miss Hillyer worked constantly to do this. Someone asked her,

"Is it here that I can learn to teach the deaf and dumb?" Her answer came quickly.

"Never, as long as you call them dumb."

In June, 1935, the schools bought the first portable audiometer manufactured in the United States, and thereafter, testing for hearing was a part of the program in all the schools. Using this for testing, the teachers found more and more hard-of-hearing children, so a new class was started. There were eleven centers. There was more community action taken on behalf of the deaf children. In 1938, the Dallas Pilot Club sponsored classes for the preschool deaf children. Miss Hillyer conducted these in her home. Dr. Tittle worked toward getting an annex available at Fannin Elementary for deaf education. Mrs. Sarah Zumwalt, school board member, was very interested in deaf education. She made several trips down to the school for the deaf in Austin and was very dissatisfied with the conditions there. She wanted Dallas to be the place where deaf children received the best education.

Dr. David W. Carter, who was also a member of the Board of Education at that time, was very interested in the programs for the deaf. Later, when Dr. Carter was president of the board, even more work was done toward developing the program for the deaf. Dr. Carter weathered some storms while he was board president, because many people thought he was too interested in the health of the children. He, in turn, thought that good health and good education went together.

The phrase, "Educate — don't medicate," was constantly thrown up to the good doctor. But nothing ever stopped him in his work toward making the children of Dallas healthy children.

The Dallas schools publicized every activity that involved the deaf children. In 1947 there was a big city-wide celebration at the Health Museum at Fair Park commemorating the one hundredth anniversary of the birth of Alexander Graham Bell, who had been an early teacher of the deaf. Southwestern Bell also did much to publicize all that was happening in deaf education. In fact, Dallas had a big part in developing curriculum for the whole nation.

Miss Hillyer retired in 1964 after wonderful years of helping the deaf children of Dallas. She was the first to insist upon having "a hearing conversation with lipreading."

The first help in education for the orthopedically handicapped came in the late nineteen thirties from the Women of Rotary. They gave their time and their money to help these crippled children. These ladies bought braces and crutches for the children who could not afford them, and finally, in the spring of 1940, they were able to hire a visiting teacher for four handicapped children. With the help of Dr. Lloyd Sheffield and Mrs. Beryl Michael Phares, School Health Director and nurse, four children were selected and a teacher, Mrs. Edna B. Reed, was hired to do the teaching of these children. A room was secured at Highland Park Methodist Church for the classes that Mrs. Reed would teach in the afternoon. In the morning she visited the homes of those who couldn't get to the class. A taxi brought the children who were able to come, and all of this was paid for by the Women of Rotary.

In the fall of 1941, the classes moved to the basement of Ben Milam School. The Women of Rotary were still paying for the teachers' salaries and the taxi fares. In the fall of 1942, the Dallas School District included classes for the orthopedically handicapped in the public schools. Two more basement rooms at Ben Milam were made available and the Dallas Society for Crippled Children bought an old bus for transportation. Another teacher, Miss Margaret Caillet, was employed. Mrs. Ruth Reeves was to come the next year. There were two classes in the morning and two classes in the afternoon. The teachers never left before five o'clock, because there was so much preparation for the teaching of these special children. The Women of Rotary were still paying the salaries of the teachers, and because of these generous women, Dallas was able to offer these classes, the first ever offered in the public schools of Texas.

The longtime dream of the Dallas schools and the Women of Rotary was realized in January, 1952, when the William B. Carrell School for Crippled Children was opened. Mrs. Edna Reed was made principal. The facility met every need for the orthopedically handicapped, and the teachers were able to extend the curriculum. There were therapy rooms as well as classrooms. Dallas had the very best for teaching these children. Dr. William B. Carrell was an orthopedic surgeon who gave so much of his time and money to crippled children in Dallas. After his death, Mrs. Carrell continued on as a strong support of this school.

Whenever a visitor came to the school, that visitor was so impressed by the spirit of those crippled children. They helped each other so much in getting around. Every one of them had such a wonderful attitude toward life — an attitude of giving.

Education has only one thing in common with business. The two share one attitude, one common goal — that of gaining perfection. And both business and education will constantly try out new methods that promise that perfection.

When Dr. W.T. White became superintendent of schools in 1945, there was a big push in education toward the Gestault theory — that of educating the whole child. So, Dr. White, grasping onto this theory, imported Mr. William Puryear from

Marshall, Texas, to be Director of Child Growth and Development. Every teacher in the system was required to take a course in Human Growth and Development. This course, naturally, would tell one how to educate the whole child. Actually, the Gestault theory is a proper theory in that the whole child is in the classroom, not just his brain, so actually every part of him should be and can be educated.

Mr. Puryear was so successful in dealing with the teachers of Dallas in stretching their teaching abilities and in fostering their creative endeavors, that Dr. White appointed him head of special education. There were not many units of special education when Mr. Puryear assumed that position, but by 1974, when he retired, there were four hundred and four teachers working in the special education classes.

There were milestones set in special education during the time that W.T. White was superintendent of schools.

1948:   A speech survey was made of all elementary school children. Speech training was given to those who needed it.

1950:   A consultant in special education was employed.

1951:   State legislation was expanded to cover deaf, blind, and educable mentally retarded. Social programs for deaf and blind were begun. The existing program for educable mentally retarded came under the state policies for helping local schools finance the services.

1952:   Program for the deaf was expanded to junior high level. The William B. Carrell School opened.

1957:   Hospital teaching was begun. A class for visually handicapped children with special learning limitations was begun.

1958:   A larger program for trainable retarded children was started.

1959:   A pre-vocational exploratory program for educable retarded boys was begun as a joint project with the vocational rehabilitation division of the Texas Education Agency. A program of teaching for homebound children was begun. Visually handicapped Negro children were separated from the group of physically handicapped at H.S. Thompson School and were given a special program at T.C. Hassell School.

1959:   Pre-vocational training for educable retarded girls was begun at the Dallas Vocational School.

1960:   Hospital teaching for non-Dallas residents at Scottish Rite Hospital was begun. Program for deaf children was expanded to senior high school.

1961:   A county-wide day school for deaf children between six and thirteen inclusive was begun. A supervisor of instruction for the deaf was employed.

1962:   A pre-school program for deaf children was begun. A class for the neurologically handicapped was begun.

1963:   Vocational adjustment coordinators for the special education department at the Dallas Vocational School and Sequoyah Junior High School were employed.

1964:   A class of emotionally disturbed was begun as a part of a pilot project in the state.

This was a first, and Dr. Ruth Turner taught this class. She is now an administrator for Special Education in the district.

When Dr. Noland Estes was superintendent of schools, more and more supportive services began to help children in special education. A school for pregnant girls was begun. These girls (who could not remain in the classrooms) could continue their education during their pregnancies. Mr. Harold Lichtenwald then headed special education and served as principal of this school.

Today, the district employs 1,061 people who bring specialized services to handicapped students from three to twenty-one years of age. First, there is the Educational Diagnostician Service. When a parent realizes that a child is physically handicapped in some way, then, at the point of detection, an educational diagnostician can be called, and the diagnostician will identify the educational abilities and deficiencies of the child. This project called KIDS (Kindling Individual Development Systems), created by Dr. Turner, is an educational program beginning in the homes of handicapped infants, toddlers, and preschool children. There is a very comprehensive booklet that was published to help parents and the early childhood teachers identify problems in the child and chart the progress of the preschool years. Then at age six the child is ready for special education that is offered by the district. KIDS is funded by the Bureau for the Education of the Handicapped in the U.S. Office of Education. It is part of a large network of early childhood programs designed for the handicapped.

The Vision program works in four areas. There is the teaching program for the visually impaired. Then there is the orientation and mobility service. Visually handicapped children learn to travel independently. There is an occupational therapist and also a teacher of Braille. Braille materials are available, and there are libraries of large-print books, talking books, and cassette tapes.

The William B. Carrell School is now a magnet school for students from grades nine to twelve. Here the physically handicapped can prepare for careers in a variety of fields. One can become anything from a building maintenance and repairman to a furniture assembler to a dry cleaner. The student is urged to do as much as he possibly can.

Happiness is Communication — is the motto of the speech, language and hearing program. Those children with speech disorders are helped. If the child has trouble in producing speech sounds, if the child stutters, if the child has an inappropriate voice quality, if the child has delayed speech, then he is screened into this program. There is a constant reevaluation, so as the speech improves, the amount of therapy is reduced.

There is a regional day school for the deaf. Here the deaf child is given sign language courses, speech lessons, auditory training, and enriched academic curriculum, counseling, and career development. There are also creative arts classes and driver education.

Teachers for the homebound and hospital bound teach all over the city. These teachers visit the homes or hospitals and instruct the students two or more times a week. They make homework assignments, they check the work, and they give grades.

All this is offered to the children of Dallas who need it. And, furthermore, right in the center of it all there is a special education resource system where the teachers can go for current materials and enrichment. The center also offers an inservice training for the special educational teachers who need to learn to effectively use new machines and new materials. This is all part of the DISD, and it all started with Dr. Kimball and one teacher in 1914 who wanted to help "unusual" children.

SEX EDUCATION

Walt Disney brought favorable sex education to the schools in the nineteen fifties. He produced two animated cartoon films on the subject of human reproduction — one entitled *A Girl Grows Up*, and the other, *A Boy Grows Up*. These films were shown to the students during their senior years in high school when they had already grown up. Until these films were shown students received sex education from talking to their parents, from hearing dirty jokes, from finding bathroom graffito, or from reading racy dime novels passed on to them by interested friends. So the real burden of sex education settled on Walt Disney's shoulders.

In high school the girls were hauled into the auditorium for the girl film, and the boys were brought in for the boy film. The films really should have been exchanged for the audiences in order to create some interest. But the Victorian-age principles abounded, so this conservative attitude held on for years.

Sex education didn't exist at all in the early days. No one felt that it was necessary, since the boys and the girls rarely saw one another in school. Until 1893, the boys and the girls were in separate rooms with separate teachers. However, it was that year when a new plan brought the sexes together and the boys and girls then sat in the same room and recited in the same classes.

"The presence of each sex exercises a wholesome influence on the other." This observation of the superintendent, T.G. Harris, was well taken, since the world outside of school had both men and women in it. However, the mixing of the sexes at the water buckets during recess remained forbidden.

"It is regretted that the construction of the central building used for the high school grades is such as to render it impracticable to use the same study hall for boys and girls," Superintendent Harris continued. Sexually segregated study halls must have been extremely dull. Lunchtime was dull too, since the boys ate on one side of the cafeteria and the girls on the other. This practice went on well into the nineteen fifties.

In the thrilling days of yesteryear, the entertainment world offered no sexual discovery whatsoever. In the silent movies, Rudolf Valentino, as the sheik lover, carried a girl off to his tent, and never spoke of sexual desires — since he didn't speak at all. He always kept the tent flap open, and besides, the actions seen within the striped canvas were purely melo-dramatic. There was no realism to behold. On radio, Fred Allen's question of the week for his friends down in *Allen's Alley* dealt with political policies and everyday problems and not with sexual dilemmas.

Children who grew up during World War II saw a lot of expectant mothers who were to bear the war babies, and these nosey children asked a lot of questions, but most of the answers from embarrassed parents dealt with a stork that hovered over Dallas delivering the babies. Therefore, the kids continued relying on jokes and underground literature for the real story.

In 1957, Dr. White brought down from New York Dr. Mary Caldrone, an educational lecturer, who broke the mold. She used words that Disney kept under wraps — words the teachers of Dallas at that time did not consider a part of education. But, after her revelations, the administrators decided sex education was truly necessary. The Disney films would be shown in the sixth grade where they made a little more sense. However, a child had to have parental permission to see the film, and the parents were invited to view the film with their child.

My sixth grader came home with the note that I was to sign giving her permission to see the film.

"Mom, it's about S-E-X."

My daughter spelled the word so that her brother who was a year younger wouldn't be unduly shocked by what was going on in the sixth grade. I signed the note, but I didn't bother to see the film since I had already seen it in high school. I was aware that the film was really just one step up from the stork, taking in the birds and the bees.

When Dr. Estes came in 1968 a new program was developed. A separate course in sex education was not offered, however. Dr. Estes felt that one could not pack sex education into a classroom period. Recognizing sexuality must become a "way of life." The teachers were urged to teach these proper attitudes.

The information given to the students dealt with not only the body but also the emotions. The chief purpose was to assist children and adolescents to develop an understanding of why they were like they were, to learn to relate to one another, and to see how a boy and a girl had certain responsibilities and obligations to their own sex and to the opposite one. The teachers led the students to see that the worth of the person was established in the light of his sexuality as well as his moral actions.

School board member, Mary Rutledge, worked closely with the PTAs on this program, and also Dr. Estes selected administrators Herman Benthul and Robert McKay, to conduct a sex education program series on Channel 13. During this program parents could call and ask questions of these educators.

Just recently Dr. Mary Merki and Angie Rose at the Humanities Magnet developed a curriculum in sex education that has gained national recognition. It's a home-school program and the PTA's are well informed about it. The teachers were carefully selected to work directly in the program which involves parents and students, and Dr. Merki and Ms. Rose train the teachers at their schools. These particular teachers in turn work with the parents and the students. Honest and open communication is encouraged between the child and his family. Finally, all the teachers in the system are exposed to the program, because regardless of the subject that one might be teaching, that teacher must urge students to have respect and understanding for one another. It's a complex, complicated, delicate, and intricate subject, and it would really be much easier to put the boys in one room and the girls in one room, and turn the clock back one hundred years. However, in today's world where the media is stark and realistic, where the children are exposed to all sorts of sexual behavior, sex education and direct communication with the home and teacher concerning this subject is a necessity. Sexual activity and the realities and consequences of it are too much a part of the life of children today to ignore it in the teaching of today.

RESERVE OFFICERS TRAINING CORPS

In the fall of 1916 Judge McCormick, an A and M graduate, became interested in bringing a Cadet Corps to Dallas. After overcoming considerable opposition to the idea, he convinced the School Board to establish the corps, and they selected Charles J. Kennerly to take charge. Commandant Kennerly appointed two young men as captains, Hargrave and Bohan, and the recruiting took place as soon as school opened that fall.

Before a week had gone by, over two hundred and fifty

boys were enlisted. Drill work started immediately, and by the time fall weather and the state fair rolled around, uniforms had arrived. It was a complete surprise to everyone, including the student body of Dallas High, to see a Cadet Corp march down Main Street in fine order as part of the big parade that opened the fair. At the fairgrounds the Cadets formed the guard of honor for the Liberty Bell that was on display there. They were highly complimented by their commandant for their platoon front marching.

The guns arrived in January, and that caused the work to quicken. The number of new applications made it necessary to form a fifth company. The young men were well-drilled in the manual of arms. They gained experience in hiking and shooting on the range. One of the most commendable steps was taken when a signal corps was formed with Captain Hargrave in charge. The men had daily practice with the wireless that had been erected, and they were also drilled in flag signaling. The new service uniforms were received in the middle of April which was a needed comfort to the men. It could get very hot in April and May.

Some Dallas citizens took great interest in what was happening with the corps. Mr. J.E. Farnsworth, vice-president and general manager of Southwestern Telegraph and Telephone Company at that time, presented a magnificent silk flag to the Cadet Corps. This active citizen of Dallas also gave a sum of money that was to be used in purchasing equipment for a drum and bugle corps.

The 1916 Dal Hi Annual pointed out that the corps really enhanced spirit. Even though it was only the first year for the corps at the school, and even though only the very rudiments of military science and tactics were covered, still the corps had helped its members mentally, morally, and physically.

"We may have been the founders, so to speak, of a great and permanent institution."

It was only a first year corps, but an encampment was planned for the spring. The young men were going to camp about seventeen miles from Cleburne near the Brazos River. For ten days they were going to enjoy the pleasures of an outdoor life and at the same time fulfill the duties expected from a military camp. All the tents, cots, and ammunition were furnished by the War Department. The War Department was a

rather negative name that was hung on the department then.
Now, it is positively called the Department of Defense. During
the camp time there would be sham battles, target practice,
and all other phases of military life. There was still plenty of
time for hunting and fishing.

The ROTC gained in popularity, and the next year there
was a corps at Oak Cliff High. Then when Forest Avenue High
opened, that school immediately had a corps with Major B.H.
Conner of the Kentucky Military Institute in charge. The
eighty-five cadets at Forest High had drill every Monday and
Friday morning at 8:15 A.M. The first public exhibition of their
cadet work came when their corps marched in the Fair Parade,
1917. Like the city, the fair parade was getting bigger and the
ROTC units helped in the growth. At Forest by midterm there
were one hundred and twenty men in the corps.

The Cadet Corps was organized not a minute too soon, because war loomed before the nation. President Woodrow Wilson issued a personal appeal too the citizens of the United
States, Monday morning, April 16, 1917. In compliance with
the request of the president to publish this appeal everywhere,
the Forest Avenue High School annual staff printed it in the
annual. Here are some excerpts from the proclamation.

> My fellow countrymen: The entrance of our beloved
> country into the grim and terrible war for democracy and
> human rights creates so many problems of national life and
> action which call for immediate consideration and settlement
> that I hope you will permit me to address to you a few words
> of earnest counsel and appeal regarding them.
>
> We are rapidly putting our navy upon an effective war
> footing and are about to create and equip a great army, but
> these are the simplest parts of the great task to which we
> have addressed ourselves. There is not a single selfish ele-
> ment, so far as I can see, in the cause we are fighting for. We
> are fighting for what we believe and wish to be the rights of
> mankind and for the future peace and security of the world.
> To do this great thing worthily and successfully, we must de-
> vote ourselves to the service without regard to profit or ma-
> terial advantage and with an energy and intelligence that
> will rise to the level of the enterprise itself.
>
> These then are the things we must do and do well, be-
> sides fighting, the things without which mere fighting would
> be fruitless:

We must supply not only abundant food for ourselves, our armies and our seamen, but also for a large part of the nations with whom we now have made common cause.

We must supply ships by the hundreds out of our ship yards to carry to the other side of the sea what will every day be needed there. Steel — out of which to make arms and ammunition both here and there; rails for worn out railways back of the fighting forces; locomotives: rolling stock to take the place of those every day going to pieces; mules, horses, cattle for labor and military service; everything with which the people of England and France and Italy and Russia have usually supplied, themselves, but can not now afford the men, materials or the machinery to make.

To the farmers: Without abundant food, alike for the armies and the peoples now at war, the whole great enterprise upon which we have embarked will break down and fail. The world's food reserves are low.

To the middlemen of every sort: The eyes of the country will be especially upon you. The country expects you to forgo usual profits. I shall confidently expect you to deserve and win the confidence of the people of every sort and station.

To the men who run railways: The railways are the arteries of the nation.

To the miner: The work of the world waits on you.

The manufacturer does not need to be told, I hope, that the nation looks to him to speed and perfect everything he can.

Let me suggest also that every one who creates or cultivates a garden helps and helps greatly to solve the problem of feeding the nations, and that every housewife who practices strict economy puts herself in the ranks of those who serve the Nation.

The supreme test of the Nation has come. We must all speak, act, and serve together.

Woodrow Wilson

On the same page of the annual that this proclamation was printed, there was also a plea for young men to join the navy.

The life offers good pay, a variety of work, and an opportunity to study and serve your country. Inquire about enlistment at the nearest Naval Recruiting Station.

The army eventually turned to conscription, but the navy always depends on recruits.

Regardless, the country did need young men, and patriotism was a priority. So with the war clouds gathering, the man in uniform was the idol of the nation.

Historian William H. McNeill in his book *The Pursuit Of Power* said that there was a "martial enthusiasm bordering on madness" that surged through the men of the United States at the time of World War I and then again in World War II. He called this behavior "bizzarre." The cadets in Dallas in 1917 and later in 1940 called it normal. Mr. McNeill blamed "an educational system that emphasized patriotism and the study of the classics" for this frenzied attitude toward heroism. The Dallas schools from the beginning taught patriotism and the curriculum was heavy in the classics, and if these two circumstances did cause the cadets to want to serve their country, then citizens should be most grateful for these two educational factors. For even though this historian reported that the men's patriotism appeared somewhat unbalanced, it certainly came in handy when the Kaiser's men in 1917 and later when Hitler's Nazis in 1940 marched forth with a vengeance to grab all land and with it the power of the world.

In March, 1918, the three cadet battalions marched by torchlight in the Annual Style Show Parade, but the really big event came on May 27, when the three corps were involved in a sham battle. THe defensive side was given to Forest High and Oak Cliff High. Bryan High was to handle the offensive alone. After a tedious march the cadet units arrived at camp, the battle grounds. There was a long wait until finally Bryan High opened the battle with a charge up the high road — on both sides of which Forest High and Oak Cliff High were entrenched. The battle lasted ten minutes with rifles and pistols in a continual roar. It wasn't decided who fared the best. Each school just assumed that their men won the war.

By April of 1918, one hundred and fifty more boys had joined the Forest corps. Actually the ROTC programs were growing in all three schools. Rifle teams were part of the corps, and awards were given each year to the team that made the highest scores. There were matches sponsored by the National Rifle Association and later a match was sponsored by Cullum and Boren Sporting Goods and Gun Store.

All this was happening on the home front during World War I. President Wilson asked the boys to stay in high school and to finish their education. Major Conner who had started the corps at Forest was called into active duty. He had managed the cadet office at the school using a U.S. Army Post as a model. There was strict discipline, and all the boys took advantage of this training so they would be better prepared for war and be of more use to the nation at this critical time. The corps men exercised and worked toward healthy bodies. All the military work with the snappy drills made them quick thinkers. The cadets also helped the nation financially, because they responded to the purchase of Liberty Loan Bonds and Thrift Stamps. Then many of the units bought their own supplies so that all military money was used toward the war effort.

A quote form the Forest Avenue Annual, 1918, showed the zeal, energy and courage of the men.

> If this war holds out, this same spirit that has brought these boys to school will carry them through the last Hun line and smash the Kaiser to terms of final peace.

The public speaking teacher at Bryan High, George Medders, was called into active duty. Before he left, he wrote this poem and recited it to the ROTC boys. It was printed in the annual.

THE KAISER
When I grow a little wiser
I'm going to get the Kaiser
I'll board a ship for France
I'll take my gun and lance
And when Kaiser Bill
Comes down the hill
I'll shoot him in the pants.

The quality of the poetry was questionable, but the spirit of Mr. Medders certainly wasn't. He was a doughboy going over there to serve. That fight for liberty was won, and finally the last Hun line was smashed. Peace did come, and with it came a large growth in the population of Dallas.

Three high schools were built in Dallas during the twenties, and all three immediately developed their own ROTC programs. The largest unit in the city eventually was at Woodrow Wilson High School. It was peacetime, but the ROTC was considered an important part of school training. Every boy had a chance to identify those requirements needed for success in later life that could not be learned from books. Courtesy and

discipline were constantly stressed in the military, and every
boy who entered the military department recognized the qualities needed for leadership. From the military come better men
to work for the country.

The ROTC struggled on as everything else during the thirties, and certainly the corps was greatly roused with the threat
of World War II in 1939. Men were once again engaging in war
games, this time at Camp Dallas in Mineral Wells, Texas. To
serve his country was the goal of every young man in 1940, and
being a cadet was expected. Everyone who was anyone was in
the ROTC in the forties. Dr. W.T. White, when principal at
Sunset High, noticed that the two percent of the men who were
not dressed in uniform displayed such a contrast to the cadets,
that these civilians actually had a "gangster-like" appearance.
One had to have a very good reason to ease his conscience if he
were not in uniform during the war years.

Former City Councilman Sheffield Kadane was one of the
most active young men in the ROTC at North Dallas High
School. He was a high ranking officer, and he looked forward to
going into the service in 1940. Unfortunately, he was a "butter
and egg man," and the troops needed butter and eggs. Sheffy,
much to his dismay, had to stay home from war, and in order to
make certain that he was useful to the country, he created
Blue Bonnet Margarine. A military career was sacrificed so
that margarine users could claim that, "Everything's better
with Blue Bonnet on it."

The ROTC went on to be a part of the school program during two wars and the intervening periods of peace. The military courses came to mean more than close order drill and the
manual of arms. There was map-reading, logistics, and communications.

More young men were enrolled in ROTC in 1949 than at
any other time. However, as the country once again settled
into peace the enrollment decreased. The shooting war began
in Korea, but this conflict never brought the numbers up to
what they had been right after World War II. Nevertheless, in
1950 applications were made for three new units that would be
placed at South Oak Cliff, Lincoln, and Booker T. Washington
High Schools.

The unpopular Vietnam war brought the numbers in the
ROTC units down to the lowest points. However, the military

survived. Some kids will always love the military and the uniforms. Adam Wyse, whose mother is Joy Wyse, Dallas talent agent, was at Woodrow Wilson during the seventies, the unpopular days of the corps. He was the only student in the history of Woodrow who served as a cheerleader, as a band member, and also as a member of the ROTC. He never had a problem as to what he would wear. He just stayed in some uniform at all times. Adam also starred in several dramatic productions, so he was costumed often for the stage. Again his wardrobe was decided for him.

Adam's older brother, Casey, who was also a member of the Woodrow Wilson corps, praised the work of Sergeant Donald Bacon, who kept the ROTC spirit going at Woodrow.

"He's one of those guys that cares, and he can really reach kids." That's all anyone could want from a teacher.

AN EVENING SCHOOL

An evening school was opened in 1902 in the cotton mills, and the program was free to all those who had not graduated from high school. This evening school was a needed addition to the system at the turn of the century. In 1904 classes were started at the high school for those who had not graduated. The students had only to buy their books and materials. The classes were held on Monday, Wednesday, and Friday evenings from 7 to 8:30 P.M.

Some of the students came for curiosity. They thought they could just come and spend an evening "frolicking on the school premises." When they saw that the school was going to require some work, many left. Some were forced by their parents to attend. These parents were clinging to that last hope that their child would receive a high school diploma. Forcing one to become educated was a useless act. The successful night school student was the one that truly sought after an education and was completely self-motivated.

Actually only twenty-five percent of the possible students were reached with the program. Many were not aware of the educational opportunity, but eventually word did get around the town that a high school diploma was there for those who wanted to study for it.

The teachers in the night school needed certain qualities in order to succeed with this group of students who were far from being like typical high school students. The night school teacher had to have a missionary spirit and had to have a large supply of the "milk of human kindness." The night school teacher also had additional duties. He had to keep in touch with the employers of the students. He had to trace down absentees. However, a school board report mentioned that the cost of the evening school was a trifling compared to the results. Actually, many of the businessmen of Dallas were involved with the funding of the school. Mr. Alex Sanger and Mr. Edward Titche both supported the evening school financially, and also they employed many of the students coming from the school.

The school continued for many years offering the courses that would enable one to obtain a high school diploma. After World War I, M.O. Mahoney was put in charge of the evening school. This was in addition to his teaching duties at Forest Avenue High. Under his direction the curriculum expanded.

There were special courses for wives in cooking, sewing, and child care. There were vocational courses started in psychology. The object of these courses was to train the foreman and superintendent in the skill of public relations. There were trade courses in automobile mechanics — and the students were taught to drive the car too! There was a class for printers. Extension classes were opened at the various businesses that offered to come under the program. This apprentice-type training was most successful.

Mr. Mahoney by 1920 was so involved in the evening courses that he was relieved of his teaching duties at Forest Avenue so he could be at the evening school. Classes for the public school teachers who were not certified to teach the Palmer System of Penmanship were added. By the end of the twenties there were courses in catering, nursing, janitorial training, pottery, foreign languages, dramatics, machinery, and bookkeeping.

In 1933 a group of German men who brought their families to Texas came to the school asking that there be a course created for them. They desperately needed to learn to speak English. Mr. Mahoney immediately started classes in English for the foreign-born.

Also in the thirties there was an increase in the attendance of women at the night school. Those were depression years, and so often it was necessary for the housewife to work if she had a skill or a profession. Naturally, she was anxious to acquire one or both.

> An age old curse put on man in the garden is gradually being lifted and a large part of his time in the future will be his to use as he pleases. Leisure should not be confused with idleness. An idle man has no leisure. Leisure is filling life with happiness.

Mahoney said this in 1937. He was ahead of his time, because his eventual plan was to offer courses that were there to be taken to fill the leisure time. Or, he wanted courses that would train one in a hobby that would fill the leisure hours. Therefore, courses in photography, parliamentary law, knitting, bridge playing, and radio were added. Radio — the new media — was eating up scripts by the hundreds each week. Many people thought that they could make an extra dollar or two by submitting possible shows. This course offered training in writing, and then a special time was set aside to inform the now radio scriptwriter where he might market the script.

When World War II came, refresher courses became popular. With so many young men gone, many older men came out of retirement to return to work. There was a "fix-it" course offered. Math courses were popular, because suddenly a lot of money could be made in the war plants. Math needed to be mastered for some of these jobs. Nutrition and war gardening were on the top of the list in popularity too. There was even a course for war brides, who were adjusting to marriages with men who were far away.

Nothing seemed to slow down the progress of the evening school. When the war was over, the men came back and picked up their education where it had been left in 1941. There were college preparatory courses. There were courses for those wanting to be electricians, plasterers, painters, cabinet makers, bricklayers, and radio repairmen.

Mr. Mahoney retired in 1950, and Walter Schiebel, principal of the day school there at Tech took over the entire vocational program. When Dr. Schiebel retired in 1964 he left a vocational high school which he had built into a model program. The vast system was assumed by Mr. B.J. Stamps who stayed at Tech until Skyline High, the ultimate in schools offering special subjects, opened. Mr. Stamps then went to Skyline as principal.

When Dr. Nolan Estes came as superintendent in 1968, the evening school was headed by Howell D. McCarley. Aside from offering typing, shorthand, bookkeeping, English, history, and government, there were adult classes in selling techniques for Christmas extras, interior decorating, how to conduct a business meeting, the Stock Market and You, grocery checking, management for owners of small businesses, gift wrapping, cake decorating, and appearance and personality development.

Then there was a night school begun with absolutely no tuition charge. In this division, Adult Basic Education Program, there were three levels of instruction. The basic level was offered to those who had no formal education or only a first, second, third grade level. The intermediate level was for those who had completed the third grade but had not completed the sixth grade. There was the upper level for those who had completed sixth grade, but had not completed the eighth grade. There were 3,000 people enrolled in this program in 1968. One hundred teachers were called to teach who had been trained and certified to teach in this type of situation.

The high school at Skyline is the largest in the nation. A very complete education is offered to anyone at the night school there who decides on a course of study, attends classes faithfully, and studies with determination to learn.

Chapter Nine

East, West, North, South, And The Grove

A couple of years before World War I a railroad was built northeast from Dallas to connect Garland (and other points east) with rail transportation. About halfway between the two cities the railway passed through a farm owned by Mr. L. Reinhardt. Fortunately for Mr. Reinhardt, a whistle-stop was arranged, a station built, a post office established, and a general store was also opened. The little town, Reinhardt, was located in the middle of rich farm land where the finest corn, cotton and small grains grew.

These farmers had children, so the Reinhardt Common School District was organized and a small wooden structure was built, a schoolhouse not too far from the railroad station. During the twenties, the community outgrew the wooden schoolhouse and so a two-story brick building was erected at the present site of the modern Reinhardt School. This first brick school built in the twenties served children through the seventh grade. For high school the students went to Garland.

In the thirties, the landowners no longer wished to farm, so they platted their acres into estate lots, and the Casa Linda Addition came into being. There had already been some residential growth in the Forest Hills Addition, for the city of Dallas was bound and determined to cross White Rock Lake and spread eastward.

In 1939 a group of enterprising Reinhardt citizens decided that their school needed modernizing and enlarging, so with a WPA grant of $66,000 they got more than they ever dreamed they'd have — a new school.

After World War II, the area, White Rock East, doubled and redoubled in population, and so in 1946 the Reinhardt School District — which included about four hundred children — was swallowed up into the Dallas system.

There was another little farming community not too far from Reinhardt. This was Bayles. The school for this little city started in a converted barn and eventually moved into a more stable building. The Bayles School by 1946, when it came into the Dallas district, had grown to a three-room school that was located just off Ferguson Road not too far from where the present Bayles School was built in 1961.

These two schools, Bayles and Reinhardt, have spawned quite a number of others in the White Rock area: Casa View, Victor H. Hexter, Edwin J. Keist, M.T. Reilly, Alex Sanger, Charles A. Gill, George W. Truett, W.H. Gaston Junior High, Robert T. Hill Junior High, and the high school, Bryan Adams.

WEST

The urge to explore the lands west of the Trinity was in the minds of most of the early settlers of Dallas. However, the Trinity was always flooding out of its banks, so the roadway, if it could be called that, was usually impassable. However, if one did get past the Trinity and up the limestone escarpment it was easy going from then on. There remains to this day a wagon trace up a draw near Seal Street contiguous to the historic Robinson residence. This is just off the Old Fort Worth Highway.

In 1858 a group of French colonists settled to the west of this area and organized the La Reunion Community. They came to build a utopia where everyone could be equal, and they worked diligently and faithfully to make their living style totally democratic. Although the French Colony failed as an experiment in community ownership, the men and women who made up this colony, after they began working for themselves, as a rule, succeeded. They left their names, and their families scattered through the city of Dallas — the Henry family of Lancaster, Ben Long, afterwards Mayor of Dallas, Reverchon, Boll, Nussbaumer, Cantagrel, Cretien, Santerre, and many other names come from the Old French Colony.

The Texas Pacific Railway built west from Dallas in 1875, and Eagle Ford, a low-water crossing on the Trinity River for the wagon trains, was the first stop west of Dallas. Population would always follow the railroad, so eventually, there was a community at Eagle Ford with two schools. One school was somewhere in the vicinity of where Sidney Lanier School stands today. The other was the Eagle Ford Community School. The best records state that these were one-teacher schools.

Industrialization picked up after the turn of the century, and the cement companies came to the area — The Texas Portland Cement and the Trinity Portland Cement. The plants were constructed and the families were moved in to work at these plants, thus the community, Cement City was founded. A few years later the Texas Company planned a large oil refinery unit about halfway between the two cement plants and the family group that ran the refinery was to be in a little community called Gates.

Just before World War I, two high schools were established, West Dallas High, now Sidney Lanier School, and Cement City High, now the Thomas Edison Middle School. There was also a little community of people living in Cedar Valley. Their school became Benito Juarez.

After World War I the area west of the Trinity became a highly industrialized district, so the residential area shrunk. The schools got so small that the principals had trouble maintaining schedules. In 1927, the schools, West Dallas, Cement City, Cedar Valley, and Eagle Ford, were annexed to the Dallas district. Later other schools were built in the area: Gabe P. Allen, C.F. Carr, Amelia Earhart, George W. Carver, Sequoyah Junior High, and the high school, L.G. Pinkston.

NORTH

North Dallas High was built in 1922 on land sold to the district by the Cole family. The land for Cole Park and for the school was originally part of a land grant issued by Sam Houston. That same year, 1922, a small independent school district just south of the new school joined the Dallas system, the

Maple Lawn Independent School District. In 1926, the Love Field district just north of Maple Lawn came in. After World War II, Dallas's residential area boomed northward, and in 1945 the Vickery Independent School District with a land area of 15.59 square miles was annexed into Dallas. Mr. W.W. Caruth gave the land in 1937 to the Vickery School District for a high school on Hillcrest Road. In 1945 the school board bargained with the Caruths for more land north of Park Lane and east of Hillcrest. The DISD business manager, Bryan Adams, wanted to buy the land as soon as possible, because this needed land was going to triple in price, and it was essential that the school district have the land to enlarge the existing high school, which was going to eventually become Hillcrest High, and to build a junior high and an athletic field. The district got the land.

A small community northwest of downtown Dallas was founded by Clement Letot, the only Crimean War veteran ever to live in the Dallas area. This Frenchman, who with his countrymen aligned with Turkey against the Russians, was right there serving in Balaklava, the place imortalized by Tennyson in his poem, *Charge of the Light Brigade*. Who knows? Mr. Letot might have been nursed by Florence Nightingale, since she gained her fame as a nurse during that battle.

After the Crimean War in 1860 Letot came to the United States and settled in Illinois. He moved to Dallas in 1876 and during the next three decades became one of the leading citizens of Northwest Dallas County. His farm had 1,200 acres, and in the middle of it he built a two-story mansion. This home stood on the hill where today rests the Calvary Catholic Cemetery.

Mr. Letot was a Frenchman who was very proud of his background, who told of his war record in the Crimean War, and who was very boastful about the magnitude of his worldly goods. He always felt that he deserved *more*. He would take his corn into Dallas and if not enough was offered for it, he would *dump* the whole lot into the Trinity River.

The little city grew and took the name of its most promising citizen, Letot. There was a merchandise store, a post office, and a whistle-stop for the Dallas and Wichita Railway. Finally there was a school built in 1882. It cost $300, a sum that was collected from the families that lived in Letot — the Taylors,

Boyds, Moonyhams, Readers, Riehns, Flynns, Andersons, Smiths, and Sparkmans. John Sparkman and A.A. Anderson were the first trustees of the school.

In 1908 the school building that still stands on Lombardy Lane was built, and in 1912 an addition to this building was made. There was a bell placed in the small tower at Letot School, and the children would hurry on to class whenever they heard the bell ringing. That bell today is on the little red schoolhouse at Channel 13. It doesn't toll anymore, but it represents a public education channel that certainly brings learning to the area. The remembered teacher at the school was Mrs. Mary Mayberry who taught for years at Letot School until 1946 when it was annexed into the Dallas system. She was then made principal.

Today the building houses the Dallas County Status Offender Project which started in 1977 as a cooperative effort of the Dallas Independent School District, Dallas County Juvenile Department and Junior League of Dallas. The school, now called Letot Academy, offers twenty-four hour individual family crises counseling, referral services and short-term emergency shelter along with classes for middle- and high school students.

SOUTH

In 1928, Dallas swallowed up two school districts in South Dallas — the Lisbon School District, and the Bonnie View School District. Lisbon was a very old little town in which my great uncle, Mr. Frank Gerlach, opened the first blacksmith shop in 1880. He use to say that it was so much classier to live in Lisbon than in Dallas. I never could verify his statement. Perhaps, it was true. Or maybe he just wanted to get that idea started so that his property value would rise. Nevertheless, he had great pride in the little town of Lisbon way out on Lancaster Boulevard.

The Bonnie View Common School District had one little rural school built on Bonnie View Road and dedicated, June 19, 1915. It burned a number of years ago, and when firemen were sifting through the ashes, they discovered a tin box in the corner stone. This box and its interesting contents are preserved at the School Board on Ross Avenue. In the box there was some wheat from the fields surrounding the building, and on a sheet of tablet paper the history of the school was recorded. The land for the first wooden school building for Bonnie View was given by Henry Diceman in 1895. The children came to school from Lisbon, Jim Town, and Honey Springs. Sarah Fitzpatrick was the first and only teacher.

In April 1914, the Bonnie View District decided that they needed a new school building. President of the school district, R.C. Day, said that some of the neighbors had their eye on Bonnie View — namely, the Trinity Heights District. Mr. Day got an attorney, Hiram Lively, to fight for the district. He did so, and on July 6, 1914, the Bonnie View District was restored and $7,000 in bonds was ready for the new school. On October 7, 1914, Mr. Day closed the deal with the builder and the school was completed in July. The dedication day, July 19, 1915, offered quite a program. First, there was a prayer given by the pastor of the First Baptist Church, Oak Cliff, W.H. Hewitt. This was followed by a dramatic reading from a former teacher, Miss Verline Peacock. I knew Miss Peacock and remember her as being very dramatic. That reading surely must have been given in a grand and elocutionary style. A song was rendered by Jesse and Charley Durham, "Olden Days." The reading of the history of the school was given by E.C. Harpold. Then two speeches followed, one by Judge Hiram Lively and another by Bay Barry Miller. The school functioned independently until 1928 when it came into Dallas.

T.K. Seago was born in 1836, Cherokee County, Georgia. His father Isaac L. Seago came to Texas to serve in the Mexican War in 1846, was killed in the war, and was buried in Matamoras, Mexico. His mother, Lucinda Seago, came to Texas in 1851 with the seven children. T.K. grew up to serve in the War Between the States, Confederate Third Calvary. After the war he and his wife, Maitland, settled in Cass County and then in McLennan County. Later they moved to Dallas County where he founded the town Seago in 1879. The ville was added in 1910 to clear up postal confusion with another town named Sego.

Seagoville had a school building (a one-room log hut) in 1867, and the first teacher was Emma Cooper. Later there was a school known as the Woodside School that was equipped with split log-seats and desks. With this sort of history, naturally in 1964 when the Dallas Independent School District annexed part of the Seagoville District, there was a bit of descension. However, getting the added tax money won out over holding on to the heritage, so Seagoville did become a part of the Dallas District.

THE GROVE

The Dallas schools grew, the smaller surrounding districts were asked to come in, the teachers, students, and the communities were in agreement with any merger, and the school quietly came into the district. However, there was one school district that didn't want to come in, no one was in agreement, and plenty happened. In fact, so much happened when the Pleasant Grove School District considered coming into the Dallas District, that the Pleasant Grove School Board accidentally shut down the schools. This whole affair made such an unusual story that *Time Magazine* picked it up and told the nation about the dilemma in the January 26, 1953 issue.

When the thought was considered that the Pleasant Grove School District would be taken in by Dallas, the big city that had just about taken over everything in Pleasant Grove except the schools, the town split wide open. Half of the population thought that the big neighboring district would be able to support the educational system much better than their local, smaller one with limited tax money coming from the citizens. Being in the Dallas system the students would have better schools with less taxes. The other half remained true to Dale Douglas, Superintendent of Schools in Pleasant Grove, and all his efforts in educating the students of that area. This half wanted to remain separate and self supporting.

Meetings followed meetings, when finally on January 10, 1953, there was an election for the purpose of abolishing the school district and the closing of the Pleasant Grove Schools. The preelection campaigns for and against the issue included angry shouting, name-calling, and small riots. The election ended with 1,650 for and 962 against the abolishment of the school system.

In the meantime the Dallas Board began running into trouble with its $24 million bond issue. By Texas law, the Dallas district could not expand an inch until all its bonds were sold, so Dallas couldn't take Pleasant Grove in its system at that time.

Therefore, the Pleasant Grove School System was abolished with no where to go and the 4,000 kids didn't like it at all. They painted jalopies with signs, "We Want Our Schools," and drove all over town. A hillbilly band was hired for a rally, the kids lowered flags to half-mast all over town, and one of the local funeral homes loaned caskets to those who wanted to use them in parades to show the death of education in Pleasant Grove. Caskets were also put on the lawns of those who led the fight for abolishment. Red paint was smeared on the houses of those who were for the schools moving on into the Dallas district. Superintendent Douglas lamented,

"I'm a chief with no Indians."

He appealed to the county first, but county help only could go to schools with populations of 125 or less. Finally with no school and plenty of worry and tears, Pleasant Grove had only one course left — to call another election and vote their school district back into existence.

This they did, and on March 21, 1953, the qualified voters in Pleasant Grove approved a $2,800,000 bond and a $1.30 per hundred valuation tax rate. This money would give the district a new high school with a large gym, auditorium, lunchroom, wood and metal shops, and more classrooms. It was obvious that the town was still split in half over the situation because 1,381 voted for, and 1,049 voted against the bond.

Nevertheless, Dale Douglas was quoted in *The Cat's Tale*, the Pleasant Grove High School paper, Friday, March 27, 1953.

> All people connected with our school in any capacity are certainly grateful for the expression of confidence as manifested by the vote of our people in the election Saturday, March 21. It is our desire to begin the erection of the buildings as soon as all the legal steps can be taken, and we hope the people understand that it does take time to sell bonds and to take all necessary steps that must be made, in order to begin our new schools.

One week later after the election forty mothers from Pleasant Grove met with Dallas's Superintendent W.T. White to ask that Pleasant Grove be annexed into Dallas. Superintendent White said,

> No! As long as they are divided as they are, Dallas is not

interested in them. Pleasant Grove has a local problem to solve before they can ask the Dallas district to consider annexing them. Both factions need to get together and work with their schools. If they ever get together so that Dallas could be reasonably certain they wanted to be peaceful and wanted to be a part of this district, their request would receive consideration. As long as they are divided as they are, I doubt if this district would be interested in them. The annexation would come after our bonds ($24,830,000) are sold. We want our district undisturbed until bonds are sold, because we want to fulfill our commitments under this program.

After one year of cooling down in Pleasant Grove and after one year of Dallas' getting its bond situation straightened out, the Pleasant Grove schools came into the Dallas District, June, 1954.

Dale Douglas became a principal in an elementary school and then principal of Woodrow Wilson. Later he was appointed Assistant Superintendent in charge of finances. Mr. W.O. Pipes, who was principal at North Dallas, was sent to Pleasant Grove High as principal. This gentleman was carefully chosen by Dr. White, who knew that he had to send a real peacemaker to Pleasant Grove. Mr. Pipes was the man that Dr. White thought could best handle the situation. Eventually, when W.W. Samuell High School was built in 1957, Mr. Pipes went there to be principal. Samuell High was beautifully designed with everything anyone could want, but for three years Mr. Pipes literally survived at the old Pleasant Grove High School.

Dr. White had certain rules, and when the Pleasant Grove schools fell under his jurisdiction, these schools had to comply with the rules. No student under any circumstances could leave the school grounds during school hours. Pleasant Grove High had no lunchroom. The kids were used to going to The Old World Eatery or to Joe's Hamburgers or to any place in Pleasant Grove for lunch. This was stopped immediately. But how could they stay on the school grounds and eat when there was no cafeteria in the old school? With Dr. White, nothing was impossible. Frances Welch, director of cafeterias, was at the school promptly at 8 A.M. the first day of school setting up a temporary kitchen, and the lunchroom was set up each day in the gym. After lunch it was all taken down — and this happened every day for three years.

Mrs. Pauline James was handpicked to go out and be dean of students. First, she had to get some of the kids out of overalls. She had to get some of the kids to start wearing shoes to school. Much of Pleasant Grove was still in the country, and suddenly the kids found themselves in a city school, and they had to dress accordingly. Mrs. James managed beautifully.

Mr. Harold Lichtenwald was sent out as music teacher, and this appointment made him also in charge of assemblies. Only Harold Lichtenwald could have faced that student body in assembly the first day that they were in the district. These were the same kids that had rolled caskets, painted signs, hung flags at half-mast, and conducted rallies. Furthermore, half of the parents of these children didn't want them there, and the other half were happy that Dallas had taken them. And now, here was Mr. Lichtenwald to lead them all (together) in joyous song. He did it! As he walked to the stage, a roll of toilet tissue followed him down the aisle. Silence fell. Mr. Lichtenwald slowly and methodically rolled the toilet tissue up, put it on the speaker's stand on the stage and announced,

"If anyone needs this during the assembly, don't hesitate to come up and get it."

He'd won over the students. This was the beginning of what really turned out to be a short and fairly *pleasant* indoctrination of the Pleasant Grove schools into the Dallas Independent School District. The climax came, of course, when the students did get to move into W.W. Samuell, a marvelous school named after one of the favorite Dallas doctors. Many, many babies who were born in Dallas in the thirties and forties, and that includes me, were delivered by and cared for by Dr. W.W. Samuell.

A few years ago I judged the one act play contest for the Dallas schools which was held in the fine auditorium at Samuell High. Speech teacher Peggy Braden was on hand to greet me, and I also got to see a favorite teacher of mine, Mr. Paul Matthews. He was then the assistant principal at Samuell. The kids fondly called him "Small Paul." Mr. Matthews gave me an alabaster apple that some student must have given to him. Mr. Matthews is no longer living, but I have an apple that I'll always cherish along with memories of his teaching at North Dallas. Not everyone has an apple *from* their teacher.

Chapter Ten

Personnel

While my husband was the band director at Greiner Junior High he was involved in a terrible traffic accident that put him in the hospital for over three months. He spent more time at home recuperating. Dr. W.T. White promised him his band directing job any time that he could come back to it, and this promise helped him in recovering.

Every day his principal from Greiner, Mr. John Santillo, stopped at the hospital to see his broken band director. This boosted my husband's spirit. Mr. Santillo didn't have to visit him so regularly. He just did, because he is a concerned and caring person.

When W.T. White High opened, John Santillo was appointed principal. Today, Mr. Santillo is personnel director of the district. He hires all the teachers, and he has a very, *very* complex job. Today there are reasons that make finding good teachers extremely difficult.

In the first place, during the seventies, because of declining student enrollment, there was a teacher surplus, so naturally those thinking of going into the teaching field went in other directions. This has created a shortage today.

Secondly, the teachers salaries remain low. This is the eternal problem.

Thirdly, there is a definite decline in the quality of working conditions. The lack of strict discipline in the homes has created an undisciplined child that is very difficult to teach.

The fourth reason deals with career opportunities for women and minorities, the two groups who in the past dominated the educational scene. The brightest among the college educated blacks and women are turning to more lucrative and prestigious careers that are offered to them today.

The final and most important reason is explained in a survey that was recently taken. It was found that between 1963 and 1980 public school teachers suffered a greater loss of occupational prestige than any other occupation. No longer are the best educated members of the communities the teachers. They used to be. They were revered and feared. This is not true any longer, so Mr. Santillo has a hard time filling all the positions.

The heart has gone out of teaching. There are still hundreds of teachers who have heart and soul in their classes. However, some have only a tolerant spirit.

Today the toleration level has risen and the heart level has dropped. One might hear, "I'm teaching for two more years, and then I plan to do such and such."

This teacher is actually teaching something to the kids, the students are learning something, but this teacher is just tolerating the situation until a better deal comes around.

The students are just tolerating the teachers. Whereas in times past, when the loyalty song was sung after an assembly or after a class meeting or a club meeting, there was almost uncontrolled spirit. Now, the students are waiting to get out. Education and learning was an end in itself, a heartfelt experience. Now, it's something to be tolerated until the time warrants a change.

At home some parents just tolerate the children. The kids have good care, but there is no heartfelt experiences in the family. By 1990 there will be more step parents in the home than natural parents. This growing situation will tend to bring about a complete change in feeling and attitude within the family circle. There are many loving step parents, but there are some that tolerate the child, since he came along with the marriage. Good care is different from loving care.

There's a drab, gray haze hanging over the schools of today. A lot of emotionalism is gone. Students used to have strong emotions for their teachers — love, hate, fear, stark terror. Today, they just tolerate.

KING TEACHER

Teachers used to rule the schools. They had the last word, and, of course, there was no question as to the fact that they deserved it. Dallas businessman Lou Harris remembered when he was in school during the fifties. He was bragging to his teacher.

"I have an A in the class."

"Oh," replied the teacher. "Think so?"

"I know so. I've made an A."

"You've made an F, and you will continue to make one until you apologize to me for such arrogance."

Lou immediately reported the action to the principal of the school who meekly responded,

"Son, I think it's best that you apologize."

This was the teacher power used to the extreme. However, all parties concerned fell to that power. Teachers worked diligently in their teaching careers. Their primary desire was to raise the academic level of every student.

Today most of the blame for the low standards in education as pointed out by the low test scores made by the students is placed on the teachers. But yesterday — there was a different story.

Idleness. Lack of interest. Sluggish. Mean and indifferent. Mentally incompetent. No effort to grasp the subject. Poor study habits. No conscious effort to get the mark. Mental slowness. Irregular attendance. Daily work always late. Careless. Listlessness. Wants to get the credit, but dislikes the work it requires. Immature and slow. Social interference — in love.

These statements were collected from high school class record books that were kept during the years before the sixties when a teacher was free to fail a student if that teacher could give adequate reason for the failure. This is a list of the reasons noted for student failures, and they were accepted by educators, by administrators, and by the parents. A teacher was not blamed for the failure. The failure rested squarely on the student. If a student came to school immature and lazy, mentally slow, in love, with no interest and poor study habits, how could he possibly pass?

Those were uncomplicated days when a child's entire school career was summed up sometimes in one word. The principal asked why the child failed.

"He's sluggish."

"What can be done?"

"He'll have to wake up and produce the work."

The teacher knew that he came from a sluggish background. His parents were not awake to his needs. He had probably drifted through elementary school barely alert to his surroundings. So, was this all the teacher's fault?

A student came to school mean and indifferent. Was it possible to teach him literature, math, history, and science? Certainly not, if he were mean and indifferent to it all. If his parents cared, he could become less mean and indifferent. If some effort was given to correct his behavior at home and the teacher was brought into the effort, the student could better his school behavior. But until that was done, and if he remained the same — he failed.

Many of the these teachers who wrote these comments were teachers and still are teachers that are described elsewhere in this book as those who gave their whole life to teaching. They were those teachers who were intelligent, who were called and dedicated, who remained most anxious to serve their students, who spent many overtime hours tutoring students, who knew their students well, and who never enjoyed failing a child. However, there was credibility in their judgment, and they were respected for their knowledge of subject matter and of human behavior. This attitude toward teachers is somewhat lacking today.

Children saw the respect that was given to their teachers and they wanted to grow up and be just like them. Good teachers bred good teachers. This breeding has almost ceased. No one wants to grow up and be a beaten down, bedraggled, and badgered teacher suffering from the Rodney Dangerfield syndrome,

"I ain't got no respect."

Teachers need a lot of encouragement. More bumper stickers should be circulated to say,

If you can read this bumper sticker, thank a teacher.

Also, for those old record books, the teacher was asked to comment on the "character" of the class as a whole. (The word *regular* was used to mean average or normal.)

> This class was not strong. Too many boys in this class. Girls, regular, Boys, weak.
>
> The students in this class are for the most part good, but they are at the age when the distractions are numerous, and they don't want to study.

The teacher was schooled in dealing with "bad ages." But as time passed, so did the age. A few students would remain immature and always have a "bad age" behavior.

"A fair class with no repeaters." This was a good situation. Repeaters caused trouble, because they knew that they were behind in the first place. A class must be homogeneous for fine teaching to transpire.

Now, there were other comments in the records that alluded to the fact that the elementary teachers had failed.

> Inadequate foundation. Poor reading ability. Needs to go back to special class. Poorly prepared.

All these reasons seem to clear the high school teachers, and place all the blame on the elementary staff. Not so!

Those elementary teachers were respected and actually feared, as I've pointed out previously. They were doing the best that they could. After all, first graders come to school in all sizes, with all sorts of experiences and backgrounds, and in all colors. Each one of these factors plays heavily on his reading readiness. These factors have nothing to do with his ability to learn, but on his readiness to learn. Some children come with vast experiences on which to draw word images. They come gobbling up vocabulary words as fast as they can, and they come with all the basic concepts for total understanding.

A teacher says, "Look at the first letter." Before that child can look at the first letter, he must know what the word "first" means. Many children come to school not knowing where "up" is. They do not know that there is a front and a back to things.

Many of the children who come from mean and deprived environments have no knowledge of "nouns." They never hear the names of things. They come to school knowing only imperative verbs. "Sit down. Shut up. Get out." No one in the home has ever spoken *about* something. Only harsh orders are given.

Some children come to school not knowing any English words. Mrs. Frances Allen, who served as reading consultant for many years in the Dallas district, guided her teachers into using the Boehm Text of Basic Concepts to ready their children for reading. Unfortunately, there are many children who enter the first grade, and who are already behind before they start.

Texts are written for children who have had experiences. The books speak of birthday parties, trips to the zoo, rides in the car. There are children who come to school never having seen a birthday cake or a zoo. The family doesn't own a car.

Mary Dillard was an elementary teacher at the Nolan Estes Center. She was a world traveler and was able to tell fascinating stories about countries all over the globe. She discovered that most of her little students had never been far from Beckley Avenue and Kiest Boulevard. They had never crossed the Trinity River to go downtown. They did not know about the bridge. They had never seen a building close by. They did not know what Dallas was. In fact, one child asked,

"What's a Dallas?"

In the sixties teachers struggled to answer, "Why can't Johnny read?" The behaviorists decided that Johnny couldn't read because his mother was working and not at home to help him with his homework. He was a latchkey kid with really no incentive to read in the first place. He had role models that were doing well and who couldn't read. Therefore, getting an education was not his goal. And, of course, he wasn't doing well, because children must see a reason for doing well. The reasons vary, but there must be at least one reason.

Now, twenty years later, the cry of "Johnny must read." Education is a political issue, and the national educational system is going to have to shape up or the country will continue to be surpassed by the other world powers.

Time magazine reported that the Dallas School System now has the nation's first computerized merit-pay plan. The director of Employee Relations, Robby Collins, stated,

> Once you have human beings evaluating other human beings, the systems produce jealousies, morale problems. The beauty of our system is that it's done totally by computer. Each school in Dallas will receive projected student scores,

based on national achievement tests. Now, in the school that can outperform the computer projections, the teachers will receive an extra $1,500.

Time Magazine goes on to state that teachers are responding to this plan with a shrug and a "So what!" Teachers want to be respected. They want recognition. They wish to be thought of as professionals.

The teacher must be trusted again.

He's careless. After working with this child after school, after encouraging him to do his best, after making the lesson relative to his world, after studying his background and discovering that his parents are rather careless with their interest in him, after working with him in spite of the fact that the odds are against him — he's still careless. He has failed.

The student has failed — not the teacher.

IT'S THE PRINCI*PAL* OF THE MATTER

The principal sets the tone of the school. He must back his teachers as they support him. Dallas has had its share of able and proficient principals. Some were and are a bit unusual, but they found delight in their jobs.

W.H. ADAMSON

In 1924 Professor Adamson marched his students from Oak Cliff High School to Jefferson Boulevard to cheer a political hopeful. Her name was Miriam A. (Wallace) Ferguson, fondly called "Ma," who was running for Governor of Texas — the first woman to run for and win the governorship.

When Ma came by in her touring car, the crowd yelled "Turkey Pan, Ma. Turkey Pan." No one knew why one yelled "Turkey Pan" at Ma. It was just something that one did. I presume it was because she represented the rural side of Texas, which in 1924 was the largest side of the state. In 1924 there were more people living in the Texas countryside than in the Texas cities, so it was appropriate to greet Ma with a hearty "Turkey Pan." Dr. Adamson with his clan loudly cheered the would-be governor that spring day when she came through Oak Cliff.

The Professor was "tough and exacting." These were the words that Dallas oilman, James D. Hancock, Sr., used to describe his beloved principal.

"I wouldn't break a pane of glass for one thousand dollars." James Hancock happened to break a pane, and Dr. Adamson made him pay for it. It was only eighty-five cents, but that was a fortune for the high school lad. Finally when he only owed five cents of his debt for the windowpane, Dr. Adamson insisted that James pay off the debt with his chili money.

"I didn't get to buy chili that day. It almost killed me. The aroma of the chili was terrific, but the nickel had to be given to Dr. Adamson."

Dr. Adamson was a slender gangling man with piercing, steel-blue eyes. Whenever a student sinned, the principal would point his long finger at the offender and glare at him silently. The student would almost sink to his knees in total respect and fear. But the professor was always fair in his punishment. He would chastise a student in one minute and then within hours invite that same student to go fishing with him.

Adamson was the only man to serve as principal of two high schools at the same time. When Sunset High was built and the students living on the west side of Oak Cliff realized that they were going to have to go to the new school, in order to get them to move Professor Adamson was made principal of the new school temporarily. He himself lived in the Sunset district, one block north of Jefferson on Montclair. The white two-story house with the pink shutters still stands proudly in the restored Winnetka Heights area.

Oak Cliff High was finally named after W.A. Adamson, a man who was known and loved by every prominent citizen in Dallas.

TRINITY HEIGHTS

Mrs. Fannie Basket was a teacher at Ben Milam Elementary School. She served as principal at the City Park School, and then in 1927 she came to Trinity Heights Elementary as principal. She was famous for her frequent visits to the classroom where she would, with only one request, tell *Uncle Remus* stories. Tar Baby, Brer Rabbit, Uncle Remus — all the characters did come to life and literally did take on human characteristics when Mrs. Basket told the tales. Children would anxiously await her visits and the stories.

When Mrs. Basket died in 1942, the principalship of the school was taken by Mr. Harrell Budd. Teachers who served with Mr. Budd said that he "squared" the school. He made everyone who was associated with the school proud that they were a part of the school and the area, both named Trinity Heights. This residential section had been an elite district in Oak Cliff, but the depression had taken its toll on the people living there. The people there were not wealthy, but they were eager for their children to learn and to rise educationally and socially. They wanted the best for their children. Mr. Budd observed this quality in the people there.

"The families in this neighborhood are not wealthy enough to make their children bored, but not poor enough to make them deprived." Lillian Stevens, who was a teacher in the school pointed out that Mr. Budd instilled pride in the children — pride in themselves, their work, and their school.

"You earn what you get," he'd say, and every teacher and student believed him.

Returning from a trip to Tennessee in 1955, Mr. and Mrs. Budd were involved in a traffic accident which took his life instantly. The PTA at Trinity Heights set out to get the name of the school changed to Harrell Budd in honor of this man who gave so much of his life to the students and teachers at the school. The name was changed.

Mr. N.B. Williams was principal after the death of Mr. Budd. A week after Mr. Williams arrived at the school, there was a memorial service held at the school for Mr. Budd. The day following the service a little boy came up to Mr. Williams, the new principal and said,

"Mr. Williams, I'm so sorry that I was sick and missed Mr. Budd's memorial service. I sure won't miss yours."
The new principal set into the scene quickly working on the same philosophy that existed in the school, "Earning what you get." Mr. Williams worked hard and earned the statement made by a little kid when he looked into the principal's office.

"So, this is where the old boy works!"

WILLIE A. PARKER

The Emaline Donohue Library, a special library of Texas history books, was founded at Forest Avenue High by the principal, Wylie Parker, in 1921. Mr. Parker was later responsible for a plan in which all of the schools in the Dallas district joined together to give a program which was written to cele-

brate Texas Week in March each year. This plan was endorsed
by the School Board. Texas and books were the greatest things
in his life. He not only read a book, but he marked passages in
the books that he wanted others to notice as they read the
books. Librarians who handled books that Mr. Parker read
shook their heads in despair. It was all right to mark in one's
own books, but marking up a library book was inexcusable to
most librarians. It never bothered Wylie Parker to draw dark,
heavy lines under memorable quotes. This very valuable library of Texas books, all carefully marked by Mr. Parker, was
given to the Dallas Public Library for the whole community to
enjoy.

Principal Parker kept a fine spirit going the whole twenty-
two years that he was in charge at Forest Avenue High. At
Christmastime he sent *every* student a Christmas card *personally* signed.

The card began, "The Season's Best Greetings to the students from the principal and the general staff at Forest Avenue
High School." The final paragraph of the four-page card
brought this message.

> The year just ahead of us has no place for the puny little
> life which is self-centered. There will be no time nor place for
> grouches and grudges and petty jealousies. I challenge you,
> even as I urge every member of the student body, to reconse-
> crate yourself to the highest and best things of life as you
> begin your work for the New Year. May you, all and each,
> renew your strength and raise your grades on each report as
> you ascend the grade curve of Mount Intelligence of Forest
> Avenue High School. May the gains you make along the
> Road of Intelligence be steady and regular throughout the
> coming year. Also may health, happiness, and as much pros-
> perity as you are able to bear be yours every day of 1924, is
> the earnest and sincere wish of,
>
> Your friend cordially,
> Wylie A. Parker
> Commanding Officer, December, 1923

In 1939 Mr. Parker called the students of Forest High together in assembly to announce the opening of the new field
house and athletic complex, Dal-Hi Stadium, later named P.C.
Cobb Stadium. It was located right off Industrial Boulevard at
Oak Lawn Avenue. He used his most demanding voice.

"Everyone will be required to attend the dedication and opening celebration of the new Dal-Hi Stadium." Then under his breath he mumbled: "I don't know why they chose to build that thing in the river bottom. Nothing else will ever be built there. Oh, well, there will always be a place to park."

Little did he know that a Woodrow Wilson High graduate by the name of Trammell Crow would develop that area to the point that eventually the stadium itself would fall to the Trammell Crow Developers.

L.V. STOCKARD

Most of the Dallas school administrators were deeply religious men, serving in their churches. This was certainly true of L.V. Stockard, who became District Superintendent of High Schools in 1925. Mr. Stockard instituted the Bible Credit Program in the district. The students could study the *Bible* at the church and receive high school credit for that study. He planned the program and saw to it that it was successful.

He was a stickler for details. Every project that he undertook was carefully planned and finished to the last, minute specification. Teachers always enjoyed his visits to their classrooms. He'd visit the class of a teacher who was doing well with her class. He would tell her so, start to leave, and then turn back and say:

"The shades aren't straight."

He was a devout member of Gaston Avenue Baptist Church. At his funeral Dr. Marshall Craig made this statement,

"He magnified and dignified every task he ever undertook."

E.D. WALKER

A feature story in the *Times Herald*, November 12, 1950, described the E.D. Walker household. Dr. and Mrs. Walker seated themselves every Sunday in front of one of the few television sets in Dallas to see son, Doak, play pro ball for the Detroit Lions. SMU football star, Heisman Trophy winner Doak brought more pleasure to his father every Sunday as the honored son continued playing the game. Today, Dr. Walker, who loves to be called "Coach," enjoys talking about his family and all the marvelous years that he spent in the Dallas Independent School District.

When Ewell Walker graduated from Austin College in

Sherman, he was sure of two things. He wanted to teach school, and he wanted to stay near Sherman. There was a beautiful young lady teaching in the junior high in Sherman for whom he had "deep feelings." Teaching school was in his soul, and the young beautiful teacher was in his heart.

"I just couldn't leave her, so when I was offered a teaching position in Whitewright, Texas, near Sherman, I took it." The principal at Whitewright urged Ewell to stay away from the big city schools like Sherman — too many politics. For one hundred and twenty-five dollars a month, Dr. Walker was teaching school and was near the lady who was soon to become Mrs. Walker. The interurban furnished transportation from his school to his love, and after one year of steady courtship, he married his love and moved to Dallas.

When Dr. Walker came to Dallas he was still anxious to teach school. "I would have taught for nothing if they would have asked me."

During that first year in Dallas, Dr. and Mrs. Walker taught at the Powell School. He taught first-year Latin, and she taught in the lower school.

"Dr. Powell couldn't tell his money from mine, so it was best that I leave his school. One afternoon in the fall of 1921, Mrs. Walker and I were driving down Haskell past the almost finished North Dallas High School. I told Mrs. Walker that I'd give my eyeteeth to teach there. I'd take seventy-five cents a month if they'd take me. Why, I'd take fifty cents!"

Dr. Walker applied to teach at North Dallas, he was accepted, and he was assigned to the new school that opened in January, 1922. He was paid $1,500 a year for teaching and for driving the school bus.

Dr. Kimball was plagued by money and teacher shortages. The only people who taught in those days were people who really wanted to teach. The money did not matter to those teachers. Dallas was growing so fast at that time, that one could make money almost anywhere. But, a teacher then, preferred teaching to anything else. This was Dr. Walker's preference.

During the twelve years that E.D. Walker taught history and commercial law at North Dallas, he was also in charge of the High Y, he was athletic manager, and he was baseball coach. In 1929, the baseball team won the city championship.

However, the event that Dr. Walker was most famous for was his minstrel show.

In 1921 a book was published by theatre man Max Stein entitled, *How To Put On A Minstrel Show*. The book contained a complete course on how one went about presenting one of the popular shows. Fine opening overtures were included along with a good selection of end men jokes and gags. It gave a listing of suitable songs. The book was sold all over the country, because minstrel shows were constantly given during the twenties. However, compared to what Dr. Walker knew about giving minstrel shows, this book was just a drop in the theatrical bucket. He was the master. He could have written not one book, but volumes on the subject of giving these blackface farces.

The first of the shows was given on March 17, 1923, in the school auditorium. There were 1300 people in attendance. *The Viking*, 1923, described the event.

> Cymbals crashed, curtain rose, and the circle of players broke into the school loyalty song. Such a selection for the opening scene was indeed appropriate, and the vast throng below the footlights was thrilled by the imposing spectacle.

Hub Adams was a student who directed the show for Dr. Walker. He wrote both the words and the music of many songs that he used; and the original acts, which made an appeal, were all the products of his active imagination. Hub had no peer in the burnt cork role of end man. Some of the songs included, *Loving Sam, She's Mine All Mine, Agravatin' Papa,* and *You've Got to See Mama Every Night.*

The humor wasn't exactly four-star quality, but the students rolled in the aisles, especially at all the inside jokes. The principal, E.B. Comstock, was always seated on the end seat, third row. In the middle of the show, there would be an actor dressed in a Western Union uniform come down the aisle calling,

"Telegram for Mr. Comstock, Telegram for Mr. Comstock."

Mr. Comstock had no choice but to identify himself.

"You're Mr. Comstock? Report to the cloak room immediately. You're overcoat is leaking."

Laughter followed. The joke was bad, but the money taken in was good — good enough to finance the athletic program for the year.

The second minstrel show given the next year drew even larger crowds. There was a parade though downtown Dallas advertising it, and because the ticket sales far surpassed the first-year sales, the show was moved down to the City Hall auditorium.

Each year the annual at North Dallas described the show as the best ever. The banjo pickers, the lovely darlings who had "startling masculine" appearances, and the hilarious end men were all part of the show.

Dr. Walker — aside from being a minstrel director — was also a good history teacher. As that history teacher, he stressed to his students the importance of reading the newspapers. He required the ever popular "current event" to be brought in every Monday morning.

There was one extremely lazy boy in the class whom Dr. Walker never seemed to inspire. The kid just sat there, and, of course, he never had a current event. In the month of May, 1926, spring fever had set in, but still Dr. Walker managed to keep his class alert, all except for the lazy boy. The semester was drawing to a close and still this particular student had not really contributed to the class. That first Monday in May, the big news that had everyone talking concerned Admiral Byrd's flight over the North Pole. The shiftless boy as usual had no current event. Dr. Walker was desperate.

"Didn't you read about Admiral Byrd? Surely you could tell us about the flight across the North Pole? Everyone is talking about it."

Dr. Walker looked straight at the boy. The boy could not look at Dr. Walker, because the boy's eyes were barely open.

"What time did you go to bed last night?" asked the determinedly interested teacher.

"Two or three."

"No wonder you don't know about Admiral Byrd." Dr. Walker was discouraged.

"Oh, I know all about Admiral Byrd. I'm a ham radio operator. I built the radio myself. At three this morning I was talking to Admiral Byrd."

Years later when Dr. Walker was principal at Bowie Elementary School, he took a group of students down to WRR Radio to present a program. There, running the big board at the station was the lazy young man who didn't have time to read about Byrd and his flight. He hadn't brought a current event, because he was dealing directly with the event.

"A part of me will always be at North Dallas," stated Dr. Walker. However, he was given a principalship — and then he was made assistant superintendent in charge of personnel.

"I thought that when I was a principal and had my faculty all lined up for the year, I'd just sit back and watch the school roll along. I had no idea that a principal worked twenty-four hours a day. Then when I accepted the responsibility of hiring the school personnel, I thought that once I got that faculty all settled into the various schools, I'd just watch the whole system roll along. I had no idea that I'd work twenty-four hours a day and then some."

But Dr. Walker loved all the work. He loved the faculty. He described Alma Williams as one who always had a great story to tell.

"Alma never married, but she wasn't an old maid. You know, there are single ladies, and then there are old maids. Miss Williams was single, but she was not an old maid."

In her language arts class, a little third grader said,

"It was so cold last night that daddy and me slept together."

"Daddy and *I* slept together," automatically corrected Miss Williams.

"You must have gotten into bed later," replied the little boy.

When Dr. Walker was the principal at Bowie School, an interested party found some schoolbooks under a house and brought them to the school. Dr. Walker played detective, checked the numbers, and traced their ownership to a Bowie student who had played hooky the day before the books were found. The boy had hidden the books under the house before he had taken off for the day. Dr. Walker called the boy into his office to question him.

The boy lamented, "I didn't have a good day. It rained, and then when I went to get my books, they were gone. I'm so scared. I know I'm in real trouble."

The good principal saw that the boy was miserable, frightened, and so sorry for his sin. The boy probably would never play hooky again.

"Well," he said, "here are your books. Now, the next time you play hooky, bring them to me for safekeeping."

Years later, this student met his bighearted and forgiving principal and introduced him as the man who kept him from playing hooky. The young man was a successful and prominent citizen.

Dallas had the best in educators in E.D. Walker. He like many educators were not paid enormous salaries for all their efforts. He was paid in love from his students and his teachers. He was paid a salary from the district, and the district never knew that he "would have taught school for nothing if they would have asked me."

DR. J.L. PATTON JR.

A miniature railroad dominated the scene in the home of Dr. J.L. Patton, Jr.

"My people made the railroads great! That's why I love the railroads."

Dr. Patton did love the railroads — and he loved the Dallas School District. There was never anyone more respected than Dr. J.L. Patton, Jr., principal of Booker T. Washington high school for almost thirty years. He was a student at Booker T. when Dr. Kimball discovered him. He was brilliant, energetic, and ambitious, and Dr. Kimball saw this in the young student. He was given a scholarship to Columbia University, graduated from that school, and came back to serve the Dallas schools and the Dallas community. His heart was with the Negro student. He was an inspiration.

Whenever Dr. Patton gave one of his memorable and affecting speeches, he would speak in parables. His choice of parables was sometimes a bit unusual but always impressive.

> Heavy burdens do have the virtue of bringing out the best that is in people. Clocks with weights have always fascinated me. Heavily they hang, but without them the clock is done for. Think of window weights; they lift the window higher. Weights often lift people to God. Weights hold things in place; the ships at anchor, or the paper weight on your desk. Those who fish know the value of the sinker, which enables us to reach the fish. Think of your weighty problems as blessings coming to keep you in place, to keep you where you can be reached, and like the clock your weight will keep you

running. Weights strengthen the spirit, sweeten the soul, stifle anger, extinguish envy, subdue pride, bridle the tongue, restrain the hand, and trample temptations.

He was well known for his "dog" speech.

Let me tell you something about dogs. I once visited a kennel in which there were big dogs, little dogs, smooth-haired dogs, and shaggy ones. There were fast dogs and slow ones; there were playful dogs and dignified ones. As I remember now, these dogs and their breeds could well serve to teach the proper use of the varieties of talent that we have in our schools. Each breed could teach a lesson in truth. The Irish setter could teach the virtue of patience and endurance. I saw the pointer. He could give direction to organization. We need pointers to direct us on our way, else we stray. I saw the retriever, the hunting dog who brings back what the huntsman has slain. We need a retriever to bring back those who stray. Next I saw the collie who is a companion and good shepherd. There I also saw the bloodhound whose chief characteristic is to search for and locate. We need to search for truth and righteousness. Truth is not to be feared; it is to be sought. Then I saw the seeing-eye dog who represents guidance for the blind. We need this guidance so much for how blind we are! Put these concepts into action and prove to the world that God's people are not 'going to the dogs.'

Dr. Patton served as one of Dr. White's right hand men. He was the needed consultant when integration plans were taking more and more priority in the public schools. Principal James C. Coalson was assigned to Booker T. Washington as the first white administrator in an all black school. He served as assistant principal to Dr. Patton.

"What a brilliant man, and he loved those kids."

PERRY FITE

When an individual works his way through college, then he cares about learning. Perry Fite worked his way through East Texas State University and cared about his education. After graduation he became a teacher, and for forty-nine and one-half years he cared about the education of the student in the Dallas schools.

He recently stated, "If I were graduating from college right now, I'd go right into the teaching field again. It's the greatest profession in the world."

Whenever Mr. Fite was called upon to speak to civic organizations, he told those doctors, lawyers, and big businessmen that they had not really lived.

"You don't really live until you teach school!"
Perry Fite claimed that he found only great people in the Dallas schools and that he never spent a day in school that he didn't love that day. He only had unhappy moments when the Tech High football team or baseball team or track team or basketball team didn't win. He was their coach for twenty-nine years.

Mr. Fite started his teaching career at Rusk School. Then he taught at Fannin School before he went to Tech as coach. In 1959 he was made principal at Rylie high School. There he worked diligently to instill self-esteem and self-pride in kids that sometimes didn't have a lot of either.

"Take pride in yourselves and this community," he'd plead. Perry Fite didn't punish a kid, he would feed him. An unruly child was a challenge. He worked to make the students see their own potential. They needed to *see* what they could do.

In 1963 Perry Fite went to Grady Spruce High School. He initiated the "I Care" system. When a visitor entered Spruce, he was greeted by a welcoming committee and given an "I Care" ribbon to wear. Every student in the school belonged to some committee which functioned to keep the school running properly. This system received national recognition when it was initiated, because the principal was able to get total cooperation from the students and the parents.

In 1979, the School Board recommended that the gym at Grady Spruce be named the Perry Fite Gymnasium in honor of the man who gave almost fifty years of his life to the schools in Dallas. He always insisted that "Everybody was somebody at Spruce." They were.

WILLIAM DURRETT

Dr. White called him the "P.T. Barnum" of the educational world. He made going to school exciting.

"Anyone can be an animal. (Referring to the animal mascots of the schools.) But it takes a real *person* to be a Kimball *Knight*," shouted the enthusiastic principal, Bill Durrett at Justin Kimball High. Barnum was a money-maker, a mover, a showman, and a man with a lot of spirit. This describes Mr.

Durrett as well. He had more money in his activity fund than any other principal in the district. He was a shrewd businessman as well as a capable principal. There were all sorts of rumors floating around the school as to how the activity money was made. The kids said that he would have popcorn popped in the cafeteria during the last period. Then after the aroma of the freshly popped corn settled in over the school, the sale of the popcorn began. Naturally there was a rush for it, because high school students are always hungry and no one could resist popcorn. When all the buttery, salted, delicious manna was consumed, everyone was thirsty. The students rushed to the drinking fountains only to discover that Mr. Durrett had cut them off and was selling cold drinks in the hallway. Naturally big sales on cold drinks followed, because no one could survive eating popcorn without a big, cold drink. This story of this moneymaking scheme is only a rumor, but the large funds in the activity account did exist.

One day Mr. Durrett left something at home that he needed at school, so he made a quick trip home in the middle of the day to pick up the forgotten item. When he entered his home, he met a thief there in the middle of his living room. He chased the thief out of the house and on down the street. The thief got ahead of the breathless principal. Mr. Durrett had just about decided to let him go, when a city bus came by. Bill Durrett jumped on the bus.

"Follow that thief," he shouted and pointed to the running bandit. The bus was soon up even with the thief.

"You'll have to get off here. I have to stay on my route," pleaded the bus driver. Bill Durrett jumped off the bus and with one flying leap caught the thief from behind.

"I put a full hammerlock on him and pulled him down. He started begging for mercy." This is what the principal told the *Times Herald* reporter who covered the story. Mr. Durrett held the housebreaker until the police arrived.

At Kimball High, the lively principal ran a tight ship. He never put a full hammerlock on anyone at the school, but several students will testify to the fact that they did once or twice plead for mercy.

Dr. White noted that Mr. Durrett never broke any rules set down for the principals.

"I visited Kimball High one day, and saw a Coke machine

in the front hall. I told him to get that machine out of the hall-way. He did. He put it in the cafeteria."

Oh, well, it made more money there.

THE WAR YEARS AND JULIUS DORSEY

I entered Robert E. Lee Elementary School on September 1, 1939.

My mother always said, "When Hitler marched into Po-land, Rose-Mary marched into Robert E. Lee."

There's nothing like giving your child something in com-mon with Adolph Hitler. However, my march was different. It brought no earth shattering change to the world — only to my life.

The two invasions were not similar by any means. Hitler's forces marched into Poland with great strength, no fear, and the plan to kill anyone who would stand in the way of their conquering the world. I invaded Robert E. Lee holding tight to my mama's hand, scared to death, with no particular plan. I just wanted to get through the day and get home to my swing in the backyard.

However, after the principal, S.M. Lloyd, called us into the auditorium and told us how much he loved us all and told us how much pleasure we would have, and after I saw that I was going to be surrounded by other second graders who were just as scared and just as lost as I was, I decided that I'd stay. And what's more, by lunchtime, I decided that my mother could go home. This pleased both her and the teacher, Maude Erwin. In fact, by the end of the day, the room was almost clear of moth-ers, and by the end of the week, there wasn't a mother on the scene. I had a happy year, and our class learned everything that second graders had to learn.

On September 5, 1940, one year after the Nazi's took over Poland, Dr. Norman Crozier died, and Mr. Julius Dorsey, who had served as principal in several Dallas schools, who served as superintendent of elementary schools and then as superin-tendent of the junior and senior high schools, took over the su-perintendency of the whole district. He came during the war years when there was no building program whatsoever, when there were shortages of paper, books, pencils, and teachers, when there was not too much manpower on the home front, and when public morale in the nation could drop suddenly as

Gabriel Heatter reported the war news on the radio with . . . "There's bad news tonight." So many of the young men dropped out of high school to join the armed forces, and all the active little children had ration stamps for only one pair of shoes a year.

But the school front was united. The art teachers taught every child how to knit, and millions of six-inch squares were knitted by the children and sewed together by the teachers and sent overseas to be used by the GIs for blankets. The kids used every scrap of paper. One would never think of using only one side of a sheet of notebook paper. The margins on the theme papers grew thinner and thinner as the paper shortage increased. The kids saved tinfoil, scrap iron, rags, thread. Everyone had a victory garden including many of the schools.

The children kept smiling during the war, and Mr. Dorsey worked hard to get his teachers to grin and bear it. He managed to get the new science building finished that had been started in 1939 at Crozier Tech High. There was a money shortage and the workers went on strike. Somehow he got the money to build and he got the men back to work, so that on February 8, 1942, the building was dedicated. Mr. Dorsey also managed to open a Dallas Defense School on 2222 Ross Avenue where men could be trained for needed positions and could be hired instantly for positions that were vacated by men called into the armed services.

Julius Dorsey made the course of study for the Dallas students a twelve-year course. A year was added in 1942 to the school life of the student. Many people who were in school during the war years often brag about being "double promoted." They were! However, it wasn't because they were so brilliant, it was because Mr. Dorsey added another grade and in order to keep the proper age in the proper class, the students were all shoved up one grade to work in the extra year.

Dr. Walter Schiebel called Julius Dorsey a sensitive "peace loving man who served in a war torn world." He had a favorite way of relaxing when he got away from the trials that he faced each day. He loved to play poker with a group of his coaches. There was never more than a dollar or two wagered during the game, but Dorsey loved to win the pot regardless of how small it was. In order to win, he always wore his lucky hat.

Now, this game never really offered a carefree situation, because Mr. Dorsey and the coaches worked with young men who played ball one year and who were on the front lines in Europe or in the Pacific zone the next. And too, there were shortages of everything but kids. Nevertheless, on Saturday night Mr. Dorsey and his friends in the coaching field gathered to play poker, and one could always spot the superintendent. He was the one wearing the hat!

PERSONALITIES

On September 11, 1842, General Adrian Woll and some 1,200 Mexican soldiers once again captured San Antonio. The intruders didn't stay long, because Jack Hays, leader of the Texas Rangers, harassed the Mexican troops until they went back across the Rio Grande. He used Sam Colt's invention, the six-shooter. Actually, the Colt wasn't a range gun, but it terrified the Mexican troops.

This Mexican invasion into San Antonio was Santa Anna's way of saying that Mexico was still a sovereignty and that the Texans were just a weak group of people calling themselves a republic. Naturally, hard-hitting Sam Houston had to speak to this, so he agreed to a demonstration of force below the Rio Grande under the leadership of General Alexander Somervell. This invasion into Mexico by General Somervell was called the Mier Expedition. Somervell left San Antonio, November 8, 1842, and headed for Laredo. He captured the little town easily, and sadly to say, some of the Texas Rangers weren't exactly polite to the Mexican citizens there. But, these men were fighters to the bone, they had come to conquer a new world, Texas, and really nothing would stop them. They were ordered back to San Antonio by General Somervell, but a few of them, about 300, including the famous ranger Big Foot Wallace, marched on to Mier, a small adobe town in northern Mexico. There they were surrounded by a large Mexican force, captured, and then marched into the interior of Mexico. Santa Anna demanded that they all be executed, but the Mexican monarch finally decided under great demand from the American ministers that in Latin fashion, he would order only one in ten to be shot. Thus, one hundred and fifty-nine white beans and seventeen black beans were poured into a pitcher and set before the men. They were blindfolded and ordered to draw a bean. The men who drew the black beans were to be shot. Their life or death was going to be left to fate, not to Santa Anna. This is where Big Foot uttered his famed instruction.

"Dig deep, men. Dig deep."
He had noticed that the black beans had been poured in on top.

Those who did draw the black beans were shot, and the others were chained together and held in captivity for over three years. Eventually they all were returned to Texas, and one of the Rangers, Richard Brown, returned, married, and had a family that produced two granddaughters who gave ninety-nine years of their lives to educating Dallas children. One granddaughter, Leland Watkins, taught in the Dallas schools and served as county educational supervisor for a total of fifty-five years. Her sister, Verbian Watkins Vaughn taught in the Dallas schools for forty-four years. When Mrs. Vaughn retired, Dr. E.D. Walker asked her to stay and teach one more year so that he could say the two sisters had given one hundred years, but Mrs. Vaughn wanted to retire when her husband did. Ninety-nine was a good number especially when it represented good teaching.

Miss Watkins almost didn't stay in Dallas *one* year to teach, because she hated the slimy black mud she had to wade through in order to get to John Henry Brown School. She and her good teacher friend, Sudie Williams, slushed through the mud together on rainy days. One day, Leland had it up to here with the mud — she was finished. She called Dr. Kimball and told him that she was going back to sandy East Texas. He persuaded her to stay at least to the end of the year. She stayed in the educational field fifty-five years and saturated her students with self-confidence.

"You can do it. You can do what you want to do." She was very proud of all of her students but she loved to mention some that were very successful — Tex Schramm, general manager for the Dallas Cowboys, Stanley Marcus, famous storekeeper, Henry S. Miller, real estate tycoon, Cecil Combs, pilot, who flew General Douglas MacArthur out of Corregidor, and Albert Bilgers, Dallas florist. These and hundreds of other students should be grateful that grandfather drew a white bean.

Roberta King was called "The Dream Girl of Adamson High." The students remember her sitting at her desk like a queen or a princess on the throne.

"We all wanted to be queens or princesses like Miss King.

She even had a regal name." Miss King taught Spanish at Adamson High, and she never allowed an English word to be spoken in her class.

Her fellow teacher and very dear friend was Ruth Ruffin. Miss Ruffin was called the "Sweetheart of Adamson." Professor Adamson always teased her about her name being so close to the word, "ruffian." In fact, he delighted in introducing her as Ruth *Ruffian*. Her charm and dignity made any association with the word "ruffian" preposterous.

The two teachers affected the personalities of everyone who was ever in their classes. Bill Sullivan, who played football at Adamson and later at SMU, returned to Adamson as principal. Many Adamson graduates returned to teach at their alma mater. Bill claimed that he could never forget the two terrific ladies. Miss King gave him a book to read, *Captain From Castille*. He was so impressed with the book and her interest, he asked to keep it. He still holds the book as a cherished memory of his favorite English teacher.

Today Miss King and Miss Ruffin share a home together. Each morning they read from the *Bible* and from a book that was sent to them by a former student who claims his success is rooted in their inspiring personalities, Maurice Acers, prominent attorney who is married to real estate giant, Ebby Halliday.

Forest Avenue High School had a Latin teacher who brought national recognition to the school. Miss Lourania Miller organized the Junior Classical League first at Forest, and then she helped high schools all over the nation to have their Leagues. Miss Miller loved Latin, and if anyone ever referred to it as a dead language, she would retort, "When Latin dies, the world will die."

She had very lively Latin classes, because she was interested in the language and her students. She never spoke anything but Latin in the hallways at Forest. If Miss Miller addressed a student with, "Quid agis?" (How are you?) The student replied, "Bene!" (Good!)

She opened her classes with, "Salve." (Good Morning.) She closed with, "Vale." (Goodbye.) Latin lived and so did the Junior Classical League.

Miss Mary Bertrand at North Dallas High was a personality I could never forget. She always kept a handkerchief on her desk that matched whatever dress she was wearing — I thought this was real class. I also thought that she was a great English teacher. Some teachers have a knack for making a fairly dull study quite interesting. Miss Bertrand could do this. She guided us through the reading of *Beowulf*. Now, one must really be an Old English scholar to appreciate *Beowulf*, but somehow Miss Bertrand could make us — not exactly appreciate it — but certainly respect the writing. We were just getting to the part about the monstrous Grendel when Miss Bertrand became ill and a substitute came in for a week. Substitute teachers are never readily accepted, because even high school students dislike change. We called the substitute Grendel's mother. We couldn't wait for our real teacher to return.

The first exchange teacher to England from the United States in 1950 was Tezzie Johnson Cox. While in England this peerless teacher gave at least twenty-five lectures. She returned to continue her matchless teaching in the Dallas system. Aside from her teaching duties, she found time to serve on the Texas Commission of the Arts, and she continued lecturing on linguistics. In her fifty years of teaching she has produced some of the finest writers and rhetoricians to ever graduate from the Dallas schools.

The kids at Forest High could never forget Ruth Barham who was dear and understanding, and who always kept a needle and thread in her desk for emergencies that might occur. During World War II girls buttoned their underpants to keep them up. Rubber was scarce and was not used on the home front. Because elastic was not available, when a girl became unbuttoned, it was all over for her — immediate social disgrace. Nila Ruth Lynn Wilhelm remembers coming unbuttoned in Miss Barham's class.

"I just sat there. I couldn't get up. Miss Barham came over to my desk and asked me what was wrong. I told her, and she came to my rescue. Do you know she gave me a silver heart for my heart bracelet when I graduated? She loved me."

At the Forest Avenue High School Alumni Association meeting, Willie Mae Berry, home economics teacher, was introduced. Miss Berry was the first home economics teacher to offer a course in cooking to the men. It turned out to be a very popular course. All the guys thought they'd be better husbands if they knew their way around the kitchen. She told of the time that one group of boys put soap powder in the stew thinking they would serve the stew to another group. Miss Berry found out about the prank, turned the tables, and the culprits had to eat their own stew, soap powder and all.

Miss Berry was late to class one day, and during the same day she was asked to punish two of her students who were late. She announced to her class,

"I'm taking the blame for this. If the teacher is late, how can she blame the students if they are late? Henceforth, I will be on time." One of the students who escaped the punishment wrote Miss Berry a note which she kept among her souvenirs.

> There is one thing I have learned from this course. It can't be put into words, but one day a couple of boys and I skipped this period. Mr. Hutchinson found us and brought us back to you, and instead of bawling us out, you took the blame. I believe after that I appreciated you more, and it also put something into my heart that will never be forgotten.
>
> Joe Epps, 1945

Today Joe is Vice President, First Texas Savings Association.

Miss Berry had a heart, and she still does. When she addressed the alumni from Forest High, she said, "Thank you for being my children. If I did anything wrong to you, please forgive me. If I did anything good for you, then God be praised." Every good teacher holds this same feeling.

WHAT A CHARACTER

"Children, get under your desks!" This was the cry of Eunice Tilly, chemistry teacher at Adamson High. One of the students working with carbon tetrachloride had poured some of the mixture down the sink (mixing with something else), and there was a possibility of an explosion. Bob Johnston, who is secretary to the Board of Education, was a student in the class and remembers jumping under his desk. Nothing happened, but the class was not disappointed. Something *would* happen in Miss Tilley's class. It always did. There were rumors that she had a still operating in the back closet and was turning out white lightning by the gallon. There was the possibility that she'd mix up a stink bomb in the lab just to liven up the school a bit.

Bob remembers the day that Miss Tilley climbed upon her desk to open a window, fell, and broke her ankle. She called for help and Principal Bill Meek came to the rescue. Six years later when Bob returned to Adamson as a teacher there, he discovered that the story of Miss Tilley's fall had enlarged. The kids now related how Miss Tilley had climbed on her desk, had fallen out of the second-story window, and had broken everything. She called for help and Principal Bill Meek looked out of the window and saw her lying on the ground below half dead.

One never served a detention with Miss Tilley. One served Miss Tilley. If a student misbehaved or didn't finish an assignment, then he cut the grass in Miss Tilley's yard. This really wasn't so bad, because her yard was a chemistry lesson in itself. She didn't water her yard with the conventional hose or sprinkler. She had large cans that trapped the rain water, and then at dry periods glass siphoning tubes allowed the water to spread across the lawn.

An elongated car — the first Lincoln Continental ever made — 1941, V 12 engine, stuck out of Miss Tilley's 1930 garage, because in 1930 garage builders never dreamed that a car would be that big. She kept the back portion wrapped up in a tarp. Miss Tilly very seldom drove the car. She just liked owning it.

When the income tax was inflicted upon teachers, Miss Tilley protested *loudly*. In fact, she objected *publicly* on the trolley car that she boarded on Jefferson Boulevard to go home after school each day.

"I didn't work very hard today," she declared with great volume so that all the passengers could hear. "The salary for today's work went to the government, so I didn't put forth much effort." Come April 15th each year, and we all have a little of the Tilley feeling.

A geometry teacher of memory had a huge butcher knife. When the class looked like it was collectively dozing, *Zipp!* he would throw the knife into his desk. The flash of that blade and the *Bong!* of the knife as it lodged itself into the desk woke up any sleeping geometry student. What a character! However, every student who ever came out of his class passed the math section of the SAT test for college entrance.

An American history teacher allowed the students to throw paper into the wastebasket from their seats provided they hit the basket. If one missed, then one got a detention. When the class appeared to lose interest in American history the teacher stopped the class and asked for paper throwers.

The paper would hit or miss the can and the class continued. It was a rather pleasant break from a deep study of American history.

We had a character teaching Latin at North Dallas, Erma Griffin, whom we all called, "The Griffin." She was stern. In fact, I thought that she found pleasure in terrifying students. My dear friend, Mrs. Ruth Ann Albach felt challenged by her authoritarian personality. I didn't. I just sat and cowered in fear of Miss Griffin like the rest of the class.

When I was teaching speech at Dallas Baptist College, I had a student who could not speak before the class. One day he gave this excuse.

"I can't speak before a group because I was terrified by a Latin teacher in high school."

"Where did you go to high school?" I promptly asked.

"North Dallas."

"Miss Griffin?"

"You better believe it," he responded, smiling weakly.

"No wonder you're scared. She scared everyone," I assured him. Then I went on to tell my class about this man who was in my high school graduation class who was serving a life sentence in the state penitentiary for murder.

"He was obviously not afraid of the law, since he went out and committed murder. However, I remember, he never moved in Miss Griffin's class. He sat there petrified, terrified and intimidated like all the rest of us were."

However, I think that I still could translate Caesar, Cicero, and even Virgil if someone scared me into it. After all, Miss Griffin was paid to teach us, not to make friends with us. One of my classmates one day said to Miss Griffin,

"I just wanted to be friendly."

"I don't need any friends," retorted Miss Griffin. Deep down inside, I think she loved us all!

One of the reasons that Miss Griffin appeared so shockingly stern was the fact that we had all come from Alex W. Spence Junior High where we had studied Latin with Ann Cochran. Miss Cochran was and still is beautiful, charming, kind, loving, and every one of us girls wanted to be just like her. She was a direct contrast to Miss Griffin. When we went to North Dallas and changed Latin teachers, that change brought trauma to our lives and shock to our study of Latin. Actually, I must sincerely admit that dealing with this contrast prepared us for the realities of life we were soon to face.

Students read Dante's *Inferno* in Kathleen Witherspoon's class. She taught English at Sunset High. Her father was a Latin and Greek professor, and Kathleen never attended a school until she went to college. Her father instructed his daughter at home. She was a good writer as well as a good English teacher, and she was extremely creative. When it did come time for the class to read *The Inferno*, Miss Witherspoon turned out the lights, closed the windows, drew the shades, got a hell-like atmosphere in the room, and proceeded with the reading.

"If we're going to read about hell, we should go there!" she declared.

Dallas has had some character "voices" through the years. Ben A. Matthews, who was principal of South Oak Cliff High from 1952 to 1964, was known as the voice of the Cotton Bowl, because he reported those games regularly. Bill Melton, Sunset graduate, who is now Dallas's County Treasurer, is the Voice of the Cowboys. Then Dr. H.H. Johns, who is Coordinator of Foreign Languages for the DISD, is the voice of the Bison. At pep rallies, the Sunset Bison speaks. Dr. Johns gives a voice to the mascot that brings victories to the Sunset teams.

WAY BEYOND THE CALL OF DUTY . . .

Deane Labenski taught math forty-four years in the Dallas elementary schools. She told her class that she loved each and every student.

"I would do anything for you," she assured them.

One little boy raised his hand to question her. "What did you have in mind?"

What do students want from the teachers? What do the parents want? Teachers are getting bitter because of all the criticism. Frank Todd, who has been a band director in the schools for a number of years made this observation.

"We're doing a pretty good job. We have a before-school program when the kids come very early and eat breakfast. We teach them all day long. Then we have an after-school program where they are kept under supervision until they are picked up by their parents. What do they want us to do — go home and tuck them in?"

Down through the years, there have been teachers that have all but tucked in the kids. Many have run a wake-up service.

My dear friend, Shirley Pollard was afraid to go to Bonham Elementary School. Annie Laurie Connally went by Shirley's house every morning to assure Shirley that she would be missed if she didn't come to school. Shirley, like all the kids at Bonham adored Miss Connally. Every doll that Shirley had was named Annie Laurie.

Shirley's mother had a baby when we were seniors in high school which made Mrs. Pollard a lifetime member of the PTA. When John, the baby, went to school, Mrs. Pollard was a little older than most of the mothers. When she enrolled John at Bonham, one little boy in John's class noticed that Mrs. Pollard was a little older than the other mothers.

"You're mother is older."

"Yeah, but she's prettier. Besides, she's had a hard life." It's great to know that some children do recognize the fact that it's difficult to rear a child.

In fact, it's so difficult that Thomas Jefferson High School counselor, Edith Cooper, served as mother to many of the girls whose parents had given up on them. One mother called. "I can't get her to school. If you'll call her, Ms. Cooper, she'll come." The counselor was not only responsible for the counseling of the student, she had to get the student there in the first place.

And Daisy Webb always said, "I taught all the little Bonnies and Clydes in West Dallas." However, she gave them love and taught goodness and righteousness, so that they didn't turn out to be Bonnies and Clydes.

Those teachers who put their efforts in teaching the extremely poor children certainly went a step further than one can imagine.

Una Kirkpatrick watched poor Mexican children take their water from a pipe that was available to them downtown. Her heart broke when she saw this situation. She started a summer program in a tent for the children. She found food and milk donors. The children came to the tent for fun and food and a little learning.

Mary Doyle taught the poor and truly needy children at City Park School. The kids looked out of the window and saw the city close at hand. She taught art and the beauty of Dallas.

She instilled in them respect for the city even though the city hadn't really given them very much.

The teachers are called to muster up all the persuasive powers that they can. John Shanks, who served as principal of several schools and then acted as director of purchasing for the school district, said that he was lazy until Coach Doc Hayes got through with him. Doc got John and all the other lazy boys at Tech moving.

"We did well for Coach Hayes."

Many Dallas graduates like to give credit where credit is due. Betty Coe, owner of Coe's Office Supply, a small but booming business downtown, said that she was successful because Daisy Boude Miller and Maureen Horton at Woodrow Wilson High took time to give her some extra lessons in confidence building.

Mozelle Welch, who is library consultant in the library and media department of the Dallas schools, was inspired by "powerful" teachers at Tech, May Stephens Fuller, Anna Henderson, and Zoe McEvay.

Emily Dorsey, the daughter of the owner of Dallas' largest printing company, who taught at Colonial School, gave little remembrances to the children she taught. Louise McFarlin still has and cherishes the little book that Miss Dorsey gave to her with the personally written love message inside. Many Dallasites hold in their libraries little books that Emily Dorsey gave as special favors to her beloved students.

Irma Hall is a professional actress who has appeared in productions at Theatre Three, the Theatre Center, and the Dallas Summer musicals. She always gets rave reviews for her performances. Much of her time is spent on stage, but most of it is spent with her students at James Madison High. She's one of those people who seem to have a talent of getting the most out of every day, because one never sees Ms. Hall without an entourage of students following close behind. She takes them everywhere — plays, concerts, lectures. She has time to be a professional actress and also a professional teacher. When she can, she sees that some of her students gain parts in stage productions. Then the whole drama class from Madison comes to see their fellow classmates perform. The kids get learning and experience from Ms. Hall.

Mrs. Ethelyn M. Chisum, a Dallas native who left Dallas

just long enough to get a degree at Prairie View College, came back to be Dean of Students at Booker T. Washington. While serving as dean, she took a particular interest in one of the girls who in time did graduate from Booker T. High. The girl came back to work as attendance clerk. Mrs. Chisum saw the potential in this girl and found a way for her to go to college. The girl, Mrs. Nocie Mae Johnson, is now one of the fine teachers in the Dallas system.

Several of the young successful black teachers in the system now accredit their successful teaching careers to two "mamas" at Lincoln and Madison High Schools. These great ladies are Hazel Holloway and Lucille McGaughey. These two teachers not only taught school, but they "mothered" thousands of kids who came through the Dallas system. These women were the only mamas that some of the children knew well.

Frank Guzick, when principal in Rylie, went to all the other high schools at the end of the semester and gathered all the forgotten gym clothes and gym shoes. He'd get them cleaned and ready for the kids at Rylie who couldn't afford to buy gym clothes. Sweat shirts and tennis shoes forgotten in the North Dallas schools were luxury items for some of the children in Rylie.

Many children appreciate the attention that even punishment gives to them. They are ignored at home whereas at school, someone cares enough to correct their behavior. Principal C.L. Duke, "dusted the pants" of a little boy who after the spanking bowed his head and left the office. Then he looked back, blinked back the tears, and said, "Thank you."

Mr. Duke's daughter, Charlotte Ann Duke, has followed in the educational footsteps of her father. She received the Mayor's proclamation as an outstanding teacher of Dallas. Charlotte includes regular skating parties and tours of the city as part of her teaching plans. Her students are learning in and out of the classroom.

On a school night Evelyn Watts takes her class from Lida Hooe Elementary School to her small farm in Waxahachie. Here the kids get a once in a lifetime experience — they milk a cow. They spend the night on the farm, get up and do the necessary chores — fix breakfast, feed the animals, clean the house — and then they get back to school on time. She teaches them about another life-style. She also teaches them how to schedule their time.

Saturday is a sacred day to most teachers, but the speech and drama teachers consider it a regular work day. So often they attend debate tournaments, hold play rehearsals, or attend one act play contests. Helen Butler who taught speech and drama for many years at North Dallas is now Instructional Specialist in Drama for the DISD. She spends many Saturdays with her drama teachers and their students as they prepare for play contests and festivals.

There are teachers who sponsor special organizations, and this sponsorship takes so much extra time. A teaching team, Mr. and Mrs. Alexander, Mike and Rosemary, never watch the clock when it comes to their school activities. Mike is a teacher at J.N. Erwin. He established the first Boy Scout Troop at that school, and Mike prepared his troop for the National Jubilee in Washington, D.C. This troop was the first black troop to attend the jubilee, and while they were there, they received national recognition for their efficiency as a troop. This group from J.N. Erwin is always on the go. They take field trips and plan all sorts of outings together. Rosemary, a teacher of remedial reading at David W. Carter High, helps Mike with the troop whenever she can.

Ms. Dede Green was selected as the outstanding Earth and Science teacher in Texas, 1979. She was not able to take her students at J.L. Long out on field trips, so she brought the field trips to the school. She had a load of dirt with fossils hauled to the school yard, and there, without leaving J.L. Long Junior High, the students could make some archeological discoveries.

At Tom C. Gooch Elementary School every morning at 7:40 A.M., Dr. Ann Kieschnick, principal, greeted her students as they got off the bus. She knew that the little ones would be frightened and even somewhat disoriented after a bus ride, so she made certain that every child saw a happy, familiar face when they arrived at school. All during the school day she stressed that the school belonged to the children. They should take care of it.

This year Ross Perot, founder of Electronic Data Systems, awarded some money and much recognition to several outstanding teachers in the Dallas system. One of these outstanding teachers was Deborah Stafford, an art teacher at H. Grady Spruce High School. This teacher had shown great interest in a girl whom she felt had much potential. However, the girl appeared to have a drug problem. The teacher did all she could to find out about the girl, her parents, her friends. She questioned the girl. She wanted so much to help free her of any possible drug problem. The teacher gave her time, was ready to spend money, really do anything to give this girl a chance to become an outstanding student and citizen. What she didn't know was that the girl was an undercover agent working with the Dallas Police Department to locate and bring to justice any drug dealers. The police honored this teacher as well as Ross Perot.

Duane Trammell, my student at Dallas Baptist College, was also selected as an outstanding teacher in the DISD, 1983. This young and creative teacher is known to stop at nothing to make his students think creatively. He even dresses in costume occasionally. The students take note, and they learn.

The financial rewards are slim, but there are those intangible rewards that teachers receive that no one else could ever receive. Miss Ruby Stevenson, who called herself a "fixture" at Ben Milam Elementary School, couldn't go out of the house without someone rushing up to her and saying, "Oh, Miss Ruby, I'd never forget you." Those are grand words to hear. And what's more, they're true. Teachers are not forgotten.

DALLAS CLASSROOM TEACHER ASSOCIATION

World War I was shaking the nation to its very foundation and thousands of teachers were leaving the profession to engage in war work and other more remunerative professions. Yet a handful of public spirited elementary teachers rose above these difficulties and held the first meeting of the Dallas Grade Teachers Conference. This was the Fall of 1917.

That first meeting was called to order by Miss Myrtle Richardson. She stated that the purpose of the organization was to "relieve stress in the teaching profession by raising salaries to a living wage." At that time the minimum salary for a teacher was $650 a year. The maximum was $950 a year. This maximum was for one who had thirteen years experience.

When Lela Lee Williams was elected president in 1918 there were certain rules set up. The dues were ten cents a month and each elementary school was to have a representative in the organization. Also, the teachers that year launched a well-planned publicity program to give the public the facts about the teacher salaries. Several mass meetings were called and the climax came with a parade staged by the schools in which *twenty-five thousand* children took part. The march must have impressed the public, because the proposed bond issue carried by the greatest majority ever recorded in Dallas up to that time. Immediately following, the Board of Education established a new salary schedule of $1,266 minimum wage and $1,700 maximum wage. There was to be an annual increase of $70. This scale remained in force for many years.

The group not only worked for better pay but also fostered a spirit of good will and helpfulness among the teachers. They wanted to raise their professional efficiency and promote the welfare of the public schools. At the annual luncheon held February 14, 1925, at the Stonleigh Terrace Hotel, several of Dallas's most outstanding citizens were present. These men definitely supported public education — Alex Sanger, Edward Titche, J.J. Taylor and Mayor Blaylock.

The depression brought, of course, the bad news that the salaries were going to be cut four- and one-sixth percent. But there was good news. The Teacher's Credit Union was established and the final passage of the Teacher Retirement Amendment was passed.

The group enlarged during World War II, and in 1944 it was called Dallas Classroom Teachers Association. The teachers all pitched in during the war and purchased $366,452.50 worth of War Bonds.

The teachers began to speak out. In the late forties, Mrs. Tezzie Johnson Cox directed a radio show, "The Teacher Speaks," that was broadcast statewide. Dallas was the scene of the Texas State Teachers Association Convention.

The group was strong enough to meet the demands of the fifties when the nation stopped to evaluate the educational system. The group went through the tumult of the sixties with the drug problems and the change in moral codes. They faced the integration problem of the seventies, and now are steeling themselves for all the criticism that has befallen education today. Merit pay is also a big issue. But the teachers will make it. Like the Psalmist said, "I have a goodly heritage." The teachers have a very goodly heritage.

Chapter Eleven

The Golden Years

What high school principal ever said *No* to a movie queen? What high school principal ever *had* an opportunity to say no to a movie queen? Dr. W.T. White did. Linda Darnell was a student at Sunset High School in the early forties, when she was discovered by a talent scout and whisked off to Hollywood. She became an overnight sensation playing the gorgeous Amber, in the movie *Forever Amber*. Linda, always a beautiful child, had modeled in the Dallas area. Mrs. Eunice Gillett designed patterns for Higginbothams, and she often used "the little Darnell girl" as a model.

After making a sensational start in Hollywood, Linda wanted to come back to Sunset and receive her diploma. She called Dr. White, her principal, and asked if she might graduate with her class. Dr. White said, "No! Graduation night is a big night for the graduates.

"She would have ruined the graduation for everyone else. No one would remember anything except that Linda Darnell was there. I mailed the diploma to her."

Later, Linda did return to Dallas to allow her friends to grovel at her feet. Her story was a typical story of the forties and Hollywood. Girls were "discovered," they became stars, they came home to adoring fans who fawned over them until they got the prized trophy, an autographed picture.

As principal, Dr. White reigned over Sunset as an exalted czar. He was so proud of that school, many said that when he walked through the halls, the buttons almost popped off his shirt. H.S. Griffin, principal, administrator, and close friend of Dr. White's, said that were he to write a book about the principal, he'd name it, "The Tender Tyrant." Thousands of people are better off today because they knew and worked with Dr. White. Students received so much from this grand schoolman.

Another possible title for a book about W.T. White would be "The Skipper From Cowhouse Creek," because it was on the banks of Cowhouse Creek, Hamilton County, that Warren Travis White spent his childhood. His great grandfather on his mother's side served with Sam Houston at the Battle of San Jacinto. His grandfather on his father's side claimed kinship with Cherokees in the Smoky Mountains.

W.T. White started teaching in a rural school in 1913 and by 1917, he was principal at Bugscuffle, Texas. He took off from his rural school to serve as a first lieutenant in the field artillery in World War I. He also married a beautiful girl that same year.

He continued his educational career as principal of a school in Wichita Falls, superintendent of schools in Fairview, Texas, principal again in Wichita Falls, and then superintendent of schools in Bonham, Texas. Sam Rayburn, the grand man of Bonham, Texas, was a personal friend. Then in 1931, he came to be principal of Sunset High School where he served until 1945 when he became superintendent of Schools.

"I helped push Dr. Crozier through 'Fat Man's Misery' and he made me principal of Sunset," recalled Dr. White. At one of the school administrators conventions Dr. White met Dr. Norman Crozier. One convention was held in Kentucky where Dr. Crozier and Dr. White took a side trip to Mammoth Cave. On the trip through the cave, the visitors saw a huge underground lake. Then they continued to a place where the levels changed. It was called Fat Man's Misery, because a fat man couldn't go through it very well. Dr. Crozier was a large man, and he attempted to go through. Dr. White was below the large superintendent, and he pushed hard on Crozier's leg and got him through. They became good friends right there in the cave, and when Sunset needed a principal, Dr. Crozier decided that the young man who pushed him through Fat Man's Misery should have the job.

"He offered me $4,500 a year in 1931, and I took it."

There were 2,600 students at Sunset the year Dr. White arrived. There was also a fine group of teachers, but no assistant principal. The system couldn't afford one. So, Counselor Pauline Warner, and Dean Virginia Durrett, with Dr. White, made certain that the school ran smoothly. Dr. White loves to recall his days at Sunset.

"The social life centered around the gym. We'd charge the students fifty cents a couple to come to the dances. The stag men had to pay seventy-five cents. After all, a stag was using someone else's date to do his dancing. The sandwiches were a dime."

At Sunset under the rule of Dr. White, there was a place for everything, and everything was always in its place — except in the physics lab. Mr. R.C. Pantermuehl never kept a neat physics lab. This bothered Dr. White at first. He walked into the lab and frowned at the disarray.

"You're going to get this all in order?" Mr. Pantermuehl left everything out for the students to pick up, handle, experiment with, investigate, and use.

"If everything were behind glass doors, no one would touch anything. This way, they finger the equipment. They investigate. I can teach so much better, because the students have made a thorough investigation of all the equipment."

Dr. White never spoke again of the lab. It stayed the way the teacher wanted it to be — available.

The faculty at Sunset was handpicked by Dr. White. There was Miss Ruth Baker. She was the mythology expert. Hattie Lee Hornback, whose father was president of Trinity University, was a world traveler.

"In those days, a trip to Europe was something that not everyone could have, so the students were not always exposed to teachers who had been to places that were studied about in the texts. The Hornback students got firsthand stories from a lady who had been there." Sarah Dinsmore was another teacher who had "read everything." Her father was a federal judge, and she had been exposed to learning and literature all of her life. She eagerly shared all this learning with the kids at Sunset.

The study of science was important to Dr. White. Ruth Morris taught chemistry. Many claim that from her chemistry lab emerged more young men who went on to medical school than from any other chemistry lab in the city.

"Miss Morris knew more than the book." At times, she did. She held the honor of Fellow of the National Academy of Science. Anyone with that honor could easily pick up an error in the chemistry text.

Mr. Nelson Hutto kept all the journalism students hopping. They reported on all the activities that were occurring at Sunset — all happening under the steerage of the "Skipper" of Cowhouse Creek.

In 1945 the city of Dallas was going to grow. With all the industry brought here by the war, and all the industry that the city fathers knew was coming, Dallas couldn't do anything else but get bigger and bigger. The educational system was going to enlarge quickly, and a man was needed to see that the quality of education was going to keep up with the enrollment. That man was chosen — W.T. White.

He assumed the superintendency in 1945 when there were GIs camped out on the lawn of the Veterans Hospital on Lancaster Road, because there was such a housing shortage. There was nowhere for the vets and their families to go. Those war babies were ready for school, and some of them poured into tiny little Lisbon School. Dr. White called Ruben Schmitt to be principal there. Portable rooms were brought in. Mr. Schmitt assumed the responsibility of finding classrooms and teachers for this sudden influx of small students.

Anson Jones School was quickly built for the kids that belonged to the LTV employees who also poured into Dallas. Wanda Barnett was assigned as principal.

"I didn't know I was principal until I read it in the paper. That's the way we found out about our assignments. I checked on the whereabouts of the school. I had the address, I drove out to the school, and the school wasn't there. I checked the address again. There was nothing at that address but a vacant lot. I didn't want to disturb Dr. White with such a small detail as a missing school that was going to accommodate several hundred students in a few weeks, so I called Dr. Walker. He and I went to survey the lot. Dr. Walker suggested that we not tell Dr. White."

"We'll have a school here by next week," Dr. Walker assured me. Portable classrooms were brought in, parents were called to help arrange the classes, teachers who were assigned to the school came to help. Miss Barnett got the offices all in order, and in one week Anson Jones school was there. Of course, a permanent building was built that year, but until then, the instant school served the educational purpose.

The growth seemed endless. Hundreds of postwar families settled in the Hillcrest area, so elementary schools sprang up all over that section to accommodate the children from these families. Also, there were many Jewish families moving into that area. Temple Emanu-El sponsored their coming. In fact, the rabbis invited the teachers of these new elementary schools to a banquet at the Temple. After the dinner the Jewish parents talked to these teachers about their religion, their families, their homeland, and about their being there in the first place. These parents wanted to establish a close relationship with the teachers, so that they, like Jewish people all through history have done, could get the most out of education for themselves and their children.

Dr. White watched over all this growth that was going to bring on the golden age of public education. Just as he had been as a principal, he continued to be as the superintendent — a stickler for details and one bound by rules.

Principal Tom Coleman was prowling around in an antique shop and spied an apple crate. It was a genuine antique apple crate, so it carried with it a genuine antique price. Tom thought,

"I wonder if Dr. White would have accepted this now treasured apple crate. Probably not!"

Dr. White was a precise, formal, structured, and exacting Superintendent of Schools who wrote a book on policy which stated emphatically that apple crates made deplorable bookcases in the classroom and that he never wanted to see one in a school used as such.

"Apple crates are an abomination to us all!" stated the academic leader. Books belonged on shelves, not in something that was used by fruit vendors.

There were certain regulations that went along with the

name W.T. White, and every administrator who served him was well-aware of every policy. In order to continue as an administrator, one had to take an annual test over the policy book. No one ever failed the test, because no one ever dared to take the test unless he or she was prepared with the correct answers. The apple crate rule showed how much appearance meant to the superintendent, how much control he had over the school system, and how much respect was given to him. His first concern was for the well-being of the students and the teachers. He felt that they deserved the very best, and apple crates were not the best. Smiles come across the faces of anyone who has ever worked with Dr. White when the words apple crate are mentioned.

Smiles also appear with the words scotch tape, hats, coat and tie, and candles. All these words remind people of rules. One did not put anything up in the classrooms, halls, administration building with scotch tape. In fact, when something was to be hung on the wall, approval came from a higher source. Nothing was stuck up without deliberate consideration. Everything was planned, and when the final decision was made as to where something was to be hung, Mr. Harold Burford, (head of all maintenance) was called in to do the final hanging. There were procedures in the White administration, and those procedures were remembered and honored during the entire time that Dr. White was at the helm.

Whenever a gentleman had desires of becoming a principal, he would go to see Dr. White personally, hat in hand. It didn't matter whether the prospective principal wore the hat or not, he just had to have one in his hand. Dr. White liked hats. The *chapeau* represented the finishing touch to any ensemble, and Dr. White wanted his personnel complete in every way. The hat wasn't the issue. It was the public showing that the man made — following the demands of the top man to the nth degree even if it meant buying a hat.

No gentleman ever went to see Dr. White without wearing a coat and tie. No gentleman ever entered the administration building without wearing a coat and tie. No coat and tie ever hung on the back of a chair — it hung on the man. Professionalism was the watchword.

H.S. Griffin, principal of Sunset from 1959–1968, jested, "I might leave the house without my trousers, but you could rest assured that I'd have on my coat and tie."

Mr. Griffin was at the administration building one Saturday morning without a coat and tie, knew that the superintendent was in his office, and knew that he didn't want to run into his leader. Still he needed to talk with Dr. White, so he phoned him.

"Where are you?" asked the superintendent.

"I'm around the corner."

"Then come in."

"I don't have on my coat and tie."

"Oh, then I'll come to you."

Whenever a dinner was planned at the schools, there were no candles on the tables. Dr. White watched out for the safety of the students, and candles were not safe. Some teachers decided that Dr. White just didn't like candles. There was no safety issue.

Certainly not all of the principals were men. There were girl principals, and that's what Dr. White called them, his "girl" principals. The girls presented a program for him once, and Dr. Mary Anna Brady wrote a parody of a song for them to sing, "We Enjoy Being *His* Girls." The chorus line included Pauline James, Frances Allen, Mary Anna Brady, Robbie Lee Mays, Wanda Barnett, and Wilma Stewart. Like the men with their coats, ties and hats, the girls had their Dr. White dresses — special attire selected just for him.

Meetings with Dr. White were very formal, and no one was ever late. There were four publications published for these administrators to follow: *Plan of Action, General Information, Policy and Procedure,* and *Curriculum in Action.* If an administrator stuck with these four rule books, then there were no problems in leadership. The morale was always high and the spirits reached peaks when at the end of meetings the group would always sing together. Dr. White opened every meeting with his favorite song, *The Eyes of Texas.* He closed the meetings with *Blest Be the Tie that Binds.*

Interest in his people didn't stop at school. Dr. White was involved in the personal lives of his school folk. He was a matchmaker. A special luncheon was planned at Sunset High by Dr. White. His guest was Colonel Bill Ackerman, ROTC officer. Margaret Boone, the home economics teacher, planned and cooked the food for the luncheon to perfection. It was during this luncheon that Dr. White realized that he had an opportunity to play cupid. He drew out the bow and sharpened his arrow. Miss Boone was still in the kitchen. Dr. White rushed out to her.

"Quick. Comb your hair and put on some lipstick and get to the dining room. I want to you meet someone."

In the dining room Dr. White introduced his good friend, Colonel Ackerman to one of his favorite girls, Margaret Boone. It wasn't long after that luncheon that Colonel Ackerman and Miss Boone were married.

Aside from playing cupid, Dr. White loved to play golf. A foursome which included Dr. White and P.C. Cobb, director of athletics, went out for a round of golf. P.C. was playing a terrible game, and Dr.White was aware of it. Cobb couldn't get his mind on the game, because that evening South Oak Cliff was playing Sunset, and the rivalry between the two schools sometimes caused unwanted trouble between the students. Such trouble could erupt that evening, and Mr. Cobb was thinking of that trouble rather than of golf. In the middle of the game, the group alternated partners, and Dr. White realized that he was stuck with P.C. Cobb for a partner. Dr. White never liked to lose, so before the round started he sternly warned his athletic director,

"P.C., forget about South Oak Cliff and Sunset for two hours, and concentrate on *this* game."
In the office he was a schoolman, but on the golf course he was a hard player and a sore loser.

Typical of the feelings held in southern cities during the fifties, Dallas held to very conservative attitudes. Conservatism prevailed in the hiring of Dallas teachers. Catholic teachers who might apply in the Dallas system were urged to seek teaching positions in the Catholic schools. The great majority of students were White Anglo Saxon Protestants, so WASP teachers dominated the schools.

Also, a graduate from a university outside the state of Texas was urged to go elsewhere for a teaching job. Coming from an outside state could bring some "foreign ideas" to the children of Texas.

This watchful hiring of WASPs was not a Dallas procedure, but rather an old southern convention. Dallas was not a large city until the fifties, and just like other southern towns the natives wanted only "their kind." Strangers were under suspicion.

Formal attitude abounded in every area during the W.T. White days. The superintendent even had the name of a school changed to make it all more formal. *Davy* Crockett School was changed to *David* Crockett. If a school bore the name of an honored person, then with Dr. White the full name was used. One did not teach at Spence. One taught at Alex W. Spence Junior High.

Always the *Bible* scholar, Dr. White used the example of Moses, leader of God's people. Moses followed the advise of Jethro, and it paid off. Always hire capable and loyal advisors — deputy superintendents in the case of Dr. White. He brought in the best assistant superintendents. As the school system grew, he turned more and more over to these dedicated assistant administrators.

The good years hit a sour note in the early fifties. The House Un-American Activities Committee strengthened its crusade against communism. Loyalty pledges were signed by the faculty members, and everyone was warned to beware of "Pinkos." Now, Americans realize that instead of worrying about communistic infiltration so much, we should have been more concerned about the advancement of Russian scientific knowledge and about those people in our midst who were not WASPs, for the happy days of the fifties were brusquely interrupted by diverse events of the year, 1957. That was the year that inflation got its foot into the door. President Eisenhower proposed the biggest peacetime budget in the history of the nation, $72,000,000,000. Both Republicans and Democrats worked together to cut it back, but that was not done. People were concerned about nuclear testing and the threat of radioactive fallout. We were constantly reassured that there was no danger, but still there was always a reason for doubt.

Later in the year, however, two events occurred of such magnitude that they made any other issue of national concern appear almost trivial. On September 4, 1957, the Governor of Arkansas refused to comply with the federal law and used force to prevent the racial integration of Central High School in Little Rock. All eyes focused on this defiance of federal authority. The nation watched on television with rapt attention the military escort that was used to protect the black children from a threatening mob as they entered the school. Then on September 9, 1957, President Eisenhower signed the first civil rights bill in eighty-seven years.

The next month, October 5, the Russians launched the first artificial earth satellite and a month later followed it with a second, heavier and more impressive "Sputnik." Americans knew Russia was ahead in scientific technology. They also knew that America would have to catch up and surpass the Soviets. On December 6, a United States rocket carrying a grapefruit-size satellite exploded on the launching pad at Cape Canaveral. What was to restore our prestige in the scientific world didn't get off the ground. It all looked pretty grim.

What happened to the United States? No longer Number One? The first thing that President Eisenhower did was to announce an extensive program to upgrade America's rocket technology. The citizen tax payers gave an affirmative nod to this, but science still had to find a scapegoat. They finally decided that the whole problem stemmed from the educational system. It was the schools! Those kids weren't learning anything. That's why we were behind! The children were just playing around. The school system needed reorganization, and, of course, the reorganization began.

That critical year the Dallas School Board agreed to work even harder than ever to deal with the taxes, the budget, and the ever increasing population of school children. The voters saw fit to return all incumbent members to the board so that experience was there in R.B. Gilmore, R.L. Dillard, Jr., Van Lamm, Mrs. Tracy H. Rutherford, Edwin L. Ripy, M.D., Franklin E. Spafford, Mrs. Vernon D. Ingram, Rouse Howell, and W.A. Blair.

Dr. W.T. White came up with the High Academic Aptitude Group Plan. This plan would extend the learning span and give more challenge to the high academic students. These students would be in an honors group and would be taught by teachers that were carefully and thoughtfully selected. The junior highs were included in the program. Now, these high academic students would only be in honors classes for the basic subjects, English, science, math, history, but for the other subjects, they would be scheduled into the regular program. Dr. White assured all parents that calling attention to the high academic group would in no way lessen the effort of the school system to give every educable child the best possible opportunity for his complete growth and development. Dr. White promised a tightening up of all classes.

The fine thing about the honors program was its flexibility. When a student qualified to enter the program, he could. Always, it was the grades and the industrious and energetic attitudes that remained the key factors that got a student into or out of the high academic group.

In the elementary schools, the top twenty percent of the pupils were grouped in certain honors classes. Their teachers were selected especially to deal with these classes whose members ranked higher than average academically.

Dr. White said that this was not a crash program. It had been under consideration for a number of years. But, the sudden realization that the Soviet Union was surpassing the country would make any good educational plan come to the foreground quickly. Superintendent White noted,

> This plan challenges the pupil by putting him on his own merits, abilities, and industry. It should go far in relieving the reported boredom of students, because their courses were slowed down by slow learners. It will spotlight the bright youngster who is not, for some reason, achieving to the top of his ability. It permits the school system to work with greater efficiency.

The new plan first touched the science department. Since 1951, science had been taught in all twelve grades. It was required in the first eight grades, and then two years of science in high school were required in order to graduate. That would stay the same, except the course of study for the elementary grades changed to include an elementary approach to astronomy, geology, biology, electronics, physics, and chemistry. There were more courses offered in the senior highs, so that actually a student could take thirteen years of science in twelve years of schooling.

Then, of course, the science fair came into existence. Every year students from all over the city of Dallas entered scientific projects. Prizes for the most technical experiments were awarded. Scholarships were given to the students who actually made scientific discoveries. Our nation was planning to top Russia right there from the Dallas Convention Center where all the winning entries from the various schools were assembled and shown to the public.

The announcement that my children had to have science fair projects brought immediate and continuing trauma to my life. I was a speech and drama teacher, my husband was a musician, and now every year for the next eight years, we had to think of two science fair projects — one project per kid. My son was one grade behind the daughter, but he couldn't inherit her project because they always had the same teachers. My children were no help with the projects, because they had gotten all the non-scientific genes, and they could only bring home the assignment for the project and stand beside me and say, "Think, mom. Think."

I will admit that the projects for the first grade were easy, but after that they were impossible. God helped me with my daughter's first grade science fair project, because a bird's egg fell out of a nest in the tree in our back yard. The *Bible* says that God knows when a sparrow falls, and I always felt like He arranged for this egg to drop at my feet so Jill would have a project. We glued the egg on a piece of cardboard, and she printed neatly, "The Beginning." The project was accepted. I had a fear that the teacher would ask Jill which came first — the bird or the egg, and I'd be in big trouble if I had to answer that. Fortunately that teacher was wise and stayed away from questions about eggs in the first grade.

For my son's first project, he glued a Hot Wheels car to a wooden board, made a gas pump out of cardboard and printed a little sign, *This is what makes us go.* His project was chosen to represent the first grade from Umphrey Lee at the convention center. He had won because of neatness. That helped me in my thinking for the next year. If neatness counted, I'd have a chance.

However, because neatness didn't count in the second grade and because second grade science was way beyond my comprehension, the children and I were forced to go to the library. Before we left for the library, I thought that we could just put a sweet potato in a jar. That's pretty scientific, but Jill said that it had been done in the first grade. There was nothing left but the library and prayer that maybe God would let — not an egg — but an entire sparrow fall. (Dissected — with all the organs labeled. No such luck.)

In all the science fair years, my husband never helped but once. He offered his tuning fork when Jill was in the fifth grade. That was terrific. Of course! a study of sound waves would be perfect. We got some material from the library on sound waves and really put together a nifty little entry showing how sound left a radio and traveled right into our ears. Her project didn't place though. Some smart kid had made a radio.

In this push for scientific achievement, someone said that all students should be taught advanced science. Dr. White, a man after my own heart, responded, "This is a myth, because all students are not mentally equipped to take advanced science."

My kids weren't equipped for science — period. It was such a relief to get them into high school and into the band program. Forcing band candy on the neighbors was so much easier than dreaming up science fair projects.

The mathematics curriculum was stepped up. The little ones in the first grade learned to court, learned to make figures, and learned to identify figures with objects. This had always been the course of study for the first grade. However, the first grade course was the only one that stayed the same. All through the other grades the program was expanded to include more problem solving. Added math courses were offered in the high school, so actually, a senior (if he wished) could take college freshman math. Usually the high school curriculum stopped with trigonometry. Now, calculus was offered.

I was always a fairly good math student. In fact, I was better than the average, and this got me into trouble once. When I was in my senior year at North Dallas, I took the college preparatory course of study. This included four years of math, so solid geometry and trigonometry were taken by students planning to go to college. All of us seniors were in Mr. Arthur Harris's trig class. We loved Mr. Harris and got to know him really well, because he always rode the school bus home with us. We never could figure how he got on the bus before any of the kids did in the afternoons. We certainly wasted no time getting out of school and on to the bus, but still he was always on first. Finally, we decided that with his mathematical mind he had discovered the shortest distance between two points, his room and the bus, and we hadn't found it yet.

My friend, Virginia Alexander, sat next to me in trig class.

She really never understood trig well, even though she was an intelligent girl. Sines and cosines were not within her subjective comprehension. She was enlightened on other subjects, but she was in the dark with trig. During a test she gave me a look of desperation and hopelessness that also carried with it a plea for help. I had no choice. I had to help Virginia. So, before I turned in my paper, I made a duplicate copy of it and slipped it to her. No one had seen me hand over the perfectly worked problems. Well, Virginia didn't have a sneaky criminal mind, because when she finished copying my paper, she threw it into the trash can. I didn't know this. I only knew that I had done well on the test, and I thought I had done well for Virginia. Just before the last bell rang that day, I was summoned into the office. There was Virginia. We were both to report to Mr. Harris. Like typical criminals we didn't look at each other. We only went to his room. There he sat with the evidence straight out of the trash can. Being a true-blue friend, I immediately stated that I hadn't copied Virginia.

"I know you didn't. But, remember, the one who keeps the motor running while the other is robbing the bank is just as much at fault."

Those words have stayed with me for thirty-five years. I knew then and there that I would never rob a bank, never keep a motor running, and never help anyone on a trig test again. Today Virginia is a fine Christian mother and wife, Mrs. Kenneth Broughton, and as far as I know she has never robbed a bank and has never again copied a trig test.

Under Dr. White's high achievement plan, the library was to become a learning nerve center at all levels of education. It had been predicted that with the advent of television, children might stop reading. This was not true according to the report of 1957. This was the year the question was asked, "Why can't Johnny read?" According to the library report Johnny *could* read and was *reading more* than ever in the DISD. Book fairs were celebrated that year, and this was a much easier fair for parents than the science fair. This fair was conducted by the librarian, and she did all the work. The children just came and examined all the new books and learned about them and their authors. In the elementary schools, the children would dress up like their favorite fictional characters. Nevertheless, the children were reading.

The big furor in the school system in 1957 developed over just how the children were taught to read in the first place. *Dick and Jane* had been around for a long time. The Dick and Jane stories were from the Scott Foresman Publishers' series of readers that taught reading by the sight of the words. That was why Spot was driven to jump so much. The child learned the words by repeating them over and over.

"Jump, Spot. Jump, jump, jump."
A group of teachers led by the master teacher Annie Laurie Connally felt that teaching reading by sight vocabulary was the best way.

However, there was another method of teaching reading that was being considered. This was through phonics, the sounding out of the letters to form the words. Houghton Mifflin Publishers created a series of readers about Tip and Mitten that favored phonics. Faye Catledge led the group that believed the teaching of reading by phonics was the only way. There was a heated debate between the two groups, and finally phonics won. *Tip And Mitten* replaced *Dick And Jane*. There was also a primer used, *Baby Ray*. Baby Ray had playmates, Will and May, and to find out just what they were all doing, the children had to sound out the words. Frances Allen, who was assistant superintendent of Early Childhood Education, felt that teaching phonics was the best method, but she felt it was always good to mix in a little sight vocabulary as well. If a child could learn a short sentence by just memorizing the words, it would give him a feeling of instant accomplishment. Sounding out the words could get tedious in time. Mrs. Allen suggested that teachers offer a short, easy sentence occasionally for fun.

"Look, Spot. Look, look, look."
Then after that the child was ready to tackle anything that Tip and Mitten might have going.

In 1957, when the public became critical of the schools and the supposed lack of good teaching, these critics at once wanted to cut out the so-called frill courses in the high schools. In the first place, electives were not frills, and in the second place, were vital to the lives of certain students. Besides, that honor student was always going to make certain that he had time for what he wanted and what he needed. The other students needed electives to guide them to career choices.

There was nothing frilly about the debate topic in 1957: Resolved, the direct United States economic aid to individual countries should be limited to technical assistance and disaster relief. The speech and debate students had to learn both sides of this vital question. A debate course has always been the best training ground for any student wishing to study law.

Girls wanting to seek careers as dieticians, gourmet cooks, or dress designers needed a course in home economics. In order to complete a project in dress design, the student so often would need to recall some algebra. The basics are part of the electives.

Miss Marion Flagg, music supervisor, brought together in that year of 1957 an almost unbelievable number of children from widely divergent school backgrounds to give a concert at the convention center. Miss Flagg did not do this to promote her music courses. She assumed that everyone thought music was mandatory in a student's life. She did this to bring to the public a fantastic showing of musical skill and art. Every choir in the city came together to sing. There were a dozen pianos playing for the voices and Miss Flagg conducted the whole thing. To be in a musical production such as this a student needed to have strict discipline of mind and body. This concert was a training ground for a well-disciplined and productive life.

Dr. White promised the citizens of Dallas that everything that possibly could be done was being done to educate the youth. He pledged that the DISD would continue to give each child the very best educational climate. The honors classes would make certain that fine minds were being challenged. The superintendent held to his philosophy that the school was only an extension of the home, and it would never try to take over the functions of the home. That would be impossible. He pointed out that creative discipline would be applied. Punishment would be given only to make certain that the child would learn from his mistakes. Harsh punishment that would cause a child to lose all interest in learning was not proper. Tests would be given to measure progress and to prompt further learning. Every child would become a self-reliant individual, a productive and successful workman in his chosen field of endeavor, and a good citizen of his country.

Dr. White's promises took care of educating children to enter the race for space. However, the integration problem was yet to be experienced in Texas.

SKYLINE HIGH SCHOOL

Sitting in his office twirling his Phi Beta Kappa key, Dr. White in 1964 came up with an idea that not only changed the educational concept in Dallas, but also made a mark on the nation's big scholastic blackboard. The superintendent was nearing retirement age, but he certainly wasn't going to drift leisurely through the last years of his service. He could do this so easily, because *Success* was written all over the results of his work as superintendent. Why should he start something new when the old was doing so well? Because Dr. White knew that innovations and new beginnings kept the old alive and brought on new perspectives. He also embraced the teaching of philosopher Will James,

"The greatest use of a life is to spend it for something that will outlive it."

So, wanting to step further into academic creativeness, he inaugurated, not only a new plan, but an entirely new school. Because Dallas continued the great growth eastward, a new high school was needed in that area. However, this high school was going to be very different. It wouldn't be just a school, a place to study. It was going to be a place to study in depth a student's area of special interest.

A steering committee was appointed by the school board, and the idea was put into the hands of the public. Trade organizations were sent questionnaires asking about the various areas where employment was needed. The Chamber of Commerce's Educational Committee and Forecast was asked to help in the planning of this new school. Presidents of companies representing major business and industrial interests in the Dallas area were invited to send representatives to discuss their manpower and educational needs. These representatives were grouped into eighteen occupational interest areas, and they then advised what training areas should be established in the new school. The Texas Educational Agency was consulted. A committee of school administrators visited outstanding schools over the nation to get ideas for facilities and curriculum. All of this information was rolled up and presented to Dr.

White and the board. Soon after, the intricate, detailed plans were on the drawing board.

The distinguishing feature of the school would be the providing for extensive preparation in a selected area of opportunity without the sacrificing of the college entrance requirements. The question, "Why go to school?" would be answered. The student would come out of high school ready for employment or ready for college or ready for both. It was all up to him.

This all sounded so good on paper, especially to the students of the sixties. Quite frequently the kids were beginning to question the reasons for attending school. The parents, too, had some inquiries.

Would this school be available only to those living in East Dallas? No, it was to be open to anyone in Dallas. Would it become a dumping grounds for those who couldn't make it anywhere else? No, there were two qualifications. The student had to have a definite educational goal and he had to have the ability to accomplish the goal. What about Crozier Tech? Wasn't that school supposed to offer all the vocational courses? This school was a step further. There would be more vocational opportunities. Also, there would be standardized tests used in the entrance procedure. The probability of success in the chosen field would be the major detriment in the acceptance of the student.

The questions poured in. This school was something *new*. People beg for something new and then they look at it with suspicion when it comes. This happened at Skyline High, the name given to the new complex. The business community had complained about the students sent to them. Now they would have better prepared workers, but they raised some eyebrows and frowned apprehensively over the whole thing.

What about athletics? They would exist to bring spirit to the school. The school would have teams just like the other high schools. Students transferring would be eligible to play on the teams.

When a student came with a particular goal in mind, could he ever change the goal? Yes, but this change could affect the level of achievement that might be attained.

Would there be foreign languages? Yes, a language laboratory was included. The study of every language would be made according to student request.

When would the complex open? September 1970, would be the grand opening.

Actually the grand opening of Skyline High School and Career Development Center has really never ceased to be. Guests from all over the world come to Dallas to see this plant that sits on a vast eighty acres. Principal B.J. Stamps opened the door of the school that featured the new cluster organization. A student spent half a day in academic work and half a day in his selected area. He could spend one-half a day with the basics at his "home" high school, and then ride the bus to Skyline for the selected area of study. The clusters included agriculture, automotive technology, aviation, beauty culture, building trades, business education, food preparation and service, electronics, garment manufacturing, graphic arts, health occupation, vocational plastics, metal trades, airconditioning and heating, wood industries, creative arts, vocational homemaking, technical music, optics, and television production.

Today, the school has twenty-four clusters and opportunities that are not offered anywhere else. It's there for the taking.

There are two complete math labs equipped with calculators and computers. When those labs opened, words like computers — data processors — were not even in the vocabulary much less in the labs. The school has kept up with the technology. There are science labs with the latest equipment.

From the homemaking cluster students come ready for employment in day-care centers, nursery schools, hospitals, and private homes.

From the agriculture cluster come the florists, landscapers, and those going into the gardening industries. The greenhouse is a prominent feature of the school.

There are mechanics and diesel mechanics. Specialized facilities are provided.

The aviation cluster provides a combination of airframe and power plant training. One learns the technical skills necessary to repair and overhaul aircraft.

The beauty culture students have two labs with all the latest equipment. The students are qualified for the state board examination that enables them to become registered cosmetologists.

There is ironwork, carpentry, glazing, plumbing, commer-

cial and residential electricity installation, carpet and lino-
leum laying, and bricklaying.

At Skyline one enters the world of construction, fashion,
manufacturing, photographic arts, hotel and motel management, and architecture. There's no limit.

Today, Frank Guzick is the principal of the high school. He
addressed his students, Fall, 1983.

"There will be no belly buttons showing here at Skyline
High." He meant that the girls would not wear halters and low
slung jeans. The guys would have shirts that were long enough
to cover the upper torso. The students would look good, would
act properly, and would learn to study as directed by the large
faculty of this nationally famous high school.

"We've never had an *incident* here at Skyline, and we
never will." After the assembly the schoolday started for students that came from the east, west, north, and south of the
city to enter a specific program of study. They can all leave
with a career if they wish.

Principal Frank Guzick, when he entered the Dallas system, first taught at Adamson. He came to love the school and
the Leopards. He'd lead loud cheers for Adamson, especially
when they played their arch enemies, the Sunset Bisons.

Then he was transferred to Sunset — enemy territory. In
the hall at Sunset High proudly hangs a Bison's head. It was
customary each year just before the Adamson and Sunset game
for a sneaky group of Adamson students to steal the Bison
head. It was not only sneaky but daring, and somehow a brazen
Leopard would enter Sunset High and get the Bison head.
After that first Adamson and Sunset football game that Mr.
Guzick attended as a teacher at Sunset, not Adamson, the
Bison head was absconded. The head was found in a field behind Sunset full of grassburrs and looking pretty bedraggled.
Principal H.S. Griffin had purchased that particular head from
an antique shop in Sunset, Texas. It was rather ironic that the
Sunset Bison came from Sunset, Texas, so Mr. Griffin was par-
ticularly attached to that buffalo. He asked Mr. Guzick to comb
and groom the head so that it could be rehung in the hallway.
Frank lovingly and patiently took each grassburr from the
woolly head, thinking the whole time of how last year he had
led yells for the Leopards and jeers against the very head that

now he was painstakingly grooming. Frank Guzick loved the kids. He loved them at Adamson and Sunset.

Later Frank Guzick was sent to Rylie Junior High as principal. Here he took care of the students and really ministered to everyone in this small community. He called himself "The law south of Loop 12." He was counselor not only to the kids but really turned out to be father confessor to the whole community helping in marital problems of parents. One of his teachers commented, "He heard confessions regularly from the whole community, not just the kids."

This was pretty good — for a fine Jewish men to serve as the father confessor of a predominately protestant community. Today, Mr. Guzick spends his whole day, of course, at the school. Then his evenings are devoted to the extracurricular activities that evolve from this vast educational plant. It's not unusual for the sedate and composed principal to be stopped by a parent who readily and proudly shares a success story of his son or daughter who had been former students of Frank Guzick. Naturally the principal is just as proud as the parent.

There are nine languages spoken and taught at Skyline. In fact, there are students from India, China, Cambodia, Vietnam, Lebanon, and Korea. The halls can have an international look at times when they all get together. Mr. Guzick noted that these Eastern students are very motivated toward math and science, and that they take every possible advantage of the science labs and computer systems, the learning tools of the school. There is the HILC, High Intensity Learning Center, for those who qualify for study that takes them beyond the high school level.

One of the teachers at Skyline, Dr. Martha Williams reflected the attitude of the faculty there. She, like her principal, teaches all day, and then spends many evenings with the students in their extracurricular activities that lead them to more learning and better career choices.

The opportunities are there. The amount of learning all depends on the amount of time and effort the students wish to give to their studies. And all of this is there because of a dream that Dr. W.T. White had in 1964 and because of the action taken by his creative school board that was led by Robert Folsom.

What is Dr. White doing today? He's answering the phone

to calls that should be made to the school, W.T. White High. Some people are not aware that there is a real W.T. White. He mentioned that someone will meet him and say,

"Are you *THE* W.T. White?"

He's teaching a Sunday School class at Oak Cliff Christian Church, a class that he has been teaching since 1931. He's still wearing super snappy-brimmed hats. He's still handsome and still a charmer with the ladies.

One lady walked into his Sunday School class just recently wearing a flat red hat. Dr. White teased,

"What's that? A Boomerang?"

Her eyes rolled up and she shook her head.

"When you've been in Dr. White's Sunday School class for fifty-three years, you take his comments without a comment."

Frances, his daughter, is in control of some of his actions.

"Sit down, daddy. We're ready to start the lesson."

The class opens with the singing of *We're Bound for the Promised Land*. Then Dr. White rises to teach the class. Before he teaches, the birthday people in the class are recognized. He gives each birthday person a dollar bill. He's been doing that for fifty-three years. Inflation has never increased the amount.

Dr. White would like to visit Greece. When he was a student he had a teacher who made ancient history live. He always wanted to visit the land he had studied about.

The retired superintendent loves to talk about his son, W.T. White, Jr., who is a school administrator for the Fort Worth Schools. He loves to talk about his grandson, Jay Ward, who happens to be a former student of mine at Dallas Baptist College.

Jay was born with one of these deep, rolling voices, so naturally he went into radio broadcasting. He worked for WRR Radio while a student, and then moved to KMEZ Radio. Jay now writes for KMEZ rather than broadcasts. The pity of this career change lies in the fact that Jay still has a deep, rolling voice. However, he prefers to write rather than speak.

When Jay was in high school at Kimball, he was working all night at WRR. He was often late to school. "Bill Durrett was an easy guy to handle. I'd come in late. He'd stop me, and then I'd immediately get him to talking about the football team at Kimball. He'd relive some game right there in the hall and forget about my being late."

Dr. White loves to tell of Jay's first day at school. "He came home not wanting to print. He claimed it was sissy. He told the teacher that he didn't need to learn to write. 'I'll have a secretary to do my writing. Besides, my grandfather can't write his name so that anyone can read it, and he's the superintendent of schools.'"

When Dr. White retired the tributes poured in. Lee McShan, Jr., who served as president of the school board from 1966–1968 said,

"He is one of the world's greatest educators and one of my dearest friends — I am thankful for both."

Marvin Berkeley, who was president of the School Board, when Dr. White retired, said,

"Whatever one might say about Dr. White, there appears to be a dominant trait that always comes through — that is, perseverance or dedication."

On Wednesday, August 28, 1968, Dr. White conducted his last meeting of the School Board. Dr. Berkeley pronounced the benediction, and at 2:47 P.M., Dr. W.T. White adjourned the meeting with the sound of the gavel and a softly uttered *Amen*!

Chapter Twelve

Tumultuous Years — Yet, Interesting

After twenty-three years of service as Superintendent of Schools in Dallas, Dr. W.T. White drove away from the administration building on Ross Avenue in his fine, gleaming gray Cadillac with the plush seats and the private phone, and the new superintendent, Dr. Nolen Estes, drove up to the administration building with his large six foot six frame crammed into a weathered Volkswagon. The vast differences in the automobiles driven by the two men easily showed the contrast in their personalities and the differences that were to be in their administrations. Gone were the days of the coat, tie, hat, and the tight ship. Coming were the days of shirt-sleeves, loosened ties, windblown longer hair, federal funding and many innovative new programs.

Dr. Estes was only thirty-eight years old when he arrived, but he had an impressive array of educational achievements. He had been a public school teacher in Bruni, Texas, at the age of nineteen. This was before he received his bachelors degree at the University of Corpus Christi. He was the first intern under a creative new program in school administration at The University of Texas in 1953–54. This was where he received his master's degree in education. He attended Baylor University as a graduate student, but he received his Doctorate of Education from Harvard University in 1959. He was an elementary teacher for one year, a principal for two years, and an assistant superintendent for six years. He went to Washington to serve in the United States Office of Education. He rose to the position of Associate Commissioner of the Bureau of Elementary and Secondary Education, before he came to Dallas.

"My entire career and training were aimed at the large city superintendency," stated Dallas's new administrator.

Dr. Estes made known that he was going to act as a "caretaker" for one year, and then he was going to work on six innovations that he felt were needed to make necessary the "quantum jumps" in education in Dallas. There would eventually be early childhood education or kindergartens, individualized instruction, occupational training, teacher training by the public schools, after-schoolhours programs, and a positive treatment of students' cultural differences.

Since Dr. Estes had been in Washington administering the innovative PACE program (Project to Advance Creativity in Education) under the Title II of the Elementary and Secondary Education Act, it was small wonder that when he came to Dallas he would bring with him the Washington influence. He came from a world of acronyms, so it was not long before in Dallas there was PEP, PIF, SAC, and PAC — programs that would involve hundreds of people and millions of dollars in federal funds. However, these programs were all a part of the swing in the nation's thinking. Where once everything was localized and controlled by one individual, the undercurrent was pulling toward strong and influential committees with powerful chairmen. Where once citizens looked at any federal control and funding with suspicious eyes, with rising costs they were welcoming all that the Washington bureaucrats could offer. Dr. Estes knew where the funds were in Washington, and he set out to get as much as he could for Dallas. More and more he was going to give his large staff control of things, and he was going to sit as the impresario overseeing the whole operation.

He felt that the students should get a "piece of the action," so there was SAC (Student Advisory Committee.) Whereas Dr. White knew and loved his students, counseled them, and served as a fine father image, the much younger Estes planned to give them the ball and let them "run with it."

Dallas was represented in the State Association of Student Councils where the student met with other council members from all over the state.

"We'll form our own district-wide student council organization with regular meetings, retreats, and worthwhile workshops."

There was to be a Student Curriculum Committee. Whereas in the past the students were told what they would study, now they were going to get a chance to select their own curriculums.

"Such a committee of students would bring a different and important view to our efforts, and perhaps would raise some questions we have not considered."
The committee could review exactly what was being offered in the classroom and make suggestions for change.

"I can also envision a Youth Service Corps — a corps made up of student volunteers who would be involved in a variety of school and civic activities. For example, I can see students helping provide day-care for underprivileged children and their working mothers — or organizing and conducting clean up campaigns or serving as tour guides throughout the city."

Student volunteers could also be used as tutors. "The major responsibility of any school system is to teach, of course, and the major responsibility of any student body is to learn. But educational research has taught us in the past few years that students can and often do a superior job of teaching too."

He spoke of making a film about student involvement that would be produced in Dallas. A governmental grant could be obtained for such a purpose. All these special projects that were federally funded needed special departments just to handle the projects. Soon they were all set up.

All this student involvement came at a time when the students were demanding it anyway. The days of "learn this" were over. The days of "why this?" were moving more and more into the educational societies. Dr. Estes seemed to have the answers to the needs of the restless and demanding students of the sixties.

PEP (Pilot Educational Program) was brought to Dallas. With this came an instant $73,000 of federal funds. In this program teachers were told that they were agents of change, not victims of change. They would have professional growth programs.

New periodicals came from the Ross Avenue offices for the administrators and the teachers, so that they could keep up with all that was being done. They applauded a new District Communication Committee. Teachers would register complaints with the members of the committee who would then see the superintendent about the teacher grievances.

A whole new department was created for the administration of kindergartens. Studies were conducted to find the proper model for the Dallas kindergartens. The little ones needed to develop good self-concepts. They needed language stimulation, especially those who couldn't speak English.

Summer schools got a working over as far as curriculum was concerned. "How to Study" was a course offered. Conversational French, creative writing, arts and crafts, physical education were soon to be included with all the basics.

The "Learn and Earn" program was brought in with a new Vocational Industrial Educational Director.

"Individual differences" were the primary concern. Each child was to be studied and dealt with in a specialized manner. Children were freed of regular schedules. The talented ones worked out of the classrooms, and there was a wide variety of exploratory experience. Choice of electives was made on the basis of intensity of purpose and aptitude. There were varied written assignments all stressing creativity. There was career exploration in all fields.

All of this was only the beginning. In the first year of Dr. Estes's administration there were forty-eight projects underway, all with administrators, chairmen, committee members, and federal funds. In one day, with one innovation, a thousand people were involved.

There were other distinctive and specific programs to come with an administrator for each one. A counseling program that dealt with the using of a male counselor in the elementary schools was forthcoming. An Innovation Coordinator for Industrial Education was appointed. The Dallas system became a free enterprise system for the teachers. If a teacher could think of something new and different in teaching, then that teacher could go on with the plan. A Sunset High biology teacher was used as a coordinator with the Museum of Natural

History at the Fair Park. There was a cultural exchange between the high schools. A teacher at Bryan Adams wrote his own textbook.

There was a lot of encouragement in these plans coming from the universities, because during these restless hippie years, the universities were anxious to study and test all the new theories. They were looking into theories on behavioral change, on perceptual stimulus, on self appraisal approaches to learning. The teachers not only had to tell what they were going to teach, but they also had to list the behavioral changes that would occur when they taught.

Television has had more power than any other media in the history of the world. It became a powerful tool in education. Each year while Dr. White was superintendent, he called his teachers together at the Convention Center for a formal convocation. Dr. Estes had his teachers gather at their schools and he spoke to them on television. Some teachers felt that they were cut off from the man who was making so many changes in their lives and in the lives of the students.

Regardless, Dr. Estes was in Dallas with three major challenges. First, he dealt with a restless bunch of kids who were not satisfied with the conventional type school. Second, some of these restless kids were involved in drugs. Drugs were deadly and illegal. Third, he faced a federal judge who handed him a desegregation order. Dr. Estes worked diligently with these problems, tried to solve them in the best way he could, and then he came up with some problems of his own dealing with the misuse of funds.

The parents of the kids of the sixties grew up in a very concrete atmosphere. There were certain established rules that were never broken. I know, because I was there. We abided by the rules set down for us, and we waited patiently to grow up so that we could get out from under the rules and do a few things.

I grew up asking for permission to do *anything*. I'd ask, and I'd get the stock answer, "Wait until you're older." Well, I'd wait a while and then I'd ask the same question. "Wait until you're older," came the reply. I waited and waited. When I was finally older, the whole sociological pattern changed, and the youth were dominating society and I had never gotten to do what it was that I was asking to do. Now I do something, and my daughter says, "Mother, you're too old to do that." I'm still waiting for my moment.

"Student rights" and "Generation gap" became familiar phrases during the sixties. They went together. We, the choiceless generation, were so successful in our drab, dull, concrete existence that we parented a bunch of kids who had everything. We gave it to them before they even asked. We were sometimes overly permissive, so the youth of America made demands, asked questions, and didn't always accept the answers that they got.

Parents in the meantime, began to look at the schools, and they decided that maybe the kids were right. There should be more educational choices. Thus, the reform movement commonly referred to as the alternative or optional educational program was offered to a society of parents and students who demanded a choice. A Gallup Poll conducted in 1973 reported that sixty-two percent of parents and eighty percent of professional educators felt that providing options for students was a good idea. The magnet schools provided the option.

MAGNET SCHOOLS

Basic skills of reading, writing, arithmetic, and the so-called competencies necessary to promote further learning must be acquired in the elementary grades. Talent identification and cultivation, whether it be in the sciences, humanities, or the arts, must start in the elementary grades and climax in the high school years. We must accept the fact that every person has a talent which can lead that person to a career which is financially and psychologically rewarding. When this happens the person can perform in a mature adult role and feel good about himself.

This process has been going on since the beginning of time, because people find careers and function in them. Those first graduates of the Dallas schools found careers and successfully succeeded in them. However, education is always looking for new ways to promote learning, so in the middle seventies the leading administrators didn't think that the conventional schools were dealing effectively with all the human diversity. It was time to bring in a "new type school."

There could be an arts school located in an art's complex

where the students could easily meet and draw from the city's artists — singers, actors, dancers.

Why not a school in the midst of a medical district where doctors, nutritionists, and researchers could become a part of the faculty?

Could a school which centered on the study of business benefit from being in the heart of the city's business district? This thought was investigated.

In 1976 four so-called magnet schools were opened. To expedite the development of these first four magnet high schools, the career clusters located at the Skyline Career Development Center were moved to the magnet schools. These students were core groups and then later 6,000 applications were received and about 4,000 students enrolled in the magnet program. This was amazing, since there really had not been too much time to promote the program in the first place. Nevertheless, the program was initiated. The idea stemmed from a sociological need for choice for the students and parents.

The Business Magnet opened first. This was housed in the old Crozier Technical High School on Bryan, the site of the first high school in Dallas, now in the heart of downtown. The program at this school began with an orientation to the basics of the business world that was taught by teachers and working professionals. Students could specialize in accounting, data processing, typing and shorthand. Later courses in marketing and management were taught. There was training in advertising, apparel and accessories, finance and credit, travel and tourism. During the senior year the students would have on the job training.

The Transportation Institute was located in a former automotive facility at 2200 Ross. The school included a repair center with the latest equipment. Roger Meier, Cadillac dealer, observed,

> It's a comprehensive classroom laboratory and on the job training program designed for students who are interested in the sale and marketing, mechanics and service, or rebuilding of motor vehicles, and will permit them to specialize in the field of their choice.

John Murchison, big businessman and patron of the arts, stated,

> We are tremendously excited by the potential for the Creative Arts Academy in Dallas, and are particularly pleased by the possibility of having Paul Baker, one of the nation's foremost theatre directors, direct this curriculum. We cannot imagine a finer opportunity for Dallas youth to train and learn in the field of creative arts.

At the old Booker T. Washington High School the Arts Magnet opened and grew. Today the school is teaching art, music, theatre and dance to students all over Dallas. Many students are paying tuition to come to this school from other school districts.

The last magnet to open in 1976 was the Health and Science Magnet. The place for this school wasn't even selected when the district knew that it had to open in just a few weeks. When the place was found a large staff got it ready in twenty-four hours.

"With the critical shortage of medical and dental support personnel, thousands of positions are open today requiring trained professionals at all skill levels," pointed out Boone Powell, director of Baylor Medical Center. The medical careers program included a thorough course in basic anatomy and physiology taught by a registered M.D. This would make way for the study in medical laboratory work, disease analysis, physical therapy, and nurse science.

Pat Kidd is coordinator of this cluster. She holds a bachelors and masters in science. Dr. Juretta Horton, Ph.D. is in charge of the cardiac laboratory. Veterinarian Bonnie Raphael teachers classes in veterinarian medicine, and then her students go on for internship at the Dallas Zoo. The students also have opportunities for work in the department of human resources. Dallas native and graduate of Forest Avenue High, Dr. Murial Brahinsky, teaches anatomy, physiology, pathology. She sends her students to medical schools and nursing schools. She commented,

> My students are ready for further study in medicine when they go to college. There are those that go on to work in the hospitals. It all depends on what they wish to do.

After the first year of developing these magnets, two additional magnets opened, the Government and Law Magnet and the Human Service Center. The Government and Law magnet prepared the student to be a police officer, a law clerk, political scientist, attorney, parole officer, court clerk. The Human Services Center prepared the student to be a counselor, a psychologist, a day care nursery teacher, youth worker, athletic coach, social worker, teacher, recreational director.

The next year, the William B. Carrell School opened as a magnet center for handicapped students.

From the 1976 bond issue came the Lincoln Humanities and Communications Magnet where students interested in languages, journalism and communications attend. Then the science and engineering magnet was built for students planning to be computer designers, programmers, systems analysts.

These are the current magnets, however, there are changes in the making. The Board of Education decided, Tuesday, December 13, 1983, that six of the district's career education programs at Skyline Career Development Center and the magnet high schools will be moved to the new Townview Center in northern Oak Cliff. The Business Center, the Health Magnet, the Human Services Magnet, Government and Law Magnet, Science and Engineering and Technology Magnet, along with the newer magnets, Talented and Gifted and the Academic Center, will all be moved to the Townview Center. The decision was made to consolidate all magnet and career programs offering the specialized curriculums at four sites: Skyline, Lincoln, the Booker T. Washington Arts Magnet, and Townview, the new facility to be constructed. Skyline will continue to provide the district's largest variety of career development opportunities.

Of course, all this hinges upon the sale of the Business Magnet in the heart of Dallas. The School Board report stated,

"The proposed facility on the twenty acre Townview site should become a jewel in the DISD's long list of special programs."

There is always an extensive recruitment program developed to attract students to these magnets and all the special education that they offer. When one considers what they offer, one might ask,

"Why would you need to recruit students into such advantages?" It would seem that students would be clamoring to enter these schools where there are facilities that private schools could never offer, and yet the enrollment in the Dallas schools dropped considerably after the magnet program was offered. It was just what parents and students wanted — a chance to pick and choose the course of study.

The magnet concept got directly linked with integration and it had a counter effect. Unfortunately the emphasis went to the attempt of racially balancing that school, rather than going to the quality of the program at the school. When Skyline opened in the fall of 1970, choice of education was the issue. When the magnet program came about in 1976, racial balance was the issue. This has hurt both races.

It's going to take time to build public confidence back into public education. The students will have to firmly believe that the best education is offered by the Dallas schools. Parents will have to be involved and will have to know exactly what is going on at the school. The word will have to get around that there are very competent teachers at these schools and that the community better give them respect for their intelligence. Bad behavior on the part of a student must mean instant expulsion. Teachers are not guards — they're teachers. Students must get it into their heads that one must *earn* a free education.

THEY USE TO CALL IT MISCHIEF

Dr. Estes came at a time when change in the curriculum was demanded. He gave the city schools that change. He came at a time when some parents demanded dress codes, others didn't. The strict discipline of the public schools was challenged by the parents who didn't seem able to discipline their own children. He came at a time when students found their desires for pleasures satisfied not at the proms or the football games, but in drugs, a *deadly* way to satisfy a desire.

Years ago, people on drugs were called "dope fiends." No one was concerned about these miserable creatures — old and hopeless. Their bodies and minds were deteriorated by the years and by the use of drugs. But, now the handsome and beautiful youth of America seemed to be needing overly exciting and exotic moments, and they were finding these moments in drugs.

Youth on drugs was — and still is — one of the serious problems in our country. The problems of the students in past years seemed inconsequential to what the drug culture was doing to the students, parents, and communities of today. Yesterday's problems could be solved!

"They're Dancing with Tears in Their Eyes."
This was the headline in the *Dallas Times Herald*, January 16, 1931, City Section. Two Oak Cliff High School girls were working in the evening at a dance hall, charging the depression price of *Ten Cents a Dance*, as the song said. The police arrested them because they were underage for dance halls. A rather loud argument erupted when one customer refused to pay, the police were called, and this was how these minors were discovered engaged in what was a major profession of the thirties. The girls planned to get an attorney, stating that they needed the job desperately. They had no money.

Passing the pocket flask around for a quick swallow of the forbidden liquor happened some on the school grounds. After all, the prohibiton days were over, and the evil drink could be purchased. However, parents were informed immediately of any drinking and the problem was nipped in the bud, before there were too many nips from the flask. Besides, at school or anywhere else, drinking was not the acceptable behavior of the popular group of kids, so there was not too much of a problem in the first place.

Being tardy, playing hooky, chewing tobacco, and smoking behind the gym were the sins most frequently committed in the early days of the Dallas school system, and actually playing hooky was by far the worst of the ones mentioned.

Frank Jordan and Clifford Perkins, now successful Dallas businessmen, left Forest Avenue High one morning on a fine fall Friday of 1923, to go to the football game in Waco. They knew that they were going to have to serve fifty detentions each when they returned, but they didn't care. A detention was a forty-five minute stay after school. When the boys returned, Frank suffered an acute appendectomy, and he never had to serve his detentions. The men are friends today, and Clifford still has never really forgiven Frank for getting sick, since Clifford, who came back hale and hearty, had to serve his detentions.

Chewing tobacco was prohibited, but since so many teachers themselves chewed, the punishment was often light. The classroom windows had been washed and shined unbeknownst to a certain history teacher at Bryan High in 1916. He thought

the windows were open and turned from his class to spit the
slimy tobacco juice out the window right on to Bryan Street.
Splat! It went right on the clean window. Now this teacher
would have had trouble sending a chewing student to the office
for punishment.

Gum was a menace. Ladies were not supposed to chew gum
in the first place much less stick a wad on the marble statues at
North Dallas High. Because the students stuck gum to the bottom sides of the desks, sides of walls, insides of lockers, and various other sites, the students were forbidden to chew gum.

Detention halls were really not so bad in the early days,
because there was always some new and creative way of making mischief. The sharpest minds in the schools were the ones
usually "kept in." The presence of an ink bottle offered a good
source of devilment. A student would casually pass by the ink
bottle, drop an Alka-Seltzer into the bottle, return unnoticed to
his desk, and the prankster with the detention hall could
watch the ink fizz over onto the teacher's desk. Also a couple of
marbles rolling down the aisle of the study hall offered some
more diversion from the drab minutes spent in detention hall.

Mrs. Pat Zang, whose family opened a fancy residential
section in Oak Cliff, recalled with a twinkle in her eyes the
days of the gang fights. The Oak Lawn boys would tangle with
the Oak Cliff boys in a friendly scuffle that might be called a
gang war, but the entanglements never led to anything serious. However, a gang did evolve during the forties that made
headlines. This gang was called the Lakewood Rats, and all the
members attended Woodrow Wilson High. The Rats were the
sons of prominent East Dallas families, and there is still controversy as to whether they were mischievous, mean, or actually criminal. The controversy remains because these Lakewood Rats are now Dallas leaders — prominent businessmen.
Some will smile and wink about their high school activities.
Others will not claim membership to the gang since there was
a question as to whether the Rats were just active little rascals
looking for a little fun or mean guys with intent to harm.

They stole cars. Or rather they moved cars around the city,
so that owners had to hunt for them. They'd walk into Sammy's
Restaurant on Greenville, order almost everything on the
menu, and then leave before the waitress brought out the huge
order. Mr. Sammy Massino, owner, complained, and it looked

like he was going to get a little nasty about the situation and take some action against their behavior. So, for meanness or for malice, they took watermelons from the watermelon stand on the corner of Greenville and Ross, and plastered the front of Sammy's Restaurant with the juicy fruit. To this day Mr. Messino doesn't have a good word for the Rats. In fact, his testimony against them is on a tape that is part of the oral history collection in the Lakewood Library.

School buses in the early days were a great spot for shenanigans. The guys would bring screwdrivers with them on the bus and attack every visible screw until the entire insides of the bus could be lifted out. All of the seats, bars, windows, heating vents were loosened by the time all the kids had been bused home. At North Dallas we lost our bus because of active screwdrivers. When the boys apologized and promised never to bring screwdrivers to school, we were once again provided transportation.

When the senior class at Forest Avenue High looked out of the east window of Miss Ruth Barham's class, they could view most of Fair Park. On a spring day just before graduation she turned to her class to remind them of their school years.

"Remember, class, these are your halcyon days."
And they were. High school days use to be calm and peaceful. Sure, there were a few gang wars, a truant student, a discovered flask. However, these were small concerns to parents and educators compared to the problem that has stolen into our educational and social scene today — the drug traffic.

The first notice of this problem came out in a headline of the *Dallas Morning News,* January 31, 1951, "Five Year Term Given Dealer in Marijuana." The police racket squad led an investigation of the report that there was marijuana smoking in the schools. At that time they found no evidence, but still, the very thought of the presence of a hallucinatory drug on a school campus was appalling.

Approximately two years later the *Dallas News* reported, February 12, 1953, "Addict Tells Why Youth Takes Drugs." Seventeen youths in the Dallas schools had access to and had taken goofballs. The article quoted a student,

"I first got fixed (a term used to identify the actual taking of a drug or goofball) on a Benzedrine inhaler at fifteen. It made me feel good."

A parenthetical explanation and definition had to be given in the paper for the word *fix*, for in 1953 the average reading public would not have known that meaning for the word. The young man quoted in the article was a student in the Dallas schools, he was from a prominent Dallas family, and he confessed to buying one hundred goofballs for four dollars. The police were optimistic about the whole affair. The Chief of Police said,

"If we can get this one ringleader, the seller, the menace will be over."

The police got the one, but it wasn't over. It was only the beginning. The drug culture that started in the colleges in the early fifties seeped into the high schools, so that by the sixties there were groups of students who continued to "get high on drugs." They "did their own thing," and they "let it all hang out." Those students who were found to be on drugs were expelled from public school immediately.

Many of these *dropouts*, a word that entered Webster's Dictionary in 1958, came from very prominent families, the so-called "straight" people of Dallas. Very proper fathers had sired these children who claimed they needed drugs to get through the day and who decided that school was a waste of time. These parents could not accept the fact that their children were not going to finish high school and were not going on to fine universities as planned. The public schools would not let them back in under any circumstances, so many private schools sprung up to accommodate these students. The private schools provided a haven for those who could not conform to the strict rules laid down by the public schools of Dallas. These kids had been expelled because of drug usage, truancy, behavioral problems that kept them out of the public schools. The student at the private schools was in complete charge of his or her own study. These "freedom" schools offered lessons that had to do with liberation struggles, the evils of a capitalistic economy and political system. There were no bells ringing, no scheduling, no dress code, and the students had the final say on the curriculum. The students came in jeans, barefooted with long hair, but at least they came to school.

Some parents protested against the public schools for their

strict policies on drugs and also on dress. These private schools surfaced as reaction to the constraints of the public schools. There were many articles in the papers about fathers who were infuriated when sons were sent home because of their improper dress and hair length. The improper dress was definitely associated with improper behavior, and the school system held on to the strict rules as long as it could. However, as society loosened its feelings toward the detached, unstrung behavior that was taking over, the schools had to relax, slacken, and curb their reign.

Most of those private schools that opened in the sixties are open today, but there is a total and complete reversal in the feelings of their administrators and teachers. The parents and the students come with totally different motives. These schools now serve parents who think that the public schools are *not* strict enough. In these private schools there are strict rules about tardiness, class attendence, dress, and certainly the use of drugs. A student with a history of drug usage is *not* allowed to enroll. Conformity is the watchword, and these schools are drawing the brilliant kids whose parents are concerned about the *lack* of discipline they feel exists in the public schools.

Of course, these private schools are also drawing the upper middle class kids whose parents would not allow them to attend the highly integrated Dallas schools.

JUDGE WILLIAM TAYLOR

"May I point out that, contrary to popular belief, federal judges do not particularly enjoy telling school people how to run their business," stated Judge William M. Taylor Jr., the federal judge, who beginning in October, 1970, became personally involved in the DISD when a multi-ethnic group of citizens, on behalf of their children, filed a class action suit seeking legal help under the Fourteenth Amendment for what they considered to be segregated schools. There were months of hearings and the submission of many plans by the school system, the plaintiffs, and outside experts. Finally, in August, 1971, Judge Taylor issued an order that called for transportation of students in the high school for integration and the use of television, field trips, and social events for the integration of children in the elementary grades. The euphemism "transportation" was used in place of "busing," the more controversial term. That August day brought screams and protests from both black and white parents.

We whites in the Southwest Oak Cliff area met with our black neighbors and political leaders to discuss the plan and to hope that our area would be left out of such an order since we were integrating naturally. However, our pleas were not heard. The terms of the plan appeared to us that the white children would be bused to black schools and the black children would be bused to white schools and integration would occur as they waved to each other when the buses passed each other.

Our meetings went unnoticed and our suggestions went unheard, so our neighborhood became almost black overnight. The houses were new, the people stood to lose very little equity, so the white owners sold immediately and went to the suburbs. The enrollment of white students in the spring of 1971 was 94,544 students. In the spring of 1972, the figure read, 85,631, a drop of approximately 9,000 white children in one year.

Judge Taylor became actively involved in the desegregation which started long before 1971. It started in 1954, three years before the Little Rock happening. The Brown decision, a decision which struck down the separate-but-equal concept, was included in the Texas State Law. In the early sixties the Dallas schools began to integrate by adopting the neighborhood concept in a year-by-year, stairstep fashion. First grade black children who lived in the district of a certain school, be it black or white, would go to that school. The next year the first and second grade black children would attend the school in their district. The next year, the third grade black children were included in the plan. This would continue until the whole system was integrated racially. However, an order from the federal government was issued. The whole plan had to be telescoped into two years, so by September, 1965, single attendance zones were established for all elementary schools, and the seniors in black high schools were enrolled in previously all-white senior highs. The faculties were integrated in 1966, and dual attendance zones were eliminated for junior and senior high schools. So, by September, 1967, there were no black and white — that is *dual* — attendance zones. However, there was little racial integration in the schools, because the residential areas were highly segregated. It was then in 1970 that the class action suit was filed, and the busing order followed in 1971.

Now, the other part of that 1971 order which included field trips, social activities, and television programs dealing with racial understanding was immediately appealed by the plaintiffs and stayed by the fifth Circuit Court of Appeals in New Orleans.

Nevertheless, that September, 1971, 7,300 junior and senior high students boarded buses and the Dallas system began implementing a plan which would last for four years. There was a drop of 28,000 white students out of the district in those four years.

In July, 1975, the Fifth Circuit Court sent the original order back, and Judge Taylor vowed that he would do the best for Dallas.

> I would be less than candid if I did not admit that, during these early years of busing in Dallas, I was somewhat disappointed and concerned about the lack of commitment toward carrying out the orders of the court. Now, don't misinterpret that to mean that people were not obeying the law of the land, for they were. But there was a great lack of enthusiasm, to say the least.

The NAACP submitted their plan. This plan was designed to bring the ethnic composition of every school district to within ten percent of the district ethnic composition. This would include the busing of 40,000 students.

Acting upon this in 1975, Judge Taylor called together the members of the Dallas Chamber of Commerce Alliance Education Task Force to participate in the court hearings. This multi-ethnic group had received a private grant to help in the finding of an acceptable integration plan. The group was visiting other cities and was looking for creative ways in which the district could be desegregated. The group came up with a plan in early 1976, the one that Judge Taylor accepted with a few changes.

In the meantime, Dr. Josiah C. Hall, a retired superintendent of schools from Dade County, Florida, was appointed by Judge Taylor as a consultant to help draft a desegregation program. Dr. Hall's desegregation plan proposed dividing the district into three catagories: naturally integrated, paired and clustered areas, and predominantly minority areas. The schools that were naturally integrated would keep the students assigned to that school. The predominantly white schools would be paired and clustered with schools in predominately minority areas. This plan would involve the busing of 23,000 students, two-thirds of whom were black. The elementary school children — regardless of race — took the brunt of the busing.

The alliance had a plan which would cut the city into five pie-shaped attendance areas of about 30,000 students each. The east Oak Cliff area would remain predominantly black.

Finally on April 7, 1976, Judge Taylor issued the Dallas School Desegregation Order. The school district would be divided into six subdistricts, four of which, Northeast, Northwest, Southeast, and Southwest, would show an ethnic population of plus or minus five percent. There would be vanguard schools for grades four through six, academies for grades seven through eight. The kindergarten through third grade would not be bused. These would be early childhood centers. There was a majority to minority transfer program that would be encouraged. A white student choosing to attend an all-black school was not required to attend school on Friday. Busing was free, and the promise of improving the buildings and facilities remained. The DISD would focus much of its interest, funding, and activity in the predominately East Oak Cliff area.

The magnet schools were created to hopefully desegregate the white areas. The success of these magnet schools was the hope of the plan. Judge Taylor stated,

> I am fully convinced that the problem of public education cannot be separated from the problems of society in general. If schools are going to succeed, new linkages have to be created with the community at large. And if the community is going to prosper and grow, the community's leadership has to provide the resources and support to ensure quality public education for its citizens.

Dr. Nolen Estes as Superintendent of Schools led the district through all these critical years without riots or dramatic incidents. He stayed close to the black community and was able to tower over all the difficulties — tower physically and emotionally. He used his large physique to gain control, he used his quiet, steady countenance to gain favor and trust, and he used his broad grin to assure success. The ethnic groups respected Dr. Estes, and he kept Dallas out of the nation's headlines as a city plagued with riots and protests. Social change could never be smooth.

The first superintendent in Dallas posted his schedule: he was very rarely in his office. He was in the schools. Dr. Estes was rarely in his office. He was in court. He needed help and he found it. In one of the meetings of the assistant superintendents, Dr. Estes looked down the long table of administrators and his eyes lighted upon Carlton Moffett, who at that time was assistant superintendent in charge of federal programs. His work was with the Title I programs in the Dallas schools. Dr. Moffett had come from Lancaster to Dallas to teach in the early fifties. He taught math. Then he had been appointed an elementary principal in several schools.

"You will be coordinator of the integration plans," stated Dr. Estes.

"I guess it was being in the right place at the right time," said Dr. Moffett. He was being facetious, because what it really meant was working far into the night and pouring over court orders from federal judges. It meant spending hours in court representing the school district. It meant studying the school district to see that high academic standards were kept during the integration problems. It meant dealing with white flight. Some would say that it was being in the wrong place at the wrong time. Regardless, Dr. Moffett called it a challenge.

Carlton Moffett's office shows evidence of his presence in court. His secretaries got the drawing of him on the stand testifying for the schools that was done by the court artist. This is framed and hanging next to two framed doodles of Judge Taylor. Judge Taylor is a doodler, and after each trial there was a rush to obtain one of the extremely intricate and complicated and entangled doodles. There have been many studies made on people who doodle, and it was discovered that when one is listening and doodling, the more involved the doodle, the more intense the listening. In the case of Judge Taylor, one can be assured that he was not only hearing like a deer in the forest, but he was absorbing like a sponge in the sea.

It has been over ten years since that first forceful and intensive desegregation order was given. The white enrollment has declined by some 54,000 students. This large mass of whites was needed for the equalization of the races. Dr. Moffett stated that the committee learned from the very beginning (along with the rest of the country) that once minority groups are no longer the minority, the whites will drop out en masse. The population must remain at least sixty percent white and forty percent minority, or the school will almost overnight become racially unbalanced in the other direction.

There is no reliable evidence found anywhere that Desegregation programs in general and busing in particular had any effect on the achievements of either majority or minority students. In fact, a report showed that minority achievement in the predominately black East Oak Cliff subdistrict is up as much or more than minority achievement in the rest of the district which was integrated.

The magnets are successful and could be even more so, if the students board buses to seek learning and not racial balance.

Because the courts demanded changes in society and education, people did come up with innovative educational programs. Now, the community will have to accept these programs as educational and not as some gimmick to racially balance the kids in the classrooms.

A change of attitude is coming since the enrollment figures show that the upper middle-class white children are coming back into the public schools. The test scores reported by the school district show that more academic achievement is on the rise. The cost of living is rising too, so more and more people cannot afford private schools. If the parents get actively involved with their children, schools will get stronger over night.

Judge Barefoot Sanders, a North Dallas High School graduate, is now handling all the integration cases and orders. He is trying to get the schools out of court and totally into the hands of professional and efficient educators. Concentration must lie on the education not on the integration of the youth of Dallas.

DR. ESTES RESIGNS

All during these turbulent times, the federal funds kept rolling into the district. However, there never seemed to be enough to go around to all the programs. Some administrators who were in charge began to look at scholarship monies, a number of which had been "in the family" for years: Williams and Read, Libby Benson, Herman Benthul, Ascher Silberstein,

Marjorie Keller, Perot Incentive, P.C. Cobb, Tetze World Peace, RIF, Partners in Reading. The Foundation for Quality Education began to use some of the special scholarship funds without proper permission.

In fact, some of the administrators began to make decisions without consulting the board chairman. Some began to bypass the system and to act toward their own interests without following proper procedural manner. The public became suspicious of the activities of these administrators as well as the superintendent himself.

Therefore, in 1980, Dr. Estes left his post as superintendent to pursue a career that he had already begun at the University of Texas. He became a professor of education at U.T. in Austin.

Mr. Linus Wright, a native of Denison, Texas, who was serving as Assistant Superintendent of Schools in Houston, was called as superintendent in the fall of 1980 to assume the duties in 1981. He publicly announced after he had served for three years that had he known the state of the educational system in Dallas, he might not have come. But he did come, and according to the teachers, he has brought about some renewed confidence and the needed stability.

Mr. Wright has put many of the administrators back into the classrooms to teach, so the top-heavy administrative force has leveled off. In an action politically praised, President Reagan cut federal funding so funds are not rolling in as they did before. The new superintendent announced that he was in complete control, and he ordered the principals to produce a more learned crop of kids, "or else." There has been some protest from the principals. Some have stated that they wished that they could select their faculty.

"I could determine what was happening in my school if I was able to choose the teachers that were there," stated one principal.

There are positive parents working with the principals, businessmen are interested in the future of the schools, and there is a growing confidence in public education. Linus Wright holds the responsibility of raising the educational level of the students of Dallas. He, with the help of his resources, must do this "or else" we're going to lose fine quality public education.

Chapter Thirteen

The Arts And Athletics — They Always Get The Skeptic Eye

Every time there is a shortage of money or there is a feeling that students are not getting enough of the hard-core basic subjects in school, the public and school administrators look at the arts and athletics and question their importance. Surely there must be a strong foundation in rhetoric, math, and science, but without athletics and the arts the curriculum would not be complete. There would be fine students neglected.

Had there not been a good band director in a high school to encourage him, my husband would never had been the fine band director he was for the Dallas schools. His students learned music as well as discipline. They acquired a sense of accomplishment in performance — self-esteem.

Had it not been for my auditorium activities teacher at Robert E. Lee Elementary School, Helen Ardrey, and my speech teacher at North Dallas, Natalie Simpson, I would never have gone on to college and majored in theatre. I taught speech and drama, and I had many successful students who came from my classes claiming that the training that they received in the art of speaking and in the art of acting was invaluable to them in their careers.

My daughter had a physical education teacher at Atwell Junior High, Betty Hale, who was such an inspiration to her that my daughter went on to major in physical education in college. After she graduated she served as a park director for the Dallas Parks and Recreation Department. Today she is a Jazzercise instructor helping people to lose unwanted weight and to get into condition for better living.

My son was encouraged by a journalism teacher, and today he is a photographer for the Tyler, Texas *Courier Times/Morning Telegraph.*

The arts and athletics are important. They give support and spirit to the schools. Like everything else, there must be a sensible balance in the basics, the electives, and the extra-curricular activities.

Beverly Benthul Renquist was listed as high profile in the *Dallas Morning News*, and she's definitely high profile at the Arts Magnet School. Beverly is a professional actress who teaches at the magnet, and she comes from a long line of Dallas educators. Her father, Harless Benthul, was principal of Walnut Hill Elementary for many years, and her uncle, Herman Benthul, was one of the assistant superintendents of the Dallas schools. She was well trained in drama by Helen Echolman at Woodrow Wilson High. Beverly played the lead in the musical *Oklahoma*, that very first Broadway musical to be produced by a Dallas high school. Now, she shares her professionalism with the aspiring actors and actresses at the arts magnet.

The administration was so pleased to welcome Paul Baker to the staff at the arts magnet. Mr. Baker was director of the Dallas Theatre Center, and now he is giving his talent to the Dallas high school drama students.

Actually, there have been professionals involved with the schools since the very beginning. The very first senior play given in Dallas was in 1901. It was directed by Mrs. O.D. Woodrow, the dean of elocutionary teachers, a true professional. She had private speech and expression classes which she taught in her studio at 1203½ Main Street. The Dallas schools hired her to direct this first senior play. The school report of that year stated that the whole point of education was to foster the tastes and accomplishments of a cultivated people.

So in Turner Hall at the high school, May 31, 1901, the senior class presented *Idyls Of The King* by Alfred Lord Tennyson. The cultivated Dallas audience was exposed to King Arthur, Sir Lancelot, Guinevere, and Merlin, via Alfred Lord Tennyson and the senior class at Central High.

Another memorable senior play was given in 1909. The medieval morality play, *Everyman*, was given and directed by Mrs. Woodrow. The 1909 annual described the rehearsals.

> The play — what a line of reminiscence the word brings to the minds of the graduates of 1909 — some pleasant, some rather otherwise. Taken all in all, the play provided a great deal of fun, but we feel sure that no one who has experienced the toils of the seniors this year in their efforts to perfect their play, will ever aspire to a life behind the footlights. Twice a week we were put through the frolicking dance of the dominoes and the dreary waltz of the Bacchanals, finishing off with the grace-creating movements of the angels. Some students were happy that they were backstage, some not.

Virginia Lipscomb played the leading role, that of Everman, in the play. Today, this star is Mrs. Lindsley Waters, and at ninety-one years of age she can vividly recall her performance and all the wonderful years that she has lived in Dallas. She mused, "I look back and think of my life as not being too glamorous. But it has been interesting." It's been interesting, glamorous, and notable.

Her father, William Lipscomb was the principal of Dallas High School from 1894–1900. He worked hard to keep his faculty and staff happy and productive. He was dealing with a particular janitor one day, and the janitor left feeling that he had been unfairly dismissed from his job. This was not the case at all. After school Mr. Lipscomb went by his church on the corner of Pearl and Bryan, saw a man coming toward him. Mr. Lipscomb, thinking it was someone asking about the church, extended his hand. It was the janitor, now very drunk. This janitor shot and instantly killed Mr. Lipscomb.

His widow, Mrs. Virginia Lipscomb was left with four children to rear, daughter Virginia and three brothers. Mrs. Lipscomb was given a teaching job at Stephen F. Austin School. Then when a school was built on Worth Street in East Dallas, the school was named for her husband, and Mrs. Lipscomb was the first principal.

Later, daughter Virginia married Lindlsey Waters, who with one of her brothers founded Tennessee Dairies. This was one of the largest milk companies in Dallas during the thirties, forties, and fifties. The little school children were supplied with plenty of milk from the Tennessee Dairies. When Mr. Waters died, Mrs. Waters ran the business until she decided that it was best for her to step out of the business world, so she sold the company to Foremost Milk.

A drama club, Sigma Delta, was organized, February 7, 1909. From the members of this club came the cast of the 1910 senior play, George B . Shaw's *Joan Of Arc*. This was a difficult play to give, and an essay in the 1911 annual verified this by mentioning the tapping of Mrs. Woodrow's stick, demanding more and more rehearsal.

In 1912, Mrs. Woodrow was not asked to direct the play, because Mr. C.S.T. Folson was added to the faculty and part of his assignment was to direct the play. He chose to do *Macbeth*. Mr. Folsom had the students in the cast sign contracts agreeing to do the play. I guess he was aware of the bad luck that always comes to any production of *Macbeth*. He wasn't going to lose a cast member. They had to sign for their parts.

In 1913, Miss Edna Rowe directed the senior play, *Vicar Of Wakefield*. She was assisted by Mr. George Medders. Later that year they gave *Rip Van Winkle*. This was the beginning of high school drama.

Across the river, Oak Cliff High had a drama department directed by Mr. Charles L. Syron. Later Mrs. Wanda Banker came to Adamson as drama coach. Miss Wilhelmina Hedde was at Sunset in speech and drama. The two ladies switched places, and Mrs. Banker then directed the drama activities many years at Sunset. Miss Hedde remained at Adamson until she retired.

Forest Avenue High School offered drama in the very beginning, 1917. The school was built with the arts in mind. The same plans that were used to build Oak Cliff High were used to build Forest. However, Forest got an extra room built on top —an art room with a skylight. The bunch at Oak Cliff High never got over the fact that Forest got a little extra frosting on top.

In the fall of 1939, the senior class at Forest Avenue gave a senior play that had questionable literary value, but which offered a lot of fun for cast and audience, entitled, "Ride 'Em

Cowboy." Mary Nell Stevenson, who is now an executive with Southwestern Bell, played the part of a Mexican maiden named Pepita. She played opposite a Mexican bandit played by a rising star from Forest High, Aaron Spelling. Several teachers at City Park School where little Aaron had attended were impressed with his dramatic ability. Now, at Forest High this fine Jewish lad was going to reach great heights playing a Mexican bandit. He and Mary Nell had impeccable Mexican accents. In fact, Mary Nell said that once she donned the rented black wig and came out with a *Si, si,* or two, her own father didn't know her.

Today Mary Nell uses her dramatic ability at Southwestern Bell while Aaron Spelling is the famous producer of *Charlie's Angels, Love Boat, Fantasy Island, Hart To Hart,* and *Dynasty* — to name a few.

"Ride 'Em Cowboy" was directed by Helen Fern Black. She was a great teacher, and fortunately her name furnished the kids with a great backstage joke.

"You look like Helen Black."

"You don't look so good yourself."

At North Dallas High, Stanley Knapp was the grand man of speech and drama. Dr. Walker may have had the money-making minstrel shows, but Mr. Knapp gave the high-class theatrical productions and also coached debate. North Dallas High was fortunate to be near the only professional theatre in Dallas during the thirties and the early forties. This theatre was located on Haskell Avenue three blocks east of the school— in a tent. These professional actors called themselves the Madcap Players, and the core of this acting troup consisted of Neil Fletcher and his wife Minnie, Toby Gunn and his wife Jeannie, and Jackie Caldwell, who played the organ before curtain time. The Madcaps were a part of theatre history. They performed when people didn't mind seeing a show in a tent, and the audience expected the show to be pure corn.

Minnie Fletcher pretended to enter the Paul Revere Hotel and become disgusted with the service.

She said, "I want to see the proprietor. I want to see Paul Revere himself."

"Paul Revere is dead," answered Toby, the bellhop.

"Oh . . . I didn't know he was sick."

The sophisticated citizentry of Dallas wouldn't take that

today, and they certainly wouldn't take what happened during intermission. Between the acts, Toby Gunn, who always played the dunce, made the ballyhoo candy pitch common to all tent shows of the period. Still wearing his show costume, he would step around the curtain with a vendor's tray slung around his neck. He frankly admitted that the few pieces of salt water taffy were not worth anything. He gained the audience's confidence with this statement.

"But, inside the box with the worthless candy is a coupon. With this coupon you are entitled to a prize from the stage."

Then the curtain would open, and displayed would be the usual carnival junk — stuffed animals, rhinestone jewelry, radios, plaster statues, multicolored plush scarfs with fringe, cake dishes, coffee pots, and anything else that Toby could muster from nearby merchants in trade for an ad in the program. Then Toby descended on the audience selling the candy with the cherished coupon inside, and Jackie Caldwell would play the organ while all of this was going on. It had a great circus effect.

Neil Fletcher lectured at North Dallas High on theatre, and the kids accepted him as a professional even though he came from this background. But then, the tent show was *theatre* in Dallas.

When air conditioning came along and Dallas became too sophisticated for the Madcaps and their antics, their tent was folded. However, Neil Fletcher did not silently steal away. He invented something that everyone in Dallas and the nation enjoys — the corny dog. He entertained the schoolchildren, he gave them acting lessons, and then he fed them. What is the State Fair of Texas without a Fletcher's Corny Dog?

In the late forties, a lady came on the theatrical scene who brought national fame to Dallas. This was Margo Jones and her Theatre in the Round at Fair Park. Margo worked twenty four house a day to establish this theatre and keep it going. However, she was always very generous with her time when it came to lecturing to the school kids. She toured the schools, and she even came to see some of the productions. What a thrill I had as a student when I was told that Margo Jones was in the audience. After our performance, she came back to speak to the cast. Her words are still ringing in my ears.

"Bless you, darlings."

And we were blessed by Margo. She brought professional theatre to our school.

At Woodrow Wilson High School for twenty years, until 1957, H. Bush Morgan taught public speaking, directed all the plays, won many one-act play contests, edited the annual, directed many clubs, handled many school activities, and was a friend of all.

I knew Mr. Morgan, and I always associated him with the one-act play contest and first place in that contest. He was strictly dedicated to drama. He was a bachelor, and many said he was definitely married to his work. He and "Pop" Ashburn were buddies, and together they promoted theatre at Woodrow.

H. Bush Morgan left Woodrow Wilson in 1957. Because of his knowledge of yearbook editing, he went to work for Taylor Publishing Company, a company that publishes more yearbooks than any other company. On his way home from work, Mr. Morgan was crossing the street one evening in front of his apartment, was struck by a car, and was killed instantly. This ended the life of an outstanding speech and drama teacher. Also it concluded the career of a man who was not only an outstanding drama teacher but a man involved in several little theatres in Dallas.

The Shakespeare Festival of Dallas founded and produced by Bob Glenn, now occupies the Band Shell at the Fair Park in the summers. Dallas audiences now enjoy fabulous Shakespearean productions where once the State Fair Musicals played. During the forties and fifties, musical comedies were produced in the Band Shell. John Rosenfield, graduate of the Dallas schools, famed arts critic of the *Dallas Morning News*, sat on the third row, aisle seat, and wrote his superb critiques of the shows. Jack Harwood, Forest Avenue graduate who went to Hollywood to teach the stars how to dance, was dancing in the chorus, and a high school lad by the name of Tom Hughes was selling cold drinks. Tom is a dear friend, but I have never believed him when he claimed that he sold drinks at the musicals. I remember these vendors being very crass and loud, yelling,

"Get your cold drinks here! Cold drinks — one nickel!"

I always insisted that the dignified and cultured Tom couldn't do that even as a high school student. "Tom, there's no way that you could have possibly yelled 'Get your cold drinks right here!' "

"I didn't *yell* that. I *announced*, 'Refreshments everyone!' "

Perhaps. Nevertheless, it makes a great story for Mr. Hughes to tell. He rose from cold drink boy to producer of the Dallas Summer Musicals. He not only produces the productions here, but now, many of the shows are cast and premiered here in Dallas, and then they travel all over the country. When the Majestic Theatre was renovated, it was a natural choice to ask Mr. Hughes to manage this theatre.

Within his busy schedule, Tom will always find time to lecture to classes in the Dallas schools. The theatre teachers of Bryan Adams, Kimball, and Carter high schools often called him to cast their shows. When National Forensic Time rolls around and a professional judge is needed, Mr. Hughes always accepts this opportunity to judge the contests.

Speech tournaments are big events. They always have been. The first Interscholastic League debate meet in Dallas was sponsored by Forest Avenue High. The topic was Resolved, that all revenues from the support of government — local, state, and national — should be derived from a single tax on land values. The topics are always timely and important. Adamson High always had a strong debate squad. Mr. C.C. Nutley joined the faculty in 1940. This gentleman did everything imaginable to interest students in debate while they were at Adamson or even before they came He got intelligence reports of the students coming in from the elementary schools and Boude Story Junior High and screened these for possibilities. If the IQ score was high enough for Mr. Nutley, he personally visited the student before he entered Amanson to see if he had speaking ability. Debate was a business with Mr. Nutley, and by 1950 the National Forensic League at Adamson was the largest club in the school. One consistent winner from Adamson, Mr. Joe Stalcup, finished his college work and came back to Adamson to cosponsor the debate department in 1951. Joe Stalcup, no longer a teacher, is an attorney and church leader. His background in debate was invaluable to him as it is to many attorneys.

When Bryan Adams High School opened Billy Mack Abbott left North Dallas to establish the speech department there. The forensics program has always been outstanding there with such leaders as Janice Weiland and Frances Clay. The Patchwork players were established by Ann Nieto. This is a group of performers who give children's plays whenever or where ever they are asked to do so. They also write special plays for special occasions.

Mrs. Mary Davis founded the National Thespians at Lincoln High School before this site became a magnet school. She was an energetic force for many years in their speech and drama department. The group there held to the motto of the Thespians,

"Act well your part, there all the honor lies."

The grand lady of forensics today is Dorothy Huffstutler at Hillcrest. She has always been a first place winner. Most of her students have been National Merit Scholarship awardees. Dorothy took over the speech department in 1965. The topic that year was Resolved: that the Federal government should prohibit the requirements of union membership as a condition of employment. This is still a debatable issue. This year there have been nineteen years and nineteen topics in Mrs. Huffstutler's coaching career at Hillcrest. She became an authority on every topic. Her students certainly were well versed. They kept winning debates. They still are winning.

AUDITORIUM ACTIVITIES

The *Dallas Times Herald* columnist, William Rogers, pointed out in his book, *The Lusty Texans of Dallas*, that

> There had been a pioneering spirit in the Dallas public Schools which had made a number of contributions to education in Texas. In 1921 they introduced into the Southwest the platoon system for elementary schools — an organization of classes which allowed the homeroom teachers to spend their entire time on fundamental subjects such as reading, writing, language arts and number work, with special teachers provided for music, art, and physical education.

But there was another special kind of teacher introduced that year not mentioned by Mr. Rogers. Not only was Dallas a pioneer in introducing the platoon system, but the Dallas educators introduced a whole new course of study to the elementary schools of Texas. This course was called Auditorium Activities. Today if one were to mention Auditorium Activities, only the Dallas natives would react to the words and know what one was talking about. Dallas was unique in offering this novel course to the children. Actually it was successfully taught in only a few school systems across the nation.

Lela Lee Williams was sent to Gary, Indiana, to study and report on Auditorium Activities, a course which had been initiated in the Indiana school districts but nowhere else in the nation up to that time. Miss Williams discovered that,

"the purpose of the auditorium period is to furnish opportunities and situations for the exercise and development of abilities for which the usual classroom does not provide."
The child would learn in the classroom and use the learning in the auditorium. If a child studied an event in history in the homeroom period, in the auditorium he would enact the event. He'd recite a poem about the event. He'd read more *aloud* about the event. He'd write an essay about the event. History came alive in the auditorium. One teacher put it this way,

"The dry bones of the past became the flesh and blood of the present in the auditorium activities class."

The same types of activities could reinforce a math lesson. The numbers became alive. Example: In a dramatic skit (visually) Mr. Number could be torn apart into fractions.The creativity that was used by the teachers,and the creativity that was squeezed from students was limitless.There is a leather bound curriculum guide — several copies of which are still on file at the school administration building — that explains the whole unusual program. It was compiled by auditorium teachers handpicked by E.B. Cauthorn to launch this creative endeavor: Blanche Smith, Minnie Bizzell, Mary Capes, Myrtle Smith, Ethel Walter, Bertha Bizzell, Florence Buryear, Callie Moffett, Annie Lee Alexander, Ethel Thomas, Blanche Brandon, Baulah Keeton, Uleta Wilhouse, Alma Dickson, Louis Paulus, and Jewell York. These teachers were paid more than the other elementary teachers, and a report plainly stated that jealously reigned among the other teachers in the schools over this so-called merit pay.

These "lovely ladies of the auditorium" really did have a little kingdom in the school auditorium. On special holidays, they were responsible for programs that would give the history of the day observed. Jewel York boasted in a piece of writing about the program.

"The auditorium classes gave the meat and bread of life to the school."
Alma Dickson noted in an essay that the teachers taught poise and brought about concentration. There was intense visualization of any event or episode. There was a socialization of the work done in the classroom, for all the subjects were correlated in the auditorium. There was a strengthening of the work done by the classroom teachers.

Helen Rogers taught auditorium for twenty-five years in the Dallas system. She stated that she always enjoyed her work at Edwin Kiest, because this was a strong middle class school. This pleased her. She said that so often people did things for the poor and the needy, but they neglected the strong middle class. These students needed attention, and too, they needed material rewards. Therefore, she made certain that in a tangible way, her students were rewarded for good programs.

Mrs. Rogers never neglected any chance of obtaining any free materials that the children might enjoy getting as handouts in class. She sent off for any free advertisement brochures of different companies and institutions. She tried to get as much material into the hands of the students as possible so that they could keep their own scrapbooks of programs and information.

A favorite play that Mrs. Rogers enjoyed giving was "Who's Who At The Zoo." Each child portrayed his favorite animal at the zoo. The stage setting was quite unusual in that
". . . each child was in his own little cage."
This really was a great play to give, because obviously there could be no disorder during the production since the cast was securely behind bars.

Miss Leta Parks, who taught for thirty years in the system, was the auditorium teacher at Alex Sanger School. She decided when she entered the program that she would always approach her undertakings from an artistic angle. Each year she vowed that she would invent a new way of using good literature and would create a new approach to teaching. Doing the same things year after year in the auditorium was not her way of being an effective teacher. Miss Parks wrote many children's plays. In fact, she said that the only way to provide the proper experiences for every child in the class was to create a specific program just for that class of particular children.

These auditorium teachers were called upon to present many PTA programs. They were united into one massive effort in 1948 by Dr. White when he asked auditorium teacher Pauline James to write, produce, and direct a program on Texas which would be a city-wide effort presented at the Fair Park Music Hall. Every elementary child in the city of Dallas was in this memorable program.

The children were taught both citizenship and parlimentary procedure in the auditorium. Also, debate was not forgotten. The students selected the topics.

> Resolved: that it is as dishonest to give help on the test as it is to receive it.
> Resolved: that it is better to tell the truth regarding knowledge of the guilt of a friend than to shield him.
> Resolved: that it is proper for girls to wear blue jeans in school.
> Resolved: that is is better to discuss our problems with our parents than to take orders from them.
> Resolved: that it is better for parents to give their children an allowance than to give them money when they need it.
> Resolved: that science has done more harm than good.
> Resolved: that TV viewing time should be limited.

The schools in Dallas were so often named for outstanding people who had served the Dallas community. The children in the school need to know about the person for whom their school was named.

Bonnie Harford, auditorium teacher, wrote a biographical sketch on each of the women for whom a school was named, and she put this material into book form. She used much of this information from her study to make these ladies come alive for the children in her auditorium classes. This produced more school spirit.

These teachers were artists in adapting their activities to the school situation. Those that taught auditorium in poor areas of town made certain that all the scenery was made by the children themselves. This would provide a feeling of self-worth. The children accomplished something, and they had pride in that accomplishment. Developing this pride was a major concern of teachers who were teaching in the poorer neighborhoods.

May Day was a challenge. Many maypole dances were held on the lawns of the schools with each class dressed in a particular costume. The first grade mushrooms gathered. The wind would blow. The wind so often was the second grade class. The daisies would sway in the breeze. Daisies were third graders. Everyone took part and everyone had to remain in perfect order for such a gigantic theatrical production to be carried off. Nothing was too big for the auditorium teacher.

Most principals approved of and thought highly of the activities in the auditorium. One cited,

> The auditorium was to the school what a well apportioned living room is to the home. It is here that the visitor gets a general impression of the school. The stage is set in a special manner. The bulletin boards speak of the seasons or of the school activities.

The auditorium activities program has been gone for fifteen years. Several former auditorium teachers, however, are still teaching in the Dallas schools. They are now teaching language arts, but many of them would like to see auditorium activities brought back into the system. Anita Elliott, former auditorium teacher who now teaches language arts at Adelle Turner, feels that the reading ability of the students would be strengthened were the program reinstated. "I taught more reading in the auditorium than a reading teacher could." The reading skills were taught in the reading classes, but practice in the reading came in the auditorium.

In 1966, the speech arts teachers met for their forty-fifth anniversary. They had been organized into a club which met for idea sharing and social purposes. However, this meeting in the spring of 1966 turned out to be the final meeting of the club itself. Dr. Herman Benthul and Mrs. Wilma Stewart, who served as superintendents over the speech arts program spoke on the projected activities. However, the changes were on their way, and the speech arts teacher, considered a frill, was to be no more. However, for forty-five years, auditorium activities in the elementary schools strengthened the learning experiences of the children.

JOURNALISM

The new subject, Journalism, was introduced at Forest Avenue High School in 1919. Seventy-three students enrolled that first year. They published the school paper, but they also received extra training in that the *Dallas Journal*, a Dallas paper published at that time, gave one of its pages each Friday to the high school news. This gave some aspiring journalists the opportunity to write for a professional newspaper even before graduation from high school. This situation exists today through the magnet school activities.

Many English teachers who teach composition state that they would rather have less students than more money. One of the reasons that students are not required to write much is that the teachers just don't have time to read what the students write. Those students who really have the writing bug end up in journalism courses. We have some fine writers who emerged from the journalism classes of the Dallas schools.

A Woodrow Wilson graduate who now is a movie reporter and editor with the New York *Daily News* is Harry Haun. Mr. Haun was recently in Dallas pushing his book, *The Movie Quote Book*. This is a great book for movie fans who like to remember favorite lines, mentally relive the scene in which the line was spoken, and then go off to quote the line thus appearing as one of those genius type people who never forgets anything. I have the book, I've read it, and I've impressed many people by quoting lines perfectly that were given years ago in a favorite movie.

Two particular columnists for the *Dallas Morning News* are DISD grads, and they are proud of it, because they frequently mention that fact in their columns. Bob St. John had the entire Dallas *News* staff and all the rest of Dallas looking for his North Dallas High School ring when he reported in his column that it was missing from his desk. Mr. St. John was sports editor of the *Compass*, the North Dallas High paper, in 1955. His reporting on the Bull Dogs got Bob off to an early start as a writer. His book on Tom Landry was a best seller in the Southwest for seven weeks. It sold over 200,000 copies. Mr. St. John has written six books, and he writes a daily column that keeps his readers both entertained and informed.

Mr. John Anders, whose mother is a teacher in the Dallas

schools, also keeps the Dallas reading public entertained and informed through his daily column. Mr. Anders loves to look back into his past, the sixties, and to remember the great green hamburgers from the Bryan Adams High cafeteria. (They were green because they were laced with relish to make for better seasoning and to make the hamburger meat go a little further.) In one of his columns he recalled, "the ultimate Bryan Adams experience" — that was engaging in a dance called "Low Life." This dance was created by the Bryan Adams crowd for the Bryan Adams crowd plus a few friends from Woodrow Wilson and North Dallas. John admitted that the sixties were gone, but "Low Life" lingers on. A journalism teacher at Bryan Adams recognized the nimble wittedness and dexterity in John Anders as a student and encouraged him to become a writer. Readers in Dallas are so much better off from reading his column each morning.

A journalist that goes back a bit in time was Miss Fairfax Nesbit who wrote for the society page at the *Dallas Morning News* for a number of years, and then later she became the television critic for the *News*. Miss Nesbit began her writing and acting career at Dallas High in 1918. She starred in the high school production of Shakespeare's *Twelfth Night*, and then she wrote the critique of the production for the school paper. Naturally she gave herself rave reviews. Miss Nesbit loved to write and act and talk. When I use to visit her down at the *News*, she did all three at once. The members of her family, she claimed, were such big talkers that at family get-togethers they all sat on the edges of their chairs ready to jump in when the one who had the floor foolishly took time to breathe. She claimed that Miss Edna Rowe and Myra Brown made her the grand actress, talker, and writer that she was.

From Forest Avenue a renowned writer and speaker emerged, Evelyn Oppenheimer. She praised Ethyl Masters, her Latin teacher, who instilled into her students the love of language and literature and the desire to read more. Miss Oppenheimer originated the oral book review that is so popular with women's organizations. During the depression years she approached Alex Sanger with an idea that she thought would lure more customers into the store. She suggested that each week in the auditorium of the store an oral book review should be given. The ladies would come in to hear the review, perhaps purchase the book reviewed, stray into other areas of the store, and buy lots of goods from every department. Miss Oppenheimer, of course, would give the review. The management of Sanger Brothers agreed, and in 1936, she became the first person in the United States to launch such a review series, and she's been in constant demand as a book reviewer ever since.

The communication field was always a part of Miss Oppenheimer's life. She has a prizewinning delivery an an extremely sharp mind. When she was a student at Forest Avenue, she became the first woman ever to win the national high school debate tournament, and she's been winning with audiences every since. In 1923, the debate topic was Resolved: women should be allowed to debate in tournaments. In 1924, girls were allowed to compete in the debate and forensic world, and Miss Oppenheimer with her colleague claimed the national title. She has written several books, one very valuable one to speakers, *Book Reviewing For An Audience*. Today she acts as a literary agent and continues to write books and articles and to orally review books all over the country.

Minette Landa, Dallas civic leader, was in the audience when Miss Oppenheimer graduated as salutatorian of her class. Seated in front of Mrs. Landa at the graduation exercises was a father with a son who was *not* salutatorian of the class. The father turned to the son,

"You let a mere girl win over you."

The boy replied,

"Evelyn is not mere."

Today there are over four hundred book review clubs in Dallas that have evolved from that original Oppenheimer series. Another outstanding reviewer today is Mrs. Bard Paul, Dallas native, graduate of Oak Cliff High. She comes from a family of Dallas leaders and communicators. Her father, an engineer, with T.L. Marsalis, laid out the city of Oak Cliff. Her brother, the honorable Judge Dee Brown, Oak Cliff High graduate, was the judge for the Jack Ruby murder trial. The characters in that courtroom drama are all well remembered, and Judge Brown remains unforgetable for his wise counsel and forceful rhetoric.

Another Forest Avenue High School graduate who made a name for herself as a writer is Mrs. Frances Sanger Mossiker. Mrs. Mossiker spent a great deal of time in France, so her histories of that country are authentic, well researched, and valuable to scholars. They're brilliantly written, so even though they are appreciated by scholars, they are quite readable and captivating to anyone who desires to read deeply about the history of France. She wrote of Louis XIV, the Sun King, in *An Affair Of Poison*. In another book, *The Queen's Necklace,* she reveals the final deed that brought about the French Revolution. Her latest book, *Madame De Sevigne*, is an enthralling story of a woman whose life touched the Sun King himself along with Madame de La Fayette and others of seventeenth century France.

These are selected writers from the Dallas schools. There are more, of course. All of these mentioned wrote when they were in school. Who is writing in school today? Is there composition work? I found some authors at Bowie Elementary School. Miss Jan Lovvorn is the teacher, and the minute that the children in her class learn some new words and gain some insights and concepts, they write books using their words, insights, experiences, and imagination. A student illustrates his own book, and when he has completed it, he, the author, reads his story to the class. Writing stories helps a child in reading stories. The class is challenged by the writing. The students are quite aware of the fact that the more words they know, the better they can write.

One of the best books that was produced in the class for one assignment was entitled, "Friday Night At The Wrestling Matches." A little girl in the class went to the wrestling matches and wrote all about the whole experience. She said she was in love with the wrestlers. Now, Dr. Kimball, were he to return to earth for a quick peek into this classroom, would go into shock over the fact that a child had been taken to such a barbaric event. He would be appalled that a little girl could experience love for anyone that gains recognition for inflicting torturous holds on another individual who in retaliation kicks his opponent in the head. Nevertheless, I read her story and she made the events quite vivid. And furthermore, she spelled all the words correctly: wrestling, match, Reunion Arena, Von Eric, iron, and claw. Teachers today must travel with the words and the experiences of their students.

Miss Lovvorn has her students as a group for homeroom all day. However, the ones whose learning abilities fall below normal third graders, the ones who cannot keep up with the rest of the class, have special classes which they attend each day. A reading specialist teaches these classes which are funded by the federal government under Title I. With a plan such as this, a child with learning problems can stay in class with his friends, learn from the teacher and from the experiences in the classroom, and then get the additional instruction and support needed. He doesn't have to give up the essential classroom friendships and experiences just because he has a learning deficiency.

"I'm a patient teacher," stated Miss Lovvorn, "because I had some great teachers when I was in school. There was Mrs. Robertson at Lakewood who made us memorize *The Raven*. This was such a challenge. I'll never forget the poem or Mrs. Robertson. She's one of the reasons that I'm a good teacher."

And Miss Lovvorn is a good teacher. She spends extra time and money on her students. She moonlights at her grandmother's well-known establishment, the Highland Park Cafeteria. With the extra money that she earns there, she buys things for the schoolroom and the kids. The class has two television sets which she bought. This teacher feels that there are offerings on Channel 13 that her students shouldn't miss. They don't, because of the generosity of this teacher.

Who else is writing? Of course, the journalism classes are. Mary Wininger, who taught journalism at Grady Spruce High was responsible for the Senior Publication, fondly called the *Senior Pub*. This little booklet is full of literary gems and puns. I saw one published in 1968 which poked all sorts of fun at Principal Perry Fite. The cover of this pub carried on it the picture of a well known bottle of beer. The title read, "Pub-Weiser, The King Of Jeers." It's shocking to some, low in comedy to others, but a lot of fun for the seniors.

The journalism class at Hillcrest puts out a fine paper each month under the direction of Julia Jeffress. Mrs. Jeffress who has been head of the journalism department at Hillcrest for the last twenty-four years, says that she has quality kids. And she's doing quality teaching in a quality school.

"I have just as many smart kids in my classes today as I did twenty-four years ago."
Mrs. Jeffress doesn't boast about her ability as a teacher, but she readily admits that she could teach in the suburbs of Dal-

las or in a private academy, but teaching at Hillcrest High is so much more satisfying. There's mutual admiration, because the students feel privileged to have her for a teacher. There are advantages at Hillcrest that just aren't in private schools. The journalism classroom looks like the city newsroom at any large newspaper, and from that atmosphere comes *The Hurricane*, a sixteen-page professional looking newspaper. Just like any good paper, about one third of it is taken by ads. This is great, for those ads pay for the editions, and the students gain experience in selling the ads. About one-fourth of the news reported involves the school and the community. Then there are interviews and play reviews; there is sports news and club news. It's a great paper, and the students at Hillcrest produce it with pride. Those writers and photographers there mean business. They gladly tell about the printer's ink in their veins, and they gladly brag about their experienced and devoted teacher who is leading them right from Hillcrest to the city desk of a newspaper, to the press box, to a news writing slot for the media, and eventually to the Pulitzer Prize. It's all there at Hillcrest — a career in journalism for the taking.

Some journalism teachers never quit serving their students. The Forest High alumni group have a newsletter that is sent to the graduates. They were seeking a name for it, so they decided to have a contest to find the most appropriate name. Mrs. Mary Smith Clark, who sponsored the yearbook for Forest in the thirties, was called upon to act as judge for the contest. She's still serving her students.

ART

In 1904 Miss Lida Hooe took over the supervision of the Penmanship and Drawing department. It is appropriate that a school which bears her name had a art teacher whose students own a distinguished award for two years. The Lung Association asks schoolchildren each year to design their seal for them. The children at Lida Hooe Elementary School designed the selected seal for the years 1976 and 1977. Their art teacher, Louise Hudgins, guided these talented children in their artistic work.

Miss Etta Harland in 1927 became the supervisor of art and the work expanded, but nothing like it did under the guidance of Evelyn Beard who was art teacher at Bowie and then assumed the supervisory position in 1953. Of course, this was the big growth time of Dallas.

Paul Harris, who was a principal, now retired and owner of an art gallery and framing shop on Lovers Lane, infuriated Miss Beard on one occasion. She held a city-wide art contest. Mr. Harris — with the help of some other mischievous principals — created a piece of art by wrapping some junk in some wire and spraying it some indescribable shade. They entered the contest under an assumed name of a child and won! Miss Beard was not too happy when she learned of the prank. However, she was a forgiving sort and gave the prize to the second place winner who was really the first place had not some principals gotten together for a little fun.

Dr. E.D. Walker had a student in one of his classes at North Dallas who doodled more than listened to lectures. His name was Fred Avery and was known to his friends as Tex. This doodler eventually went to Hollywood where he became one of the top artists for the Walt Disney studios.

The Dallas schools have always had fine artists teaching in the classes. In the evening school for a time, professional cartoonist John Knott from the *Dallas News* taught some classes.

Joe Day taught art for thirty-one years in the elementary grades. He posted the children's art work all over the school. He was proud of each and every picture created in his classes even though the art came from small, inexperienced and sometimes shaky hands. It was art. It was creative. And it came from a learning situation.

THE MUSIC PROGRAM

A heart specialist took notice of the fact that many symphony directors lived to be very old men, Toscanini being a prime example. Why was this? He found that the waving of the arms strengthened the heart muscles and gave the ribs an extra workout. The choir and band directors in the Dallas schools have lived long, happy lives. Let's hope the program continues to do so.

When money ran short music was cut from the schools. As I've already related, the Mother's Club saw to it that Miss Birdie Alexander, music director, was reinstated. Music classes continued. Miss Alexander had the mothers behind her all the way. They even furnished pianos at the schools.

> The rhythmic marching made possible by the pianos has greatly improved the rhythm of the schools and has reduced disorder in the lines to the minimum. The greatest sympathy and leniency are exercised toward boys whose bodies are in a transition stage, and toward those who have no inherent musical abilities.

This was Miss Alexander's way of saying that marching to music improved the discipline in the hall. This makes sense. Whole bodies of troops are kept in perfect order on parade with a band blaring away in the rear. The kids could be kept in perfect order as they marched through the halls with the piano playing in the background. However, woe to the clumsy klutzes. They could throw off the whole rhythm of the school.

Birdie Alexander, who people said sang like a bird, was music supervisor until 1913, when another lady arrived on the scene, Miss Sudie Williams. She had studied music at Chapel Hill Female College, at Southwestern University, and at SMU. She had also studied with Hans Kreissig, the first conductor of the Dallas symphony orchestra. While she was supervisor of music, she came up with some very creative activities for the children. She, like Miss Birdie Alexander, felt that music classes taught the children way more than just music. The minds and bodies were also touched by the beautiful sounds. The activities in her music classes taught the students how to organize materials, how to best commit something to memory, how to evaluate ones feelings, how to think creatively, and how to have a better imagination. She came up with a music memory list. She sponsored contests and programs. The children were always busy.

However, the project most pleasing to Miss Sudie and the project most remembered by her students dealt in the keeping of the Walter Damrosch Music Notebook. Walter Damrosch came from Germany with his father, Leopold Damrosch, who was to establish the German opera at the Met. Later Walter assisted his father, and eventually succeeded his father as conductor of the New York Symphony. It was then that Walter Damrosch started a series of concerts just for young people, and when radio was invented and became popular, he saw an opportunity of reaching all the young people in the nation. Therefore, he gave up his other work in broadcasting and founded the NBC "Music Appreciation Hour." Every Friday morning at 10 A.M., all the children, including those in Dallas, heard,

"Good morning, my dear children."
The program was on its way toward informing and entertaining children all over America.

The notebook was for the children themselves to illustrate and explain their own feelings about the music. Mr. Damrosch wrote,

"This is your notebook, because you are to write and illustrate it for yourselves. The questions are not like examination questions, given to find out what you remember. They are questions that will set you thinking, so this book will really be your own work rather than what you remember of what others have told you."

Every student in the Dallas schools regardless of age, kept a set of Damrosch notebooks. These books, published by the NBC Radio Symphony Orchestra, were purchased by the kids. They listened to the program on the radio and then they filled out their notebooks. Each grade had a notebook geared to that age. There were blanks to fill in, pictures to draw, conclusions to make, and feelings to express. The children learned music, but they learned to keep their notebooks tidy. They learned to listen effectively. They learned to draw. They filled in the pages the way they wished. Some children cut pictures from magazines and pasted them in.

Mrs. Margaret Ann Whittelsey Templin, daughter of John Whittlesey, the principal, shared her notebook with me. The October 9, 1931, lesson dealt with the study of four pieces by Schubert. The *Military March in D* was played. Then the children underlined the appropriate word to finish the statement.

"Schubert's Military March in D is Slow, Sad, Thrilling, Alarming." Margaret underlined "thrilling" which I guess it was to her. The other questions read,

> Mr. Damrosch calls his orchestra a Musical Family. Give a reason for this.
>
> How may some of the orchestral instruments be compared to different persons in a family?
>
> On the opposite page write down what you wish to remember about the concert, or paste in any pictures or poems

that seem to you to fit the music. Better still, draw your own pictures or write your own poems.

Margaret Whittelsey chose to draw pictures of the Military March.

Walter Damrosch made this observation.

"There has never been a country whose musical development has been fostered so exclusively by women."

This was certainly true with Miss Sudie Williams, the devoted fan of Walter Damrosch. On July 6, 1938, the Dallas Symphony Board met in order to disband the orchestra since there just wasn't enough money to keep the group performing. Miss Williams cast the only dissenting vote on the board. She rose to her feet and announced,

"We will raise the $65,000 that is needed for the 1939 budget." She felt that the citizens of Dallas would give even though there was still a deep depression. She was right. The patrons gave the money, and the symphony had a fine season with Jacque Singer conducting. When people enjoy the symphony today, they should silently breathe a prayer of thanksgiving for Sudie Williams. She kept it going when no one else thought that it could.

Miss Sudie died the next year, 1939, and John Rosenfield in his column in the *Dallas News* said,

"Dallas will have to make it without her. It will be hard."

That same year, 1939, a train was heading west and stopped at the Union Station in Dallas. A tall, stately lady alighted on the platform to be greeted by her good teacher friend, Lulabelle Pitts. The traveler was Marion Flagg. She had been teaching music at Horace Mann in New York, and she was now headed for a position in California. Her friend, Miss Pitts, mentioned that the music supervisor job was open in Dallas.She felt that Marion should apply. As the visit continued so did the talk about Miss Flagg's possibly applying for the music job. She did send the application, she was hired for the job, and Marion Flagg never got to California. She stayed in Dallas to see that music was ideally taught and lavishly exposed to the public in productions that sometimes included every child in the district.

Miss Flagg encouraged each teacher to be extremely creative in teaching. Still, there was a united spirit amid the ranks of music teachers, because gigantic, city-wide music festivals were given and all the teachers worked together creatively.

At the beginning of each year, Marion Flagg met with her choral teachers, and "heaven help you" if you missed the meeting. She introduced herself by spelling her name.

"Please note the O in Marion. There is no A, since my mother didn't know the difference in the male and female endings to that name."

Her music teachers spelled her name correctly, they respected her, and some feared her. At Robert E. Lee, our music teacher, Miss Nellie Althouse, always asked the tone-deaf children and the unmusical children to just move their lips when they sang on the day that Miss Flagg was going to visit. She always sighed,

"Miss Flagg must not hear a sour note."

Marion Flagg was a fine supervisor, but she was a teacher at heart. Whenever she visited a classroom and the music teacher really wanted to please her, that teacher would ask Miss Flagg for a critique. Then the smart teacher would turn the class over to Miss Flagg and let her do what she loved to do the most — teach.

Miss Flagg worked closely with the Dallas Symphony, and all the Dallas children attended one symphony concert each year, sometimes two. She conducted the audience of children in singing with the orchestra. Naturally she conducted the symphony too. This she adored. For almost thirty years, Dallas students attended the symphony and watched Miss Flagg conduct. It was an experience!

Toward the end of her life, she depended more and more upon Louis Sturkey, a music teacher with the Dallas schools. When death came to Marion Flagg, it was discovered in her will that she had her entire funeral planned.She had written the funeral devotion and had selected the music. This was a typical action on her part!

The Broadway musical came to the Dallas schools in 1958. In an essay entitled, "Our History, Our Heritage," former drama director at Woodrow Wilson, Helen Echolman, remembered,

> Opening night was March 20, 1958 — the night we had
> been preparing for all those long months. The house was

completely sold out for three (we had originally planned only two) performances; old basketball tickets had to be sold for standing room only. At 8 p.m., the nervous cast in full stage makeup and costumes waited in the wings! The house lights dimmed, the first notes of the overture were heard and the curtain slowly opened on *Oklahoma* about which people are still talking. At the end of the performance, the huge audience, spontaneously rose to its feet and applauded! Never before had I seen a standing ovation for a high school show. Never before had a high school given a Broadway musical. There had been operettas and follies presented in the past, but never until March 20, 1958, had there been a musical given. The students at Woodrow led the way.

Today, a musical is given each year by almost all of the high schools, and they are extraordinary productions. Several years ago L.G. Pinkston High gave a black version of the musical *West Side Story*. Instead of the conflict lying between Latins and whites, the show was cast so that the conflict existed between Latins and blacks. This was a brave undertaking dramatically as well as socially. The production was a total success and the show had to run several extra nights to accommodate the vast number of people who wanted to see the show.

William (Bill) White who is the choir director at W.T. White is noted for his extravaganzas. He directed the first musical at Sunset High in 1963, which starred Sally Saldo, well-known actress in Dallas today. Two little children, a boy and girl, were needed to complete the cast, and because I had been in college with Bill, and because we knew each other quite well, and because I had a boy and a girl, he borrowed my children for the show. I readily agreed to have the children there for the first rehearsal, and fortunately the children wanted to go. Fraternizing with high school seniors was a big thrill for a nine-year-old little girl and an eight-year-old little boy, so the whole experience was terrific.

I discovered Bill was a professional director. The kids had such respect for their teacher and musical director and producer. Bill sang in the Dallas Summer Musicals for twenty years. He knew all the musicals so well, having performed in every one of them at the music hall. He was often selected to do supporting roles in the summer musical shows as well.

Colton Erwin, choir director at Bryan Adams and his wife

Hildegarde Erwin are both former chorus members of the Dallas Summer Musicals. These people have the sensitivity to teach and the professional experience to bring the best type of training to the Dallas students.

There is not one mention of country music in the curriculum guide of the Dallas Independent School District, but some good country came out of the music classes. Furthermore, this good country music came out of one graduation class, the class of 1963, Adamson High. Hailing from that group is Ray Wylie Hubbard, whose classic, *Up Against the Wall Red Necked Mother*, was high on the charts for weeks. His father, Royce Hubbard, was principal of Martin Weiss Elementary School. Larry Groce, from that same class, wrote, *Junk Food Junkie*, for the "country lovin' " bunch. He lives in Nashville and still composes. B.W. Stevenson (Chuck) is known for *I Want To Be On My Own*, and he's certainly gone out on his own to much fame in the country music world. And last, but not least, concert singer Michael Murphy, who made it big first with *Wildfire*, came out of that class. He continued to make one hit after another in the country music world.

THE INSTRUMENTAL PROGRAM

There's a false rumor floating about that band directors hate football games. This is not true. Band directors love football games, but they're not so fond of halftime shows. Sometimes band directors put over one hundred kids out on a field and expect them to march in the same direction. This is courting disaster right off. Then the situation is complicated by the fact that sometimes the drills call for the band members *not* to march in the same direction, but to march in all directions and then somehow end up in an organized mass. The scene is further complicated by the fact that the students must all be dressed alike, must have instruments in their hands, and must be able to play those instruments in tune while marching. The complications arise more so when suddenly one student in the rank is ill or has a funeral to attend and is not there at all to fill in a spot that is left in the mass. And to make matters even worse, it rains on the whole affair ruining the uniforms and the instruments. The formation is thrown off even more when a mother calls and insists that her child cannot march in the rain. That makes for another vacant spot.

Football is fine, it's the halftime shows that can be catastrophic. And to make matters worse for the band director, most people think that the only thing a band director does is prepare for the halftime shows, so when a halftime show is bad, some viewers in the stands think the whole year is a total failure. People are not aware that band directors actually teach music, and would really sometimes prefer to be only music teachers rather than halftime producers. However, most of them are good sports and put the whole thing into perspective, and keep smiling.

Band directors have a great love and respect for the instruments that are in the hands of the students. They like the kids, but kids can be replaced. Sometimes the instruments cannot. One of my husband's tuba players almost fell off the top of the stands at the game. He was saved. The students were so relieved that their friend had not fallen. My husband was so relieved that the tuba had been saved. Tuba players are a dime a dozen. Tubas are very expensive.

When the David W. Carter Stage Band was playing in a concert, trombonist Mark Seibert, whose father Bob is a music publisher in Dallas, scooted his chair too near the edge of the stage. My husband, as he was directing, realized that Mark and his trombone were falling off the stage, so he yelled,

"Hold up the trombone."
Mark could fall off the stage, break a few bones, and recover. The trombone could be permanently damaged.

Actually, band directors have hearts for their students. It's just that students come easily. They enroll. But the uniforms, instruments, music, must all be purchased, and the budget is never large enough for it all. So, in order to finance the whole program, the band must go out and sell the well-recognized and ever popular "band candy." The candy vendors were making such a mint off these sales, that other salesmen got into the act. The band now sells light globes, magazines, Christmas candles, toothbrushes, bulletin boards, and shoe polish. Rex Lewis, a salesman for the *Dallas Morning News* and Dallas school graduate, told of the year that the Thomas Jefferson High School Band sold shoe polish.

"We all bought the polish to support the band. We used it and our shoes disintegrated. You could easily see that the school was behind the band program, because every student had on such ugly shoes."

One band director after a big sales push on toothbrushes signed,

"The things we do in the name of education."
That year he retired and joined the company that was selling toothbrushes to the bands and made more money than he ever did teaching school.

An irate father whose child came home with crates of Christmas candles to sell sent a note to the band director.

"If I wanted my child in sales, I would keep him home and let him work for me in my company. I sent him to school for an education." Regardless, of all the trouble in the sales and the flak from the parents, the sales will continue. The band will always need uniforms and instruments.

The first band director in the Dallas schools was Colonel William Herzog. His bands were military bands that were attached to the ROTC units at the schools. Colonel Herzog was a well-trained musician and he taught music to the band members, but he also taught them marksmanship and military tactics. He also had to serve all the schools, but there were not many then right after World War I.

The Colonel had a glorious war record. He had fought in Columbus, New Mexico, in 1914, against Pancho Villa. It was in New Mexico that he served under General Pershing in the Sixth Field Artillery as band director. Colonel Herzog and General Pershing were personal friends. Later General Pershing asked Colonel Herzog to audition the musicians and form the AEF band during World War I. Colonel Herzog used his friendship with the great general in another interesting way. There was an order during World War I that required all officers and soldiers in the AEF whose names were of German origin or whose ancestors were German be sent back to the United States. Colonel Herzog thought this was ridiculous. He protested to his friend General Pershing who put an end to such procedure.

The instrumental program was enlarged in 1931 when E.B. Cauthorn employed George Enoch Hurt as band director at Dallas Technical High. This was the first school with its own instrumental music teacher. Colonel Hurt conducted the whole music program.

Then in 1934 the band program grew when George Royster came to teach band in the junior highs. He was one of the last directors to be called Colonel — the end of the military atmosphere in band directing.

Colonel Royster had to carry the instruments and music stands with him from school to school in his car. The children knew what time the Colonel would drive up to the school — and they would help their band director carry in the needed equipment. Then when the band period was over, they carried everything back out to the car, so that the Colonel could travel to the next school for another band period.

There were orchestras. The just recently retired concert master of the Dallas Symphony Orchestra, Zelman Brounoff, was a member of the Forest Avenue High Symphony under the direction of Lois Wilcox. The orchestra won four state championship awards. Mr. Brounoff loves to tell of the time that he was concert master of the Forest High symphony. He was playing for the production at the high school of *HMS Pinafore*.

"I started the orchestra off in a fine tempo, then I ducked out of the pit to run backstage to put on a red jacket so that I could sing in the chorus. Then I came back to the pit to finish the first act playing in the orchestra. Then for the second act, I once again started the orchestra off, left for the second time, this time to sing a solo on stage. I returned to the pit and finished the show . . . I was a triple threat."

Pem Davenport was the pianist in that orchestra at Forest High. He went on to become a Broadway conductor, conducting the hit show *Guys And Dolls*.

Jack Glatzer, internationally known concert violinist, was a student at Forest Avenue High. He won first place in the Dallas Symphonic Festival, 1940. This entitled him to compete in the national contest held in New York. Jack played in the contest, returned to his hotel room, decided that he had not won, and went to the station to board the train back to Dallas. Someone reached him just before he boarded the train to tell him that he had won — he thought it was a joke. He was still determined to board the train. Finally, convinced that he had won, he stayed to receive the coveted award. There was a cartoon in the *Dallas Morning News* depicting the situation. It showed Jack leaving prematurely with the caption, "Going . . . gone!"

Jack went on to Oxford to study. He was one of the hundreds of extremely talented students in the Dallas schools.

Henry Brahinsky started Jack Glatzer on violin when he was six years old and taught him all through his school career. Mr. Brahinsky has trained many professionals. He is himself a professional musician playing with various orchestras in the area.

One of the outstanding Dallas musicians to come out of the orchestra at Woodrow Wilson was Chris Xeros. This fine violinist is the conductor of the Richardson Symphony.

In 1954, there were more children in the first and second grades than in *all* the senior high school grades. That year, there were 1,773 graduates from the high schools with 11,000 first graders coming into the system. Obviously, these increased numbers affected the whole school program, but the elementary band program really boomed. The outstanding elementary band directors at that time were Marshall Head, Steve Bayless, Frank Todd, Charles Meyers, Ralph Utley, Wally Roberts, and Bill Wartes to name a few. They did well scholastically speaking as well as financially speaking, because at that time the elementary instrumental music teachers enjoyed what was the closest thing to merit pay that has ever been offered by the district. These teachers were not on contract. They just went out and sold their music programs to the children and their parents. The more they sold, the more money they made. They were paid for their ability to sell music, to teach music, and to keep the parents and students satisfied. Of course, one determining factor was the area in which they taught. The wealthier the area, the more students they had. Nevertheless, these elementary band directors could make more than any teacher in the district regardless of the amount of experience or the amount of education. Eventually, they went on contract like all of the other teachers.

The men mentioned that joined this program (like most of the band directors) were band directors by day and professional musicians by night. They would come and direct a concert in a tuxedo, because immediately after the concert they were off to the nearest country club or hotel to play with one of the outstanding dance bands in the city.

Reigning over the instrumental program for the Dallas schools was a beautifully organized and talented lady, Marjorie Keller. She recruited some of the finest musicians for her program. There were city wide music festivals and concerts. The Orbit concert given in the sixties featured Doc Severinsen. Once again the kids got to work with a professional.

Today Mr. Karrell Johnson is heading the music program for the Dallas schools. He proudly sent the Maurine F. Bailey Concert Choir from Lincoln High School to Russia last year. The choir didn't win first prize, but the experience for the students was invaluable. The kids raised most of the money for the trip themselves, and the money they couldn't raise was given by Dallas businessmen, who stand behind the Dallas schools. Support will always be needed for the arts. Let's hope that it will continue.

ATHLETICS

In the early days there was no formal athletic program. However, in 1908, an athletic association was established to give some structure to the already present physical activities. Superintendent J.L. Long said,

> All city children need more exercise than they usually get. The lack of opportunity to engage in outdoor sports is largely the cause of juvenile misdemeanors, youthful loafers, and nervous girls who cannot stand the strain of schoolwork.

He displayed a bit of chauvinism there by implying that girls were not equipped emotionally or mentally to handle academic work. It made them "nervous."

Nevertheless, the Dallas High School football team was organized and got right into play in 1909, one year after the league was established. In a game with Sherman High School in Sherman, Texas, the Dallas team broke all records by scoring ten points in a minute and a half of play. This they did under great handicaps — for the crowd of students who traveled to Sherman for the game was so excited over the whole affair that the gang didn't stay off the field. The players were hampered by the students who just couldn't stay on the sidelines. Even the spectators actually got into some of the plays and hindered the players.

One report of this game stated that the captain of the Sherman team was not only a football player, but he was also a fine gentleman. Several times during the game he righted the umpire and saved the Dallas team some penalties.

E.P. Craig was the coach in 1909, and at the sports banquet on January 9, 1910, at the Oriental Hotel, he stated that the Dallas team was so much better than the team down at The University of Texas. One source said that the players were so honored by this statement that they actually stopped eating long enough to cheer for themselves. The teams did all this fine winning with no gym in which to practice and work out. So, the students were urged to keep making noise about the lack of a gym. The teams had earned a gymnasium, but unfortunately the citizens of Dallas had not moved on the issue.

The track team in 1909 won five first place trophies, and they did this with no place to practice. The baseball team did well. The budget showed that they only had seven dollars to spend on the team that year. The basketball team survived with no gym at the school. They were forced to play in the nearby park.

In 1909, the editor of the year book made this plea.

> Nothing appeals to the heart of the average high school student so much as a well equipped gymnasium. Although the preparatory schools of this city and high schools of other cities of its size have satisfied this desire for physical training in a very great degree, yet Dallas High School has been singularly lacking in this line. Under these conditions which have prevailed at high school and the rival schools of this city, the victories our team has achieved are astonishing. Nothing but the do-or-die spirit which has characterized Dallas High School men could have won out. But we should make some allowances for the exceptional superiority of our men this year; every year will not be so favored. Each year, as our rivals increase their training advantages, our victories are won at an ever increasing cost. It is now time that the public spirited men who send their children to Dallas High School were taking some action on this point? Compare our own and our rivals' advantages. The Dallas High boys come in from hard track practice, perspiring, dirty, wearied. They board the cars in this condition and go home. Holy Trinity boys under the same conditions go to a live gymnasium where they are treated to a shower bath and rubbing down. Dallas High teams have to practice basketball on slippery grounds in misting rain and any other sort of disagreeable weather. Terrell's boys have a large and dry gymnasium.

Could we achieve our success under more unfavorable circumstances?

Surely men who spent their four years of high school life
in D.H.S., surely they do not wish to see the old school so
outstripped by its new rivals. Can we not now start a campaign for a gymnasium in interest of those who come after
us? We could do nothing which would win their everlasting
gratitude more than this. Let us talk this question whenever
we can, before all men who have a vote in our government.
Keep it before the public until we are rewarded with as noble
a school gymnasium as ever was built by loyal and devoted
students of any institution.

That same annual mentioned the fact that the girls were
playing basketball. The game was putting roses in their cheeks
and making them strong and healthy. In fact, the strength of
the girls was weighed. And the strength of the basketball girls
was astounding. This crowd didn't fit into that nervous cate-
gory that couldn't stand the strain of school.

"Can you imagine," the annual asked, "What would happen if the girls should join the ranks of the woman's suffrag-
ists?" It seemed that the writer of the essay in the annual saw
one of the "fair damsels" toss a book at one of the boys.

"The only reason the boy did not have a concussion of the
brain was because he didn't have any brain in the first place."

In 1912 a physical training supervisor was appointed, B.C.
Tapp. With Mr. Tapp came more competitive games between
different schools. Also a woman instructor came into the high
school to hold classes in physical training. There was a girls
league formed under the direction of the supervisor at the
school and the supervisor at the YMCA. The girls signed to
play on the teams, and then they signed to help the boys morally. The girls promised that they would discourage the boys
from using tobacco and profane language. Their feminine
charms were to be used to keep the men in line. Here was a bit
more chauvinism creeping into the scene.

Still without a gym but with a positive spirit, the students
organized an outdoor club. The 1912 annual simply stated that
"on account of the inclement weather, the outdoor club could
not go outdoors." They did finally get to go hiking around
Bachman Lake and later they went on an all-day hike to the
gravel pits on Hutchins Road.

In 1915 the athletic program got a big shot in the arm when Mr. G.L. Ashburn (whom the guys called "Pop") came on the scene. This gentleman kept the spirit of the teams and the fans going even though the competition got stronger each year.

The coming of Dr. Justin Kimball finally brought the gyms. He stated,

> The ancient Athenians built few school houses, but centered the school life around the gym and produced a race never surpassed.

The new Oak Cliff High got a gym in 1916. Forest High in 1917 was built with *two* gyms, one for the boys and one for the girls. Now the women libbers of today would cheer this move on the part of Superintendent Kimball. However, were they to read further into his report, they might just withdraw a few of the cheers.

> No nation is ever stronger in physical constellation or in moral fiber than the race of women who are its *mothers*. So often in the South I see feeble underdeveloped physiques of its women who must give physical constitutions to the coming generations. Thousands of girls in well-to-do homes in this country grow to womanhood with flabby muscles and delicate underdeveloped bodies that have never had an hour of vigorous, hearty, red-blooded, whole-bodied exercise in their lives. What little exercise they do is languid walking and household tasks. Nothing to build up the torso, strengthen muscles of back and chest for good constitutions. No wonder the stress of womanhood breaks them down. Add this neglect to the foibles of dress and footwear to which fashionable womenhood in America are susceptible, and you have invalid women. No virile race was ever born to invalid women.

Here Dr. Kimball viewed women only as mothers needing strength— not corporate executives.

The gym was coming to Dallas High School, now called Bryan High because there was more than one high school in Dallas, in 1921. This coming encouraged the students no end. They still had all sorts of excuses for any loses that they suffered in 1920.

> We would have won the basketball championship this year if the team had not had to trot over to the YMCA to practice. Just watch us next year in our gym.

The football team at Bryan High lost to Forest and Oak Cliff in 1920 — again because there was no gym. However, they had a player who attracted a lot of attention. This was "Crack" Dubois. He was center and guard. The *Dallas Morning News* stated,

"Crack is the most popular and dependable player on the team. When the big piles are uncovered, Crack is always on the bottom."

In 1921 the teams at Bryan High did win over every team they played except Cleburne High. The gym did make a difference. Also, the annual reported that there was "poor officiating" at the Cleburne game, so actually the Bryan High team really won.

The girls were introduced to organized sports in 1924. Until then, they had only calisthenics. Now, there were volleyball teams and softball teams. And if one didn't play on the team one could try out for cheerleader. These cheerleaders led the earliest organized cheers.

> *You haven't got the pep.*
> *You haven't got the jazz.*
> *You haven't got the team*
> *That Bryan High has.*

The acceptable dress for the girls in the gym was a middy blouse, black bloomers, and black hose. A whistle would blow, silence would fall, the piano would play a lively tune, and the exercise would begin. Miss M.B. Smith was the first physical training teacher for girls at Forest High and Miss A.B. Henry played the piano. After the exercises,

> You will see girls climbing ropes with all the agility of their ancient jungle ancestors. Here and there a maid over-burdened with too much bottom is laborously endeavoring to accomplish the feat of standing on her head.

One day out of every two weeks was devoted to the teaching of personal hygiene. Posture, correct treatment of the body, and other information was discussed.

> You can tell our girls have had physical training. The girl's carriage, her attitude towards her studies, her school spirit, her whole being is changed — she is more energetic, she has more animation about her. Yes, she is the sort of girl

that every high school needs and is proud of.

There wasn't a nervous one in the lot.

There was no lolling in the gym — no gossip time. It was a time to don the bloomers and work out. The workouts varied. There were days devoted to games. Two days a week were devoted to dancing. The girls were all endeavoring to acquire the art of Irene Castle or Pavlova. One girl wrote an editorial.

> Usually when we go to our physical training class, we have gone through a hard period of school work, perhaps a trying period in the laboratory or a period in which we have been concentrating on mathematics, or else, we have become fatigued from passing an examination. Our minds have become stale, our circulation bad, and the proper quantity of blood not being sent to the brain — then how good it feels to jump into our gym suits, and spend twenty-five minutes in actual physical work.

The girls' activities were shared with the community. Each month there was a physical training party. The gym floor was packed with girls and the parents watched the action from the sidelines. The program opened with a game played between two selected teams. A whistle blew — silence. Then there was a rush for places. The parents saw drills, dances, and exercises. Mom and Dad would crane their necks to see just how agile their daughter was. Hopefully, she wasn't a klutz. However, those teachers, as it was reported, made ugly ducklings into swans. And it all happened in the gym. After the program the girls gathered around the instructor and gave a cheer. They sang the loyalty song together, and this ended an evening of fun and frolic. This happened every month in every high school for many years.

Through Dr. Kimball's platoon system, physical training was introduced in the elementary schools. The teacher led the children in Swedish gymnastics. This brought muscular development of chest, shoulders, neck, back, and abdominal muscles. The children engaged in rhythmic exercises as well. They played indoor and outdoor games. Every minute was planned. Teachers did not just turn the kids loose for an hour. The time was beneficial to the body and mind of each child.

At Robert E. Lee School we played a lot of Red Rover, Red Rover. One particular friend (very agile and athletic) who was constantly called over and who was already a star out on the field, was Texie Jane Waterman. It was all that playground activity that made her so able to choreograph the Dallas Cowboy Cheerleaders. Dr. Kimball probably never had the Cowboy cheerleaders in mind when he planned the physical activity for the little children of Dallas. Nevertheless, they are an indirect result.

The little children were playing, the high school girls were striving for grace, beauty and comeliness, and the guys were out on the field gaining strength, courage, and endurance.

Meanwhile, the athletic departments were growing and with their growth the spirit of the schools increased. Dr. Kimball appreciated all the spirit shown in athletic competition between the classes in the high schools. He thought that this rivalry was good and wholesome, and that it developed a strong love in the students for their school. However, he was fearful of the enormous competition that was building between the schools. The whole country was becoming more and more sports minded, and Dallas minds were turning in the sam direction.

Dr. Kimball insisted that the athletes make good grades in order to keep playing. He kept things in tight control, but he was noticing the overt display of spirit at the games. The cheers were getting louder and louder at each game. The spirit was getting more and more intense. Cheerleaders were now present, and the superintendent really wondered where it would all stop. He finally decided that the spirit came from the native Texan coaches. It was they who stirred the students into the frenzied behavior at the games. They had the spirit, and it had mushroomed into the stands. So to offset this he brought in some coaches from out of Texas, P.C. Cobb, Howard Allen, and Alfred Loos. Dr. Kimball didn't realize that a coach's spirit was the mark of the trade. These men became Texans so fast, that the spirit, instead of waning, increased. The records showed that there was an increase in the number of schools, and this brought even more rivalry and spirit.

When North Dallas opened in 1923, Principal E.B. Comstock had so much spirit for the first game that he dismissed school early so that everyone could get to the game on time. That first game was with a Fort Worth School, and Mr. Comstock urged the kids to drive carefully. Later he heard that several of his best and most mature students had been stopped for speeding through Grand Prairie. He was distressed over this, and later he became the moving force in the development of driver education in the schools.

"Pop" Ashburn was the cool member of the athletic department. He never seemed to get rattled over anything. When he left coaching and became principal of Woodrow Wilson High, he accepted the duties of the principalship with the same even temper.

Howard Allen was the beloved coach. Years later after his death, some vandals broke into Adamson and tore up the school. H.S. Griffin was called from the administration building to inspect the damage. He saw the broken trophy cases in the hall at the school.

"Where are the trophys? They can't be gone."
He was told that they were all locked up in one of the rooms. Mr. Griffin wanted to see them. He was taken to the room where he silently let his eyes travel over the silver cups. He lifted one, and tears streamed down his cheeks.

"Here it is. The 1924 State Championship Trophy. Nothing must happen to Coach Allen's trophies."

In 1923 at Forest Avenue Alfred Loos was given an assistant coach, Herschel Forester. When Woodrow Wilson High opened, Mr. Forester went to coach there. He always felt like he was called into the teaching profession. Just as Adoniran Judson was called to be a missionary to India, he felt he was called to coach and teach at Woodrow Wilson High. He loved the kids, he loved coaching, he loved the school. After he retired from coaching he stayed at Woodrow to teach. One day while teaching the students whom he loved so much, he suffered a stroke and died. In telling this his son commented that his father had "died with his boots on." But that's what he wanted to do.

While at Woodrow Herschel Forester coached two Heisman Trophy winners, David O'Brien and I.B. Hale. He also coached his sons, Herschel, Jr. and Bill, who were outstanding players at SMU and then went on to play professional ball. Herschel played three years with the Browns and Bill played eleven years with Green Bay. Coach Forester's grandson, another Herschel, was captain of the W.T. White High School team in 1979 when that team was all district and all city champions. At the all district game with Hillcrest High, Herschel ran the winning touchdown. The kids at Hillcrest were disappointed at their loss, but as one Hillcrest parent and fan put it,

"His grandfather surely would have been proud."
All the Foresters are community leaders and supporters of the Dallas schools.

W.W. Bushman came to Dallas to coach in 1926 at Sunset High School. The correct spelling of his name was Buschman, and in order to get the "c" in his name, he would have to spell it. He grew tired of doing this, so he legally changed his name to read Bushman with out the "c". Two years later his brother Al Buschman arrived in Dallas to serve as Director of Health and Physical Education. Al never dropped the "c". The names are spelled differently, but the family is the same.

Bill was made principal of Sunset in 1941, but when war was declared, the much loved and respected man said that he could not ask those boys to volunteer without going himself. So Bill went to war. He was lost flying the Hump through the Himalayas from India to China after the Burma Road was closed. He never got back to his Sunset High School. In 1948 an elementary school was built and named for W.W. Bushman.

Al Buschman, as director of Physical Education, was credited with turning the Dallas athletic program into a money-making program as the district grew to twenty senior high schools and twenty-three junior high schools during his forty-one years of service. In 1963 he succeeded Mr. P.C. Cobb as Director of Athletics and remained at the head of the vast program until his retirement in 1969.

As the director of the physical education department he made certain that there was a gym in every elementary school. He organized an after-school program for the boys and girls in the grade schools. He formed square dance clubs throughout the system. One of his pet projects was the Christmas Basketball Tournament now known as the Dr. Pepper Tournament. It's been popular since it's inception in the late forties.

Mr. "B" wrote an athletics manual that has been used by other athletic departments as a pattern. The Alfred J. Loos athletic complex was designed by Buschman, and it has been used as a model for other field houses all over the country. He did all this and never made an enemy doing it. This was quite an accomplishment for someone who worked with thousands of people and thousands of dollars.

Mr. Buschman often moonlighted as the official basketball timer for the college games. He was also the timer for the Cotton Bowl games.

He was a natty dresser — always looking as sharp as a pin. The guys used to ask him when he visited the schools,

"Hey, coach, do you polish the bottom of your shoes too?"

The very first night football game that was ever played in Dallas was between North Dallas and Sunset in 1931 at the Cotton Bowl. This was a big step forward in athletics. Until then there had been after-school gatherings at grandstands. Now it was big time. However, Dallas needed its own stadium, so one was built. The stadium (which was originally named Dal-Hi) was the last educational complex to be built with WPA funds. It was the pride of the athletic department. No one but maybe Wylie Parker was concerned that it was built in the river bottoms,but there was always concern about the railroad track that ran beside it. Students were warned about crossing the tracks at Oak Lawn and Harry Hines. Trains would run by during the games, and smoke often drifted over the field, but this never bothered the fans. In fact, I remember us cheering students (wanting any reason to cheer) cheering the trains as they passed by. They always responded with a large blast of the whistle.

During the opening celebration of the stadium on 1939, each Dallas team played a short quarter. No scores were kept but the rival schools were paired against each other. Sunset played Adamson, Woodrow played North Dallas, and Tech played Forest.

Later the name of the Dal-Hi Stadium was changed to P.C. Cobb Stadium to honor the man who was called "Mr. Athletics" of Dallas. Other field houses were built, some named for the men who spawned the enormous athletic program that exists today: Herschel Forester, Alfred Loos, and John Fouts. The Sprague family was honored when the athletic complex was given the Sprague name. Dr. George Sprague was the first president of the Central Dads Club, and his son played ball for Adamson. Mrs. Sprague organized the PTA at Adamson.Today there's a new athletic complex just completed. It is named for P.C. Cobb. Once again Mr. Athletics is honored. The complex is by the Fair Park on Robert Cullum Boulevard. It's situated on a street named for a gentleman who played football for North Dallas. The story goes that Bob Cullum was knocked out on the field during a game. When he returned to consciousness, still on the field, the first face that he saw was that of his mother's. She had frantically run from the stands out on the field to see that her boy was all right. There was no damage to Bob, because he finished the game. Later he rose to become Dallas's great grocery man, Tom Thumb. Today, a Woodrow Wilson athlete and former mayor of Dallas, heads this vast grocery business, Mr. Jack Evans.

There are sports stars all over the horizon that came from the Dallas schools. Davy O'Brien is listed in the Texas Sports Hall of Fame. There is another sportsman in the Hall of Fame, golfer, Don January, who began playing for Sunset High School in the late forties. He went on to win the PGA and other major tournaments. Golf was introduced into the system in 1926, and this was certainly good for pro golfer January and others who, even though they didn't make golf a career, received college scholarships in that sport.

The Golden Gloves shone in Dallas with Johnny O'Glee. Boxer O'Glee eventually put down the gloves after college and served as a principal in the Dallas system for many years.

As E.D. Walker said,

"In the beginning there was one coach at each high school. He coached everything. Now, there's a coach for every sport and also teachers for physical education. It's big."

Every coach has a desire to win games and a desire to make their team members play good ball. This takes discipline, and that's what coaches teach. It's a needed subject.

Presently, John Kincaide is head of athletics for the district. He is assisted by Ralph Fulton, Charlie Dyer, and Loie Harris. Ms. Harris is the first woman to hold such a prestigious position. He also has another assistant, Kedrick Couch, who won so many games as coach that he wrote a book on winning. He shared his secrets with other coaches.

The Actions Of the Past Are The Strengths Of The Future

One hundred years ago some interested citizens of Dallas came together for the purpose of bringing public education to the city — to offer everyone an education regardless of color or class. These interested parties had to lure intelligent people into the teaching field by offering special teacher training programs and the promise of good wages for a good job. They had to convince the Dallas society that public education would offer more opportunities to their children than any privately-funded school. They had to generate excitement in the hearts and minds of the parents so that they would send their children to the public schools of Dallas. They had to convince parents that public education would offer the best education to their children. And they had to do this with very little money and a few shacks that they called schoolhouses.

Today, school administrators, school board members, and interested citizens are just about in the same condition as those early school board members and interested citizens were one hundred years ago. They have the same selling job on their hands. Except today, there are classrooms, labs, libraries, athletic fields, gyms, rifle ranges, shops, auditoriums, theatres, greenhouses, cafeterias, video and audio equipment, and computers available for all the students if they will use them.

Today, however, there are thirty times more people in Dallas, some homes are very unstable, the undisciplined child can do as he pleases, more people *have* things, more people do *not* have things, more people think that they have the *right* to have everything, rudeness and incompetence and poor workmanship are the norm, winners are loosing, loosers are winning, and envy is the feeling for the day.

People read and write history for two reasons. One reason is for the pure enjoyment of learning about and reflecting upon the past. The second reason is to look at what has been, evaluate the happenings, and see what conclusions can be made about those past activities. I feel that the enjoyment is here in the anecdotes, the reports, the recorded feelings and thoughts of those who were — and who are still — involved in public education in Dallas. Now, what conclusions can be drawn from these?

The concern over public education is a national issue. We read that the students are mediocre and unprepared for the future. We're told that the other nations in the world are surpassing us in their knowledge of technology and science. We hear that teachers are dropping out of school more than students ever did. We're informed that the ones that are staying are not the best teachers. Some say that the low salaries are causing more and more teachers to leave the profession. A college professor exclaimed off-the-cuff,

"If the low salaries haven't gotten them, then the sex, drugs, and the abominable behavior in the kids have."

What can the nation do for public education. First, the federal government must keep a closer watch on the money that is given to education. Mass governmental handouts are disastrous. There are block grants given. Some educators feel that these are better than the catagorical ones that had been given in the past. The local administrators can determine the use of the money in the block grant. Nevertheless, each grant should be handled like a precious gem that gleams in the dark when a special light is focused on it. The right people must receive the money.

This country must glorify education. It must give tribute to the great minds of our country. Learning must become popular. Those who achieve must be rewarded with praise. Great minds, academic, scientific, and literary, must be set before the youth of America as favored role models.

Education, not wealth, must be praised. Some of our governmental leaders have failed the kids. They are so full of envy and greed that they have lost their "public servant" image.

Our state and community must continue to study the budgets for education. Teachers need better salaries. Merit pay has never worked in the past. Maybe there is a plan somewhere in someone's mind that would work. A continuous study needs to be made on the acquisition and the distribution of funds.

Regardless of how much the teachers are paid, they must have more respect and appreciation from the students, the parents, and the public. The teachers use to rule. They have been dethroned, and this is bad. They must be once again given the crown and scepter and be trusted with the power to teach.

Of course, those teachers must be worthy of this power. The colleges must grant teacher certification only to those having the knowledge to teach. Teachers must be monitored in their classrooms by trusted administrators. This was done in the past. Good teachers never mind being watched.

"The whole success of our activity depends on our personal honor and on our academic integrity. If we should appear to our students as men who take their oath lightly, there would be an end to any good we might be able to accomplish by our teaching."
These are the words of a master teacher. All teachers must feel this way. Teaching must not be taken lightly.

Parents must send their children to school with self-respect and self-esteem. Only then will the child get along in school. The eternal truth will always be,

"Love your neighbor as yourself."
A child must love and appreciate himself, or he will not love and respect others.

Each parent must show the child his assets and guide him toward using them. Parents must make their children see their potential and develop that potential to the utmost. This attitude must be started in the home. Teachers can only develop it as they teach.

There is so much greed and envy, and we have all the reason in the world to believe that it will accelerate and grow. Parents must work toward making their children proud of who they are. Thomas Jefferson said, "All men are created equal." The *Bible* didn't say this. God speaks of the poor which "we will have with us always," the lame, the discouraged, the widow who was poor, the ruler who was rich, the one with everything, the one with nothing . . . When God spoke of these people, he didn't apologize for their presence. He *did* challenge those who had abilities and had health and had money to get out there and help those who didn't.

Good teachers feel called to help, to enlighten, to guide. They feel that they must bring every child to their highest point of achievement. They need encouragement and praise as they are doing this.

Dallas is no longer a small Southern town that opens its doors to only a certain "kind." We're a big city holding all kinds of people coming from various states in the United States and various countries from all over the globe. This is good. It denotes growth in business and industry. It brings growth socially and educationally.

Gone are the days when the schools were filled with students who were almost identical in background and financial status. Our schools hold a mix of people, but the students hopefully are all there to learn. However, they must be grouped according to their level of academic achievement. The schools can be mixed, but the classes must be academically homogeneous or learning cannot occur. The teachers must be trusted to group these students for concentrated learning. The teachers must recognize the individual differences in their students. Good teachers can do this.

The parents and the teachers must work closely together. If a child is not doing his work, the parent must know this. He must be told of the problems in learning and accept the teacher's decision about the child's academic standing.

If a child becomes a *major* disturbance in the classroom, the teacher calls the parent immediately. The parent and the teacher discuss the disciplin for the child. The unruly behavior must cease. Teachers cannot teach in a mass of disorder. The administrators, obviously, must stand behind their teachers in these judgements.

Hopefully, with more respect and more prestige and more power, there will be less turnover in the teaching profession. Children need to have the same teachers each day. This gives stability to their life, for children cannot endure too much change. They must know where they will be and with whom they will be. If the children are secure, then they can use their minds to learn and not to worry. Stress is a hindrance to their academic achievement.

Shifting children around must stop. In looking at the past, one can easily see that abrupt change caused a mental and emotional problem in the child. There are enormous changes made in the homes today. Parents divorce. Families move. Too much rapid change is going to create a child who cannot or will not learn.

When Alvin Toffler was here in Dallas, I was privileged to speak with him. This is the man who predicted all the change. He was proud to report on all the advancements that the changes brought. I asked him about the emotional trauma that comes with so much change. He shook his head.

"That's another story, and a vast problem."

There are great teachers teaching today. They need to be encouraged. Of course, there are bad teachers in the classrooms too. There always have been. We had a teacher at North Dallas who did nothing but polish her nails. However, we sat quietly while she did this. I don't believe we learned anything, but on senior day, when we girls got dressed up and wore nylons, whenever we got a run in our stockings, at least we knew where to get the nail polish to stop the run. This bad teacher was just *one* in a group of many terrific ones. The whole faculty wasn't condemned because one teacher had polished her nails.

Good teachers teach because they want to impart knowledge. They really don't think of the pay. They never have and they never will. Teachers have living testimonies walking around all over the earth. Awards, trophys, medals become rusted. They get lost — they are forgotten. But the living testimonies speak.

"I would have never made it if it hadn't of been for this teacher." That's a big payment!

Harry Haun, the writer from Woodrow Wilson High, included in his *Movie Quote Book*, the lines from a scene in George Cukor's movie *Born Yesterday*. They're very appropriate in a book about education. William Holden was teaching Judy Holiday, and she was gratefully absorbing knowledge like a sponge. She asked him why he was teaching.

"It's sort of a cause. I want everybody to be smart. I want 'em to be as smart as they can be. A world full of ignorant people is too dangerous to live in."

INDEX